ALSO BY DAVID RITZ

BIOGRAPHIES:

Divided Soul: The Life of Marvin Gaye

Faith in Time: The Life of Jimmy Scott

Respect: The Life of Aretha Franklin

with Tavis Smiley: *Death of a King: The Real Story of Dr. Martin Luther King, Jr.'s Final Year*

AUTOBIOGRAPHIES:

with Ray Charles: *Brother Ray*

with Smokey Robinson: *Inside My Life*

with B. B. King: *Blues All Around Me*

with Etta James: *Rage to Survive*

with the Neville Brothers: *The Brothers*

with Jerry Wexler: *Rhythm and the Blues*

with Aretha Franklin: *From These Roots*

with Walter Yetnikoff: *Howling at the Moon*

with Robert Guillaume: *A Life*

with Laila Ali: *Reach*

with Gary Sheffield: *Inside Power*

with Felicia "Snoop" Pearson: *Grace After Midnight*

with Lang Lang: *Journey of a Thousand Miles*

with Don Rickles: *Rickles' Book*

with Don Rickles: *Rickles' Letters*

with Jerry Leiber and Mike Stoller: *Hound Dog*

with Paul Shaffer: *We'll Be Here for the Rest of Our Lives*

with Grandmaster Flash: *My Life, My Beats*

with Tavis Smiley: *What I Know for Sure*

with Cornel West: *Brother West*

with Archbishop Carl Bean: *I Was Born This Way*
with Natalie Cole: *Love Brought Me Back*
with Janet Jackson: *True You*
with Scott Weiland: *Not Dead and Not for Sale*
with Ralph Branca: *A Moment in Time*
with R. Kelly: *Soulacoaster*
with Bettye LaVette: *A Woman Like Me*
with Scott Stapp: *Sinner's Creed*
with Buddy Guy: *When I Left Home*
with Nik Wallenda: *Balance*
with Joe Perry: *Rocks*

NOVELS:

Search for Happiness
The Man Who Brought the Dodgers Back to Brooklyn
Blue Notes Under a Green Felt Hat
Barbells and Saxophones
Family Blood
Take It Off, Take It All Off!
Passion Flowers
with Mable John: *Sanctified Blues*
with Mable John: *Stay Out of the Kitchen!*
with Mable John: *Love Tornado*
with T. I.: *Power and Beauty*
with T.I.: *Trouble and Triumph*

INSPIRATIONAL:

Messengers: Portraits of African American Ministers, Evangelists, Gospel Singers, and Other Messengers of "the Word"

GLOW

THE AUTOBIOGRAPHY OF
RICK JAMES

RICK JAMES
with David Ritz

ATRIA BOOKS

NEW YORK   LONDON   TORONTO   SYDNEY   NEW DELHI

ATRIA BOOKS

A Division of Simon & Schuster, Inc.
1230 Avenue of the Americas
New York, NY 10020

First Atria Books hardcover edition July 2014

ATRIA BOOKS and colophon are trademarks of Simon & Schuster, Inc.

For information about special discounts for bulk purchases, please contact Simon & Schuster Special Sales at 1-866-506-1949 or business@simonandschuster.com.

The Simon & Schuster Speakers Bureau can bring authors to your live event. For more information or to book an event, contact the Simon & Schuster Speakers Bureau at 1-866-248-3049 or visit our website at www.simonspeakers.com.

Interior design by Kyoko Watanabe
Jacket design by James Perales
Jacket photograph © Ron Slenzak Photography, Inc.

Manufactured in the United States of America

10 9 8 7 6 5 4 3 2 1

Library of Congress Cataloging-in-Publication Data

James, Rick, 1948–2004 author.
Glow / Rick James with David Ritz.
pages cm
1. James, Rick, 1948–2004. 2. Funk musicians—Biography. 3. African American rock musicians—Biography. I. Ritz, David, author. II. Title.
ML420.J233A3 2014
781.644092—dc23
[B]
2014004137

ISBN 978-1-4767-6414-6
ISBN 978-1-4767-6416-0 (ebook)

ACKNOWLEDGMENTS

Editorial assistance by Aaron Cohen and Harry Weinger.

Thanks to Jeff Jampol for making this book possible—and to the estate of Rick James for continuing to honor his legacy.

Gratitude to David Vigliano, Malaika Adero, Todd Hunter, Will LoTurco, and Arron Saxe.

Much love to my family—wonderful wife, Roberta, and Ali, Jess, Henry, Jim, Charlotte, Nins, James, Isaac, Esther, and Elizabeth.

To the Tuesday morning gang—Dennis, Skip, Ian, Dave, Kevin, David, Herb, Dejon, Juan, and Dan—and all my friends in and out of the meetings who keep me sane.

And love to my dear brothers Alan Eisenstock and Harry Weinger for helping me in so many ways.

—*David Ritz*

GLOW

INTRODUCTION

I met Rick James in Marvin Gaye's studio on Sunset Boulevard in Hollywood in 1979. Marvin was forty, Rick was thirty-one, and I was thirty-five.

Rick was riding high. His *Come Get It!* album, with the hits "You and I" and "Mary Jane," had gone double platinum. Rick later described this time: "[My royalties] bought me a mansion once owned by William Randolph Hearst with a sunken living room and a dramatic fireplace that looked like it came out of *Citizen Kane.*" His second album, *Bustin' Out of L Seven*, was a runaway smash, and in the kingdom of Motown, he was the newly crowned prince.

Once upon a time, Marvin had been a prince himself, but in the late seventies he was struggling to regain commercial success. It had been two years since his last hit, the nouvelle disco "Got to Give It Up," an autographical meditation on his reluctance to dance.

That night Rick was dancing all over Marvin's studio. He wore a tiny silver cocaine spoon around his neck and, dipping into his bag of blow, he freely offered up samples.

I was there as Gaye's biographer, learning as much as I could about Marvin's life, which, in those days, revolved around the studio. Marvin was low-key, but having recently completed the autobiography of Ray Charles, I was accustomed to a supercharged personality. I was not, though, accustomed to anyone as supercharged as Rick. His energy was outrageous. He spoke in streams of consciousness that revealed a brilliant mind. He spoke nonstop. He was respectful of Marvin, whom he referred to as "the Master." But knowing that Gaye was self-conscious about having hit forty, he also liked to needle him by calling him "Uncle Marvin."

When Rick asked to hear what Marvin was working on, Gaye played "Dance 'N' Be Happy" from the unreleased *Love Man,* an album that would be reworked several times and finally issued as *In Our Lifetime,* an uncompromising view of an impending apocalypse.

Rick liked what he heard, but Marvin didn't.

"It's superficial," said Gaye.

"Sometimes superficial sells," said James.

"But substantive sells even more," Marvin argued.

"I like substantive," said Rick. "What do you think about this substance I have right here?"

Marvin laughed. "It's good," he said.

"It's all good," Rick agreed.

Marvin's tracks played over the banter.

"The funk is deep," said Rick.

"Substantially deep. But I haven't gotten the story straight. That's why this man is here—to help me figure out the story." That's when Marvin formally introduced me to Rick.

"When that book comes out," said Rick, "I'm going to be the first to read it."

When, six years later, the book—*Divided Soul: The Life of Marvin Gaye*—did come out, Rick was among the first people to call me with his reaction.

"Marvin's story is incredible," he said, "but wait till you hear mine. My story will blow you away."

It did. When we got together on several occasions, I started taking notes. I couldn't write fast enough. Rick's story was off the charts, an epic of music, crime, and sex. He didn't give me the whole picture, but enough to whet my appetite. Rick had great musical focus but limited conversational focus. He'd start stories, build them up, and then, reminded of another story, switch tracks. At times he'd have four stories going at once. He might not finish any of them. One thing, though, was clear: he contained stories like the oceans contain fish.

Reading *Divided Soul*, Rick was more motivated than ever to write his own book.

"Marvin's story ends in tragedy," said Rick, "but mine will end in triumph."

There were, to be sure, more triumphs in store for Rick, and in the coming years he called me several times to make sure I took note of them. "The book will get done," he said. "I really want to get started."

But that didn't happen until the nineties, when a prison sentence gave Rick the literary focus he might otherwise never have experienced. I was asked to write an essay to accompany a multi-CD overview of James's career. I readily agreed, seeing it as a chance to reconnect with Rick.

A long series of prison interviews ensued, many in person, many more on the phone. During the first, Rick told me that he had been studying biographies and reread the ones I did on Marvin and Ray Charles. He was finally and firmly committed to do one of his own.

Would I help? I was only too glad. I used this eight-week period of face-to-face encounters with Rick to form the basis of what I hoped would be his autobiography.

While he was still incarcerated, the CD set came out (*Bustin' Out: The Best of Rick James*), along with my essay "The Musical Memoirs of a Superfreak," largely written in Rick's voice. He sent me a message that he liked the essay and had high hopes for the book that we would write together. I was optimistic about completing the project, based on not only the large amount of intimate interview material I had accumulated but also Rick's willingness to bare his soul.

When he was released from prison in 1996, he had served two years and twenty-three days of his five-year sentence. He was elated and called me a month later, eager for us to get together and work on the book. He mailed me several hundred pages of notes and partial chapters that he had written in prison. The story was not organized chronologically. There were major gaps and more than a few breakdowns in logic. Yet I was encouraged because there was so much to work with. Rick was serious about telling his story.

Another year passed before he called me. He was ready to release a new album, *Urban Rapsody*, and wanted me to come to the studio to hear it. The music was great, and, like your typical writer, I was gratified to see that on the studio console were copies of autobiographies I had written with B. B. King and Etta James.

"I haven't disappeared," said Rick. "I've been keeping up with you through your books. I just had to get this music out. We'll get to work. I'll call you in a few weeks." We had several long conversations after that, during which we discussed the structure of the book and several new passages he had written. Then his calls stopped.

I tried contacting him dozens of times. A couple of those times we connected, but he sounded increasingly remote. The prospect of our putting his autobiography in publishable shape seemed more and more distant. Through mutual friends, I heard that his struggles with drugs had deepened.

In 2004, he called to ask whether I had caught him on *Chappelle's Show*, where Dave Chappelle, playing Rick, uttered the immortal line "I'm Rick James, bitch!" I had watched him, and though the skit was funny, I saw tremendous pain in Rick's eyes. He looked like a defeated man. He said that because he was back in the public eye, it was time to do more work on his book. He was depressed because his marriage to Tanya Hijazi, the great love of his life, had collapsed. Their divorce became official in the summer of 2004.

On August 6 of that year, a friend called to say that Rick had passed. The papers called it "pulmonary and cardiac failure." I thought of what Rick had said, twenty-five years earlier, about avoiding what Marvin Gaye did not avoid—a tragic end. I went to the phonograph and put on "Standing on the Top," the song Rick had written and produced for the Temptations' *Reunion* album. I had a happy memory of watching Rick rehearse that group, his favorite, back in the early eighties when the record was cut. The session had been chaotic but creative, with Rick in possession of his full musical powers. That day he experienced tremendous satisfaction.

Rick James was a major player in the highly competitive game of rhythm and blues, where only the most talented survive. In that earlier essay, I wrote, "Between Parliament and Prince, Rick carried the banner of black pop over that fertile territory known as funk. As the seventies melted into the eighties, he was bad, superbad, the baddest of the bad. His orchestrations were brilliant, his shows spectacular. He worked in the celebrated R & B instrumental tradition—percussive guitar riffs, busy bass line, syncopated horn punches—extending from Louis Jordan, Ray Charles, Ike Turner, James Brown, the Memphis Horns, Johnny "Guitar" Watson, Sly Stone, and George Clinton. Rick honored the tradition—and added to it. His funk was high and mighty while his attitude stayed down and dirty. His eroticism was raw. He was an early gangsta of love, calculatedly insane, unmanageable, both benefactor and victim of his own inexhaustible energy."

A half-realized unauthorized version of a James autobiography appeared after his death but fell woefully far short of achieving Rick's goal—to write a book worthy of his musical and literary intelligence. The last thing Rick told me was, "The material is there, but the book still needs lots of work." Until now, that work has never been done.

Glow: The Autobiography of Rick James represents the full expression of our original project. It is based on not only my interviews with Rick but also the material Rick gave me. It is written entirely in Rick's voice—our intention from the very start of our collaboration. It's all Rick, all the time.

My hope is that in reading this book you will hear Rick, see Rick, and feel Rick revealing his heart. He was as creative as he was conflicted, as driven as he was diverted by his demons.

This is, I'm convinced, the book that Rick wanted—a memoir that is startlingly candid, fearless, and informed by the notion that confession is the most sincere and powerful form of prayer.

David Ritz
Los Angeles, 2013

PART ONE

BREAKING OUT

LOCKED UP

'm having these crazy dreams in jail. The dreams are so vivid—so wildly creative—that I know God is in charge of my imagination. I couldn't dream up this shit without God. God has to be the author of my dreams. In one dream, I'm with Miles Davis. We're dressed like African princes. Our robes are blue and gold. Miles is singing and I'm playing trumpet. Black angels are surrounding us. We're bathed in sunlight. We're on top of the Empire State Building and everyone in the city of New York can hear us. The people are assembled on the street; they're hanging out their windows and waving flags from office buildings. Helicopters are flying over us, but our music is so powerful that we drown out all noise. Our music is some symphony that has the angels dancing in the sky.

"Didn't know you could play jazz so good," Miles says to me.

"Didn't know you could sing so funky," I say to him.

The music is so beautiful I start crying through Miles's horn.

Someone says, "The hospitals are clearing out. The patients are healed."

Someone else says, "The churches are clearing. The congregations are in the streets."

"I told you," says Miles. "I told you we could do it."

When I put the trumpet to my lips again, the horn turns into a megaphone. When I start to speak, I hear the voice of my mother.

"My son has the answer," she says. "Miles gave him the answer. Listen to my son."

I turn to Miles, who rarely smiles, and see that he is smiling.

When I wake up from this dream, I am smiling.

But I'm still in jail.

✦

This long stay in jail is the first time I'm remembering my dreams. I'm not even sure I had dreams before they put my ass behind bars. My mind was clogged up with cocaine—not just any cocaine, but cocaine strong enough to fuel jet engines. I was a jet engine that got dislodged from the plane of my brain. I crashed to the ground and broke into a million pieces. When the pieces magically came back together, the engine could work again. But the fuel was no longer cocaine. The fuel was something I hadn't used since I was a little boy. I'd call it natural energy and natural drive. It's a natural restlessness to see and explore and learn. Couldn't do any of that exploring when I was ripping and running through the world of intoxicants. Didn't wanna explore. Just wanted to stay high.

So ain't this a bitch? My highs are my dreams. My dreams are my escape. And my imagination is my way out of prison. If you break down the word "imagination," I guess it means manufacturing images. Dreaming is the purest form of that process—so, for as long as I'm locked up, I'm gonna write down my dreams.

I'm also gonna write down my life.

I've always wanted to write my own life story. But outside of prison I could never sit down and be quiet. My energy was scattered. I was always going in a dozen different directions at once. But now I got no choice. Got nowhere to go and nothing to do. I'm forced to read. And in reading—especially about the lives of people I relate to—I get excited. I read about Charlie Parker, Nat King Cole, Bob Marley, and Malcolm X, and I understand exactly why their lives went the way they did. I see their fuckups as my fuckups; I see their talents as my talents. Sometimes talent is so big it takes you to places that you don't understand. Super talent doesn't take you to the Land of Peace; it takes you to Crazyland. And if you ain't emotionally grounded in something rock-solid, you gonna get annihilated.

I got annihilated. Now I'm getting healed. And part of the healing is dreaming, remembering, and writing.

I can write in peace because I don't have access to my lethal vices. Being a celebrity in jail also means I have protectors who keep the bad cats away from me. They see I'm serious about writing and form a shield around me.

In prison, I've gravitated toward the bookish brothas. I've met Muslims who have taken me deep into the Koran. I love and respect Islam. I was raised Catholic but never really studied the Bible till late in life. The Christian brothas in prison have given me a new way to look at the Word. A Jewish man has been talking about Kabbalah, mysticism with wisdom of its own.

Don't worry. I ain't gonna shove no religion down your throat. I'm not using this book to win converts. I'm just using the book to manufacture images from my past. I just wanna look at old pictures, lay 'em out there, and, like a jigsaw puzzle, see if I can make the pieces fit. See if I can make sense of a life of nonsense and understand how I got to be caged up like an animal.

I am an animal, a fuckin' wild animal. I lost my human soul. I lost my human mind. But in this animal cage, my intention is to win back my humanity. Animals can't write.

I can.

I will.

Here goes . . .

STANDING ON THE TOP

This ain't no dream. This shit really happened:

Nineteen eighty-two. Ronald fuckin' Reagan in the White House turning this country more conservative than it'd been since slavery, and me telling my manager, "I gotta get outta here. Gotta get to Europe."

"Beautiful," said my manager, "because Europe has been calling. Europe wants the funk."

"Well, let's funk 'em up," I said. "Let's freak 'em out."

"What do you think of Germany?" asked my manager.

"They're the biggest freaks of all. Let's fuckin' freak 'em!"

Next thing I know I'm at the airport, where, as the cats in my band are boarding the plane, I'm standing there popping quaaludes in many of their mouths. I take two. We're getting fucked up 'cause we're scared shitless of flying over the ocean. We drink ourselves into oblivion.

When we land, an army of funk fans is waiting at the airport. We're treated like conquering heroes. They're waving all my albums—*Come Get It!, Bustin' Out, Fire It Up, Street Songs*—and breaking out in a spontaneous version of "Super Freak." Chicks are stuffing joints in my pocket. One fine bitch slips into my limo. Her blond hair is the color of sunlight and her big beautiful breasts are practically busting through a T-shirt that says something in German I don't understand.

"What does that mean?" I ask.

In heavily accented English she answers, " 'Fucking is fun.' "

She calls herself Greta and says she's my biggest fan.

"Are your songs about things that really happen to you?" she asks.

"My songs are fantasies."

"Can I be a fantasy?" she asks.

"You already are."

The fantasy gets fatter:

I'm onstage in front of the cameras for *Rockpalast*, a German MTV-style show that's broadcast to one hundred fifty million fans across Europe. My opening acts are the Kinks and Van Morrison. I get out and fire up the funk to where the riot squad is lined up in the front of the stage. Doesn't matter that the audience is German; those motherfuckers know every word to my every song. They're mouthing along like they grew up in the hood. They're flashing me the funk sign and won't stop screaming till I give 'em five encores.

That night in my suite, Greta is demanding encores of her own. I'm giving, giving, giving, loving, loving, loving, riding high and riding low, riding Greta into the land of pure ecstatic pleasure, where nothing can stop us, not even the light of morning sunshine that creeps in our room and casts a golden glow over her voluptuous body, this German angel sent to welcome me into the womb of her funk-loving motherland.

Renewed and ready to take on whatever awaits me in Reagan-land,

I don't need a handful of quaaludes to get back on the 747 home. After taking Europe by storm, I can keep the plane flying on the fuel of my energy alone. There's no way I'm gonna fall outta the sky. No way I'm ever gonna fall.

"That 'Standing on the Top' song you did with the Temptations," says my manager soon as I land, "that jam is tearing up the charts."

I think back to when I was a teenager running the streets of Buffalo while listening to the Temptations on my tinny transistor radio. Never thought I'd be the one who'd help put them back on top. Yet that's exactly what I'm doing.

"You got the Midas touch," says my publicist. "That 'Fire and Desire' you did with Teena Marie is the bomb."

Teena's my protégée, a deeply soulful white girl with a voice big enough to scare off the baddest sista. Teena's become a star.

"Your star's so bright right now," says a friend, "all you gotta do is shine your light—shine it on anyone—and you create another star."

"You're the one keeping the lights on at Motown," says my business manager, referring to the label where I've been recording since 1977. "You're the whole fuckin' franchise, baby."

I'm rolling up these compliments and smoking 'em like joints. I'm snorting 'em like they're blow. The compliments are getting me higher than the actual weed and cocaine that I'm ingesting in massive quantities. On Monday I see myself as Ivan the Terrible. On Thursday I'm Alexander the Great. On Saturday I'm Napoléon Bonaparte.

The world is about to crown me emperor. I will rule. I will exceed whatever meager dreams I once had and move into the real of immortality. My funk will transform the material into the eternal, the conventional into the cosmic. The planets will resonate with these rhythms coming outta me. The universe will bounce to the beats of my Stone City Band.

I'm above earthly notions like right and wrong. I'm above the danger of human mistakes. As long as the hits keep coming—as long as I keep hitting the dope, as long as my people keep hitting me with the news of my success—I will fear no evil.

They say Jesus died when he was thirty-three. Well, I was taught to love and respect Lord Jesus. And when I was thirty-three, I worried that would be the year when I, like the Savior, would meet my worldly end.

But now I'm thirty-four. I've endured the hardships. I've paid my dues so I can spread the news. My news is all good and getting better every day.

I'm where I need to be.

I'm in charge.

I'm it.

BROTHA GURU

've met a man in Folsom State Prison who talks about the Me Monster. I call this man Brotha Guru 'cause that's what he is. If you ask him if he's a Christian or Muslim, he won't say. All he says is, "You ain't gonna define me by no category. You ain't gonna limit me to no label." Brotha Guru has darkish skin and says he's a mix of many races, including African-American. He won't specify what went into the mix except to say, "A little bit of everything." "I am," he says, "whatever you want me to be." He's short and solidly built, but he doesn't show off his muscles. At the same time, there's no ignoring two tattoos written up and down his forearms in bold black ink. The right one says ANARCHY and the left one says DISCIPLINE. Ask him what that means and he says, "I'm the meat in the middle." Ask him how he wound up doing hard time in Folsom and he says, "Following the Me Monster." Brotha Guru likes to break down the Me Monster.

"The Me Monster," he explains, "ain't hiding in no closet. He ain't lurking around the corner waiting to mug you. He's inside you. He is you. He ain't all of you but he wants you to think he is. He wants you to think he's the only thing that makes it safe for you to walk through the world. He telling you that the bigger he gets, the more food you feed him, the safer you are. But that's a lie. He ain't taking care of you at all. And even though he's acting like he's your champion—your cheerleader, your biggest fan—he's really your murderer. The Me Monster wants to see you dead."

"You really think my ego wants to kill me?" I ask.

"Shrinks call it self-destructive behavior," says Brotha Guru. "I just call it what it really is—suicide."

I scratch my head. I'm not sure I agree.

"You're a smart motherfucker," Brotha Guru tells me. "But I'm guessing that you're too smart for your own good. I'm guessing no one could ever tell you shit. You had all the answers. Hell, you wouldn't even be listening to me if you weren't behind bars. Took these bars to convince you that your shit stinks like everyone else's. I suggest you start listening to someone besides the Me Monster."

"I'm listening to you, Brotha Guru."

"That's all I got to say today. If you wanna meet in the yard tomorrow we can get talk more. I wouldn't mind hearing more about your life. Have you started that book you been talking about?"

"I have."

"How much you written?"

"First few chapters."

"They any good?"

"You tell me. I'll start reading 'em to you tomorrow."

GOOD ROCKIN'

The excitement of the music was always there. It was there in Mom's records. It was there when I heard the voices in the dark night coming off those records—Dakota Staton talking about the "late, late show," Billie Holiday looking for her "lover man"—but the excitement got all over me on the night that Mom took me on her numbers run.

Mom was sweeter than sugar and the light of my life. I never have or will love anyone more. She was also smart as a whip. She had to be. She had to house and feed eight kids on her own. That's why she worked as a cleaning lady by day and ran numbers by night. She kept her two day jobs because they were a good cover for her gig for the Italian Mafia, the major crime force in our hometown of Buffalo, New York. As a numbers runner, she didn't make big bread, but enough steady bread to keep us from starving. She had twinkling eyes and a loving nature. She cared for her children like a mama bear cares for her cubs. Don't even think about messin' with any of her kids.

And even though she was tiny in stature and had this little overbite that could make her look naïve and harmless, she was neither of those things. Mom was one of the toughest ladies in iron-tough Buffalo.

Because my dad had walked out, Mom was all I had. So naturally I wanted to be with her every minute of every day. When she asked me on a Saturday if I wanted to come with her, my little heart started beating like crazy. I practically started to cry, "Yes! Yes! Yes!"

"Just keep quiet," she said, "and do what I say."

"Yes, ma'am."

It was one of those freezing Buffalo nights, with snow falling heavy and fierce wind howling off Lake Erie. Mom had me bundled up in wool. I slipped twice on the ice. The bitter cold had me shivering. When we reached the nightclub, Mom had me hide inside her big overcoat. I loved that. I felt so protected, so secure. Once inside the door, I loved feeling the heat of the room with the chatter of the people and the clanging of glasses and musicians warming up their instruments. In a back room, Mom took off her coat and then showed me where I could hide under a table behind the bandstand. "Stay here until I come for you," she said.

I stayed. I watched. My ears blew up. My eyes popped out. I was so excited I nearly peed my pants. I was so happy I nearly started screaming. I couldn't contain myself.

"Star time!" said the emcee, a tall fat cat with slicked-back hair, lime-green suit, banana-yellow shirt, skinny black tie, and pointy-toe mirror-shined alligator shoes. "This little lady is tearing up the country from coast to coast with hits like 'Roll with Me, Henry' and her latest, 'Good Rockin' Daddy.' All the way from Hollywood, California, let's meet and greet the hottest star on the scene, she's bad and she's mean, ladies and gentleman, bring her out with a big Buffalo round of applause, for your viewing and dancing pleasure, Miss Etta James and the Peaches!"

Etta James came out in a fishtail sequin-sparkle gold dress. She had a blond wig on her head. Her skin was light and her body was buxom. She wore purple eye shadow and long eyelashes. I thought she was beautiful. One Peach was to her left, the other to her right. They were dark-skinned ladies in black dresses with wide smiles. I also thought they were beautiful. It was all a vision of beauty like I had never seen before. And then when Etta started singing, the vision became an epiphany.

Her voice had a growl that I felt deep inside my body, in my stomach, under my skin, up and down my spine. It wasn't that her voice was strange. I recognized it as the voice of my mother and a hundred women I had known growing up. It was the familiar voice of my neighborhood. But because she took that voice—that raw, honest, supercharged voice of real ordinary life—and put it to music, I saw the ordinary world turn exciting and new. It was that moment in *The Wizard of Oz* when Dorothy leaves black-and-white Kansas and goes to Technicolor Oz. Etta James took me to Oz. Crouched under that table, taking in her every move, relishing her every note, I discovered an excitement that I had to possess, an excitement that would change everything about me, drive my life, and turn me upside down.

I also saw something else that would forever shape the boy who became the man who became the artist himself. I saw that music— the power of Etta's voice—made everyone happy. I saw that the music made everyone want to drink and smoke. And the drinking and smoking—the beer and wine, the cigarettes and the reefer— were all part of the music, part of that other world that Mom was showing me.

Mom moved through that world with grace and style. That's one of the reasons I loved her so much. She wasn't afraid of that world. She worked in that world. She carried those betting slips from customer to customer, she did her job of working the underground lottery for the underworld bosses with the same slick efficiency as when she ironed our clothes or fixed our fried eggs for breakfast.

"You liked the music?" she asked me when she was through making the rounds and ready to move out of the club.

I was so happy I couldn't even speak.

"I see it in your eyes," said Mom. "Your eyes are smiling."

When Mom saw how deeply the music penetrated my soul, she made a habit of taking me with her when she had to run numbers at the nightclubs. I got to know the Royal Arms, the Pine Grill, and the Bon Ton.

In those days Buffalo was still alive. The Bethlehem Steel mill was going 24/7. There were jobs in the black community. There was action. There was music. And not just rhythm and blues. There was jazz, sophisticated modern jazz, that Mom heard and loved. She gave that love to me. She'd sneak me into clubs to hear Miles Davis when John Coltrane was his sideman. I got to hear Wes Montgomery play guitar and Jimmy Smith rip up the Hammond B3 organ. I got to hear cats like big-baritone Arthur Prysock sing "Misty" and doo-woppers like the Moonglows sing "Sincerely."

Before I turned ten, I knew where I wanted to live—in those clubs—and I knew what I wanted to do—make that music. Outside the music, the world was boring. But inside the music, the world was magic. Mom had brought me inside, and inside was where I was determined to stay.

◆

Don't know why my daddy decided not to stay with us. My memories of the man are cloudy. I see him as a handsome dude. He liked to boast that he had Indian blood running through his veins. At night he'd slip a woman's stocking over his head to keep his process in place. Sometimes he and Mom would go out at night. When they came back, she'd be crying. He didn't like to hear her crying, so he beat her. Seeing him slap around my mother, sometimes even punch her with his closed fist, got me crying and swearing that the minute I got big enough I'd grab a butcher's knife and slit his throat. The happiest moment of my childhood came when he left and never returned. Mom never mentioned him again—not for the rest of her life.

Strange to think that he gave me his name—and nothing else.

I was born James Ambrose Johnson Jr. on February 1, 1948, the third of eight kids. Brother Carmen came first, then sister Camille. Mom was only thirteen when she had Carmen with a man we never met. Camille also had a different dad than us six younger kids. His name was Homer, a half-white, half-black dude, a serious drunk who, when Mom kicked him out, got deep into drugs and disappeared down the back alleys of Buffalo.

I was third born. Then came Roy, Cheryl, Alberta, William, and Penny. We were cramped into a small apartment in the Willert Park projects for low-income/no-income families. Mom kept the place spotless. She also made sure we went to church. She thought the Catholic church would put us in a higher stratum of society. And if we joined the church, we'd get to go to Catholic schools that were, in Mom's view, better than the public schools. I understand Mom's thinking: she wanted to advance her children. Just as she was willing to run numbers to keep us in food and clothing, she was willing to bypass the Pentecostal churches where she was raised to put us in a religious setting she saw as more cultured. She also liked how the priests and nuns were strict, just as she had to be strict with us.

Like most kids, I hated strict. I was naturally wild, and it took a lot to keep me in check. That was sister Camille's job. Because Mom was either out on her day gig or running numbers at night, Camille was the enforcer. Sister was small but strong as an ox. She didn't mind using muscle to keep us in line. There was always a line of boys looking to make it with Camille, a sexy lady with good hair. In the ghetto good hair meant waves, not kinks.

My own kinky nature was there early. For all I know it was there at birth. Maybe Mom saw it and thought by putting me in Catholic school the nuns could cure me. For a while I walked the straight and narrow and even became an altar boy. That didn't last long. The streets were calling and so were older girls. I was nine or ten when Nancy, a fourteen-year-old girl, called me down to a basement in an abandoned building. She was the teacher, and boy, was I the eager student! I learned my anatomy lesson in a hurry. She was quick to show me how the parts fit together. I didn't understand ejaculation, and just before coming I pulled out and ran to the bathroom. I thought I was about to piss.

"Hell, no!" she said. "Get back over here. You ain't through."

I did what I was told. Her screaming got me a little scared until I saw it wasn't pain screaming, it was pleasure. Can't say that I experienced that much pleasure. It was more like an initiation rite. Nancy invited me back down several times, and each time, intrigued by the phenomenon of inserting myself into a girl, I became better at pleasing her and, in due course, pleasing myself. As a preteen, I was well on my way to becoming a man—at least in the fine art of fucking.

Fantasies and fucking went together. The more I fucked Nancy, the more I imagined I was fucking someone else—say, a woman in her twenties with a wide booty and big titties. The nuns at school saw me looking over the girls. They saw my lascivious nature and tried to scare me.

"Sex is for older people," said one of the nuns when she caught me playing with myself behind the playground. "Sex is for married people. God doesn't like it when kids touch themselves and think about sex. Those thoughts disrespect God and his son Jesus Christ. Do you understand?"

"Yes," I said.

"Do you believe me?"

"Yes," I lied.

"Are you going to do it again?"

"No," I lied again.

"Good," she said, "but to make sure you don't here's something to remind you."

With that, she took a ruler and whacked my hand.

That night in bed I touched myself again, thinking about what it would be like if the nun was wearing nothing under her habit.

My own bad habits got worse—talking back in class, cracking jokes, never bothering to do my homework. I was a quick learner, though, and one of the priests, Brother Timothy, took an interest in me.

"You have an exceptional mind, James," he said. "But you lack discipline."

"What's discipline?" I asked.

"Making yourself do things you don't want to do."

"Well," I said, "I don't want to do discipline."

"That's just the point. Without discipline, there's no achievement."

"What's achievement?"

"Getting things done. Finding a way through the world."

"Making money?"

"Yes."

"My mom makes money."

"She has discipline. She's a hard worker."

"She's good at math. She can add up figures in her head. She never forgets a number."

I was about to tell the priest that of all the number runners in our neighborhood, Mom got the most respect from the Mafia because she never made mistakes. Better sense, though, told me that the priest didn't need to hear those details.

"One of the beautiful things about the Catholic Church," said the priest, "is our confession. Through confession we can purge ourselves of bad deeds and thoughts. With a clear mind, discipline is much easier to attain. Have you been to confession, James?"

"Not yet. I don't know what to confess."

"Everything you've done wrong."

"And that'll make it easier for me at school?"

"A million times easier," the priest assured me.

"And I can say anything?"

"Anything, son, and God will forgive you."

I liked that idea. I went to confession, where I told the priest the truth. I told the priest that I'd been drinking wine out of the tabernacle and thinking about putting my prick inside the nuns. Next thing I knew I was kicked out of school.

"What happened?" Mom asked me.

"I did what I was told. I confessed."

"That wasn't a good idea," she said. "Certain things no one needs to know about."

The mixed message: the church says tell it all; Mom says keep it on the down-low. Now I understand. Now I see that the church was thinking about the soul and how it needs to be free of sin. Mom was a practical lady who had to stay free of the law. As a kid, though, the disagreement between my mother and the church was unsettling. Rather than let the confusion linger, I took Mom's advice to heart. She was feeding me. The church wasn't.

If I had crazy thoughts, I would keep them hidden. If I did crazy things, no one had to know. If sex was on my mind more than it should have been for a preteen, well, that was my business and no one else's. If Nancy kept calling me down the basement, where I had learned the right rhythm of riding her to a frenzy, I wasn't about to tell a soul.

Mom showed me how to deal with the world on the world's terms. She knew who to approach and who to avoid. She was savvy, a quality I learned to appreciate early on. Her numbers running had gotten so good she saved enough to get us out of the low-rent projects. I was still a preteen when she told us we could say good-bye to funky town. We were heading over the Swan Street Bridge to a classier situation, the Perry Projects, where the apartments were not only bigger and cleaner, but where everyone was white as the first snowfall of winter.

HOUND DOG

The white/black tension in American life and American music all came down on me around the time we moved to the Perry Projects.

Mom had this 45 rpm record that had a red label with a picture of a peacock. She played it all the time and everyone in our household loved it, me more than anyone. The singer was Big Mama Thornton, whose voice was like Etta James's—big, brash, and sexy—and the song was "Hound Dog." I loved the lyrics that said, "You ain't nothing but a hound dog crying all the time." I wasn't even sure what they meant. They sounded so good coming out Big Mama's mouth.

Then one day we were watching our little black-and-white TV and there was this white boy called Elvis Presley, with slicked-back hair and a sneer on his face, singing the same song. I couldn't quite figure out who he wanted to be. He looked a little bit like a juvenile delinquent, but he was also trying to sound black.

"How come they don't have Big Mama singing this song on TV?" I asked my mother.

"'Cause Elvis is the most popular thing since sliced white bread."

"What's so good about him?"

"The girls like him. He's pretty, and he don't mind shaking his booty."

"Won't he get in trouble for stealing this song from Big Mama?"

"Anyone can sing anything they like."

"Well, I can sing as good as that guy," I said.

Mom laughed, "I bet you can. I bet you will. I want you to."

"And then will they put me on TV instead of him?"

"By the time you grow up, maybe they will."

When I started public junior high, I saw a lot of guys who looked like Elvis. They had the slicked-back hair and the sneer on their lips. They were the guys who were quick to call me nigger. They were the guys who made me realize that, although Mom wanted to give us the advantages of living in the white world, the white world didn't want us.

My main running partner was my brother Roy. He and I were the only blacks in school. The white gangs chased us home every day. If we weren't so fast, we wouldn't have made it. Every day it felt like we were running for our lives. Same thing was true with Camille— only she didn't run. She stopped and fought. She'd fuck up anyone who called her a nigger.

One day Mom happened to be home when me and Roy came running in. She looked out the window and saw the white gang. She grabbed us both, opened the door, and told the boys who'd been chasing us, "Ain't no harm in fighting—long as you do it fair and square. Which of you two boys wanna fight my sons?" Two guys jumped out. "Fine," said Mom. "Go at it."

Maybe it was because Mom was looking. Maybe her confidence

filtered down into us. Whatever the reason, Roy and I had no problem kicking their asses. We beat them into bloody submission while
Mom beamed with pride.

That didn't solve the problem, though. It wasn't just the
greased-up Elvis Presley/James Dean–looking thugs at school who
came after us. It was our neighbors as well. Like Boston, Buffalo is a
black-hating racist city.

Every week someone would lob a rock through our front window
or burn a cross in the little patch of grass in front of our apartment.
We were scared. We wanted to move back to the old projects and be
with black people. We wanted to be with our own. We begged Mom
to get us out of there.

"No way," she said. "We deserve to be here. It's our right. No
one's gonna drive us outta our house. We staying."

"Why?" I kept asking.

"Because I worked damn hard for this place, and the law is on
my side. Law says long as we got the money—and we do—we can
live damn well anywhere we please."

Our neighbors and schoolmates didn't see it that way. They
thought we were invading their territory, and they weren't going to
have it. When Camille came out the corner grocery store holding
big bags of food, a motorcycle gang was waiting for her. Their leader
was a muscle head called Toby. He gave his boys the high sign, and,
just like that, they started knocking over Camille and stomping on
her food. There were too many of them for her to fight. When Mom
heard the story, she grabbed a long kitchen knife and headed down
to the grocery store. The gang was still there.

"Touch one of my kids again," Mom told Toby, "and I'll put
this knife through your heart. I'll go after you and every one of you
motherfuckers—and I won't be alone."

The look on Mom's face and the tone of Mom's voice stopped

the boys in their tracks. They knew it was best to keep their mouths shut. That night when I heard her call my older brother, Carmen, I knew it was on.

Carmen was fierce. He'd just gotten out of prison for the third time. I didn't know all the reasons he'd been sent to jail, but I assumed they involved violence. Carmen was a violent man. He was short, five foot seven or eight, but built of steel. His dark brown eyes looked right through you. When Roy and I were misbehaving beyond normal amounts, Mom would threaten to call Carmen. He was her enforcer. A beating from Mom was one thing—the cord from her iron hurt like hell—but a beating from Carmen was something else. He used his fists.

When I asked Mom the details of whether Carmen would go after Toby, I never got a straight answer.

"You go on and mind your business, son," said Mom. "That's something you don't need to worry about."

Roy and I talked about it all the time. A few days passed, and then a few weeks.

"Wonder when Carmen's getting here," said Roy.

"Wonder what's gonna happen when he does show up," I said.

We didn't have to wonder for long. One night I was asleep in the bed that I shared with Roy when I heard this commotion outside.

"Fuck you, you nigger!"

"Fuck you, you punk-ass cracker!"

I ran to the window. The streetlights had been shot out and it was too dark to make sense of what was happening. Clearly, though, a blow-to-blow struggle was under way. I started to run out and see for myself, but Mom was blocking the door.

"Get back in your room," she said. "Carmen's taking care of this."

Not many minutes later I heard the door and saw Carmen walk in. He was with a prison-mate friend and a third man who I hadn't seen in years—my father. The three of them had some bruises and bloody knuckles.

"You take care of business?" Mom asked Carmen.

Carmen was quick to answer. "Toby and them ain't ever gonna bother you again."

And they never did. Word went out that the Johnson gang was the baddest in Buffalo. Toby and his boys were in the hospital for a month. And when they finally got out, they never said another word to us. "Nigger" was no longer in their vocabulary.

Funny, though, that Mom, who hated the word "nigger" when white people used it against us, used it herself when she'd punish me. If I got caught stealing or telling a lie, she'd put me over her knee, whip out that iron cord, and let me have it, all the time saying, "Little nigga, you ain't ever gonna do that again, are you?"

"No, ma'am," I'd cry. "Never ever."

With Mom said "nigga," even though she was about to whip me, she used it with love. When Toby said "nigger," even though he was also looking to put a beating on me, he said it with hatred. Mom wanted to hurt me so I wouldn't be bad again. Toby wanted to kill me so I'd be dead.

When Carmen took care of Toby, a good feeling washed all over me. I lived through Carmen just as I lived through Mom. They were both tough characters who walked through the world without fear. They were both fighters, and they were my family. Carmen taught me and Roy how to box. We both proved to be fierce fighters. Carmen also taught us how to wield a switchblade. "Don't matter how you win a fight," said Carmen, "long as you win."

Mom bought a ten-speed bike for me and Roy to share. "Don't go off without the other," she said. "Make sure you got each other's back."

I'd ride while Roy walked or ran beside me—then vice versa.

We had our game down tight. Then came the day when, instead of sharing the bike with Roy, I decided to go bounce on Nancy down in the basement. Roy didn't mind. He had the ten-speed all to himself. When he didn't come home, though, we all started to worry.

"Where's your brother?" asked Mom.

"Out riding."

"Why ain't you riding with him?"

"I was too tired," I lied.

Then came the call from the hospital. An ice cream truck ran a red light and smashed head-on into Roy, dragging him for blocks.

"Is my baby gonna die?" Mom asked the doctor when we all rushed over to the hospital.

"It's gonna be close."

Our family huddled together in prayer. The prayer was answered. Roy was spared, but remained in the hospital for two months. For two years he had to wear a cast that covered both his legs up to his waist. Mom became his nurse. In spite of her day job cleaning houses and her night job running numbers, she found time to care for him. Whenever she wasn't working, she was with Roy. I felt like I had lost her. I also felt like she blamed me for the accident. Why hadn't I been there? If I had, maybe I could have pushed Roy out of the way. Maybe I could have prevented the whole thing. Naturally I never told Mom the truth—that I was too busy fucking Nancy to worry about Roy—but I detected that Mom had guessed the truth. She didn't come out and accuse me of anything, but I felt a strange vibe. I felt a distance between me and Mom that was never there before. And rather than try to decrease that distance and move closer to her, I went the other away. I widened the gap. Rather than subject myself to what felt like Mom's scorn, I avoided Mom altogether.

I got bitter. I thought back to those times when Mom took me to the nightclubs and I'd get to play drums during the breaks. I had natural talent for percussion. The grown-up party people would gather round me and dance, applaud, and sing my praises. Mom would beam with pride.

"My boy's special," she'd say. "My boy's got him some genius talent."

After Roy's accident, though, Mom didn't offer to take me to the clubs. Those private nights between me and Mom were over. Roy was the one who got all her private time.

I tried to focus on school but couldn't. The teachers kept telling me I was smart, but no one knew how to handle my reading problem. No one knew how to get me to pay attention to words on the page or numbers on the blackboard. I was good at all the sports—I was a scrappy YMCA boxer and got a reputation as a tough brawler—but I was never the best athlete. If I couldn't be the best, I'd rather play. My best friend became music. In music I was easily the best. I could sing in a deep rich voice, sounding older than I was. I could pick out harmony notes and give them to the other guys who liked to sing doo-wop with me. I could pick up a guitar and, just by instinct, play a blues riff by B. B. King or a rhythm riff by Bo Diddley.

When I came home to show Mom what I had learned, she said, "Later, son, I got to tend to Roy tonight."

Well, I had my own affairs to tend to. I had turned thirteen and had me more than one girl. I'd put the lessons that Nancy taught me to good use. A lot of the older girls—ones who were seniors in high school—got the idea that I had special talents. One of the nastier girls—I'll call her Charlene—had a body that wouldn't quit. She was known for giving it up easily and quickly. One day at school, she whispered in my ear, "I hear you a pussy pleaser. Is that right?"

Before I could answer yes, my dick was already hard. That night, in the backseat of an abandoned car on the outskirts of the city, my dick was deep inside her.

"For a kid," she said, "you know how to last long."

"I ain't no kid," I said. And to prove it I went back for seconds, lasting even longer than the first time.

When Charlene told her best friend, Brenda, about my prowess, Brenda made her wishes known to me. Brenda was an only child who lived alone with her mother, and her mother was gone for the weekend.

Brenda liked it from behind. Did I know how to do it that way?

"This way, that way," I said. "All ways are my ways."

From then on, I called her Backdoor Brenda.

I got busy in a hurry. Pleasing girls was good work. Pleasing girls was a lot more satisfying than schoolwork. Even on those occasions when I made a good grade or wrote a report praised by my teacher, Mom was too preoccupied with Roy to acknowledge me. So I found ways to get that acknowledgment from other females.

One Friday night I was with a girl who kept me busy till the wee small hours. After our marathon, I fell asleep and didn't wake up till ten A.M. I'd never been out all night before. I thought Mom would kill me. But when I got home, Mom was feeding Roy. She didn't bother to look up and say hello. She hadn't even noticed that I'd been out all night. That crushed me. That also got me to thinking that she didn't even care. And if that was the case I could go on and do whatever the hell I wanted to do. I could steal some money out of her purse and hop a Greyhound to New York City.

CHASIN' THE TRANE

The Greyhound was cheap. The ride was long. I was bored to death. With all the stops, it took from ten in the morning to ten at night for the bus to make its way from Buffalo to the New York City Port Authority Terminal on Forty-Second Street. When I got out, the energy hit me hard. The lights were blazing. The city was alive. The city was screaming. I started walking faster than I usually walk. I started thinking faster than I usually think. I remembered one of my girlfriends telling me that Greenwich Village was the spot for jazz. I asked a brotha which way to Greenwich Village. He pointed to the subway. I bought a token and a half hour later was standing in front of the Village Vanguard. JOHN COLTRANE APPEARING TONIGHT. Great, but how do I get in? The line is long and the admission is high.

All my time with Mom had taught me how to slip into clubs without being noticed. I waited till there was a little discussion at the door between the ticket taker and a ticket holder. When the ticket taker was distracted, I slipped under the rope and stood by the kitchen door. There were a few empty seats. I chose one back in the dark shadows. It was a small club so it didn't matter where I sat. I was in. I was four hundred miles away from home. I was about to hear John Coltrane tell the good news.

I'd heard Coltrane back in Buffalo when he was still with Miles. But this was the newly liberated Coltrane, Coltrane the leader, the Coltrane of *Giant Steps* and *My Favorite Things*, the Coltrane that all the hip cats in Buffalo had been listening to night and day. Among them all, I'd be the first to say I'd seen that Coltrane live and in person at the Village Vanguard. I was in a privileged position, and I damn well knew it.

I remember the name of every man on the stage. I studied each musician like a jeweler studies a watch. McCoy Tyner was the pianist. Reggie Workman played the upright bass. Eric Dolphy blew the bass clarinet, an instrument I had never seen before. Elvin Jones changed forever the way I viewed the drums. He gave the drums a voice—like the drum was a trumpet or saxophone. All these men were masters who understood they were there to serve their master, John Coltrane.

Trane switched back and forth from soprano to tenor sax. On his soprano, his voice was high and crying. On tenor, his voice was manly and moaning. He didn't say a word to the audience except to introduce a song. "This is 'Spiritual,'" was all he said. He did all the explaining with his instrument. It wasn't a regular song that lasted three or four minutes. It seemed to last thirty. Trane seemed to go on a journey, like the journey I took from Buffalo to Greenwich Village. He kept on riding, kept on looking out the window, kept on describing everything he saw. Except the window was a window into his own mind. I felt like he was opening up his mind for me to see inside. And his mind was filled with ideas. One idea led to another. The gears were in motion and meshed together. I understood how his mind was working 'cause mine worked the same way. It was a spirit that was moving him. That's why the song was called "Spiritual." That spirit was moving me. That spirit had finally let me focus on something for a long time without getting restless or bored. I could see where I could ride that spirit all the way to the end of the line.

The line called the A train led me to Harlem and the Apollo Theater, which had haunted my imagination ever since Mom started bringing home *Jet* magazines with pictures of the stars posed in front of its big marquee on 125th Street. When the Coltrane set ended, I ran up to catch the last show at the Apollo. The big star was Jackie Wilson. If Trane was heaven in the sky, Jackie was heaven on earth. He was down-to-earth, down to where women got wet just watching him move his hips and do his splits. Jackie Wilson made Elvis look like Howdy Doody. The Jackie Wilson I saw that night at the Apollo was prime Jackie Wilson, "Lonely Teardrops" and "To Be Loved" Jackie Wilson, the Jackie Wilson of "Talk That Talk" and "Doggin' Around," the Jackie Wilson who, when he asked the audience, "Am I the man?" had a sista screaming, "Yes, Daddy! Hell, yes! You all the man I need!"

During my trip to the Vanguard and the Apollo, I had me an epiphany. Brotha, I had me a vision. I wanted John Coltrane's sacred spirit and Jackie Wilson's sexual energy. I wanted Trane's imagination and Jackie's syncopation. I wanted to be honored like Trane as a great artist and be worshipped like Jackie as a great lover. I wanted it all.

"What you gonna get," said Mom when I came back to Buffalo late the next day, "is a whipping like you never got before."

The whipping was serious, but the trip was worth it. I had been in the presence of genius. The standards had been set. Now I was on the move. Every few weeks I'd scrounge up some money to hop the bus back to New York. I needed to hear Art Blakey and the Jazz Messengers do "Moanin'" at Birdland and see Chubby Checker doing "The Twist" at the Peppermint Lounge. The pattern set in: I'd come home, get a beating from Mom, then go back out again. Finally, she had enough. She sent the cops after me. They found me hiding in the tiny bathroom in the back of the Buffalo Greyhound station and hauled me off to a juvenile delinquent home. Mom came to visit.

"Why?" was the first thing she asked. "Why you always running, son?"

"I don't know," I said. "I get antsy. I need to get out and see the world. There's music I need to hear."

"There's music in Buffalo."

"Not like New York."

"But your family's in Buffalo. Your family's all you got. You know that, don't you?"

"Yes, I do."

"And you know I love you."

"I know that too, Mom."

"Then stop all this nonsense before something real bad happens."

I stayed quiet.

"Did you hear me, James?"

"I heard you, Mom."

"And you'll listen to me?"

"I will."

I didn't. I got into deeper devilment. I started running with one of the gangs at school. I did that because the danger excited me. I did that to show the tough guys that I wasn't scared of nothing.

It was all about action and music. I didn't have an instrument to play so I took Mom's broom and strummed it like a guitar until all the straw fell out on the kitchen floor. When Mom saw what I had done, she broke out the iron cord. Another whipping. I took that anger and put it into a gang fight. In one of those rumbles, a kid got shot. I wasn't the shooter, but, along with three others, I was arrested and spent three months back in the juvie. When I got out, Mom was so furious she went for the iron cord again. But by then I was too old for a beating and far stronger than her. I caught her hand and held it. This look of bewilderment came over her eyes. Then came the tears. I couldn't stand seeing Mom cry. But tears or no tears, that woman wasn't going to beat me again.

The mood of our household—reflecting the mood of my mother—went from low to high in a New York minute.

"Guess what, baby?" she said one Sunday when she and her boyfriend, Al Gladden, came out of her bedroom.

"What?"

"Me and Al are getting married. Ain't that wonderful?"

I didn't know what to say. I felt like I was losing my mother to another man. At the same time, I'd been noticing that the more she was with Al back there in her bedroom, the less angry she was with me. Al helped her moods. Al also got her pregnant and got me a little baby sister, Penny. Penny brought joy to the family—she was everybody's baby doll—and Al brought us to our first real house with a front and back yard. It was on Ferry Street, in a better black hood than we were used to. The only drawback was that Al's mama, daddy, brother, and sister lived on the second floor. Each of them weighed at least three hundred pounds. It was like living under elephants. Every time they took a step, the ceiling shook like it was about to cave in. They were also Holy Roller Christians who looked down at us as sinners. Mom's marriage was working out—except for his heavy drinking, Al was a cool guy—but the living arrangement was all wrong. I was still looking to escape.

Other than my gang exploits, my big escape was music. At Bennett High, I was a decent jock but I could never compete with someone like Bob Lanier, the star of our basketball team, who'd go on to NBA glory with the Detroit Pistons. In music, though, I figured I could compete with anyone, even the great John Coltrane. I just needed a sax of my own. But Mr. Hillard, our music teacher, said all the saxes were taken. So I went to a set of drums and started banging away. I must have been playing for ten minutes before Mr. Hillard came over and said, "Not bad, James. Where'd you learn to play?"

"Taught myself."

"Let me hear you do a double paradiddle."

"A double what?"

"It's an essential drum rudiment. You have to learn the rudiments."

"Why? I can already knock out a killer groove."

"Strong rhythm is essential, but it isn't everything."

"Well, I wanna know everything."

"Then stick around, James."

I tried but couldn't stick around for long. Mr. Hillard, a Juilliard graduate, had a lot of information that went over my head. Even the words he used—like "polyrhythms" and "complex time signature"—got my head to swimming. I didn't have the patience to learn out of a book. I didn't want to spend my time exercising the muscles in my fingers. I just wanted to groove!

Mr. Hillard and I went back and forth. He said the groove wasn't enough. I said the groove was the magic: that's why Trane could keep riffing for a half hour on the same song. Elvin Jones's groove locked him in. Same thing with James Brown. His grooves were monsters. I was also deep into the Latin grooves of Mongo Santamaria and Willie Bobo.

The midsixties, my teen years, was the time that Motown, just across Lake Erie from Buffalo, was grooving like a motherfucker. Those huge hits by the Supremes, the Four Tops, the Temptations, the Miracles, Martha and the Vandellas, and Marvin Gaye came out of the great grooves of a rhythm section that I later learned was anchored by bassist James Jamerson and drummer Benny Benjamin, cats called the Funk Brothers. I knew I was a natural-born funk brother and didn't need no book learning to prove it.

Mr. Hillard was a good guy who put up with my arrogance as best he could. Hard as he tried, though, he couldn't get me to study. I might have eventually listened to him were it not for a decision I made during my sophomore year at Bennett. I entered the talent contest. I was nervous as hell, so scared that the night of the show I had to run to the bathroom and throw up. But I was also confident enough to face an auditorium filled with all my teachers, friends, and family. The world was watching me.

My plan was to kill the crowd by keeping it simple. I went on-stage with nothing but a drum and a couple of sticks. I set a funk beat and stayed on it a long time before opening my mouth. The groove, accented by rim shots, got the crowd going. Every crowd loves a groove. I decided to sing a song everyone knew—Stevie Wonder's "Fingertips." That number has a bongo beat of its own, but I added to that beat—I put my own hurting on it—and gave it a new edge. "Fingertips" is a sing-along-type song, making it easy for me to get the crowd going. It was easy to get them on their feet and shouting, it was easy to get them up dancing in the aisles, easy to get them to make me sing the song a second and third time. Took the principal ten minutes to calm them down. I walked off with first prize, and musically speaking, no one could tell me nothing. Sorry, Mr. Hillard, you're a cool guy, but I won't be needing those books of yours. I can make the world dance without 'em.

Came to find out that singing onstage made the girls love me more. After my victory, they were coming after me like moths to the flame. Beautiful butterflies were fluttering around me. From the minute I became a little jive-ass star in high school, it was never enough to have one. Sure, I liked the blue butterfly, but the yellow one was cool and the orange one even cooler. They were all so pretty that I had to have me a collection. And naturally the cats I ran with had to know about my collection. In their eyes, that made me a bigger man. The bigger my collection, the more time I spent studying their beauty. I skipped a lot of school until Bennett kicked me out.

Welcome to East High, notorious for its juvenile delinquents. I fit right in until I got kicked right out. While I was there, though, I took on another challenge. East had an all-black marching band called the Brown Cadet Corps with riflemen, bugle blowers, and long-legged majorettes. I wanted to see whether I could cut it as a drummer in the corps. I also wanted to wear the super-sharp uniforms—this unit was cleaner than the Board of Health—as well as score some of that juicy majorette pussy. Proud to report that I accomplished both my goals: Marching around the football fields of Western New York, I didn't drop a beat. And diving into those majorettes, I got me the honey I'd been dreaming of.

East High let me go. My lousy grades, poor attendance, and disrespectful manners with the teachers—who I saw as stuffed shirts and old maids—were too much. I was too bad even for the bad-boy school.

Grover Cleveland was my third and last-stop high school. It was a mix of Italian and chocolate, and the tension was high. They called us niggers and we called them guineas. It wasn't exactly a level playing field because a couple of the guineas had fathers in the mob. That meant our fighting equipment—mainly switchblades and baseball bats stolen from the gym—didn't have a chance against the serious handguns holstered under their leather jackets. When Mom caught wind of the coming wars between the black and Italian gangs, she pulled me out of that school before I could quit. She may have saved my life. Two weeks after I was gone there was a nasty rumble where one of my partners got shot through the heart.

My school history came to a screeching halt. I told myself that I'd never have to see the insides of a classroom again—and I was glad. But I was also without a clue. No school, no job, no future.

Sixteen-year-old black boy running the snowy streets of Buffalo, looking to break out.

But what does he make of the world around him? Barry Goldwater is running for president against Lyndon Johnson. The Vietnam War is firing up and the draft is on. Civil rights legislation is being passed and Martin Luther King is in the news, but the hipper cats on the corner are talking about Malcolm X.

Where do I go?

What do I do?

How in hell am I ever gonna get over?

THE CULTURE

We finally got out from under the Gladdens and moved down the street to another house on Ferry. Roy had healed up and turned into an honor student. Carmen had fucked up and was back in prison. Camille had two babies and was living over a fish store with her old man. Cheryl, Alberta, and Penny were growing by leaps and bounds. Brother William was almost tall as me.

I was out on the streets, picking up part-time jobs but mainly gangbanging. The big race riots didn't happen till 1967, but when I was fifteen in 1963 the rumblings had begun. There was an incident on the East Side where some brothas broke into a big electronics store and started looting. Me and my partners followed them and ran out with a big-ass stereo that we dropped off at my house. We went back for seconds and hauled off three TVs. Next day we pawned off the merchandise for enough money to buy a summer's worth of weed.

"Smoking all that weed is turning you into a full-fledged knucklehead," said Malcolm Erni, a black minister who knew Mom 'cause he liked to the play the numbers.

"Weed makes me creative," I said. "It stimulates my mind."

"Weed makes you horny," he said. "It stimulates your dick."

I couldn't argue. My stash of girlfriends was up to four—my all-time high.

"Do something useful with your mind," said Malcolm. "Learn your culture."

"What's that?" I asked.

"Books, literature, politics, history. The black culture is a beautiful culture. Did you know that Jesus was black? Before Jesus, black people's roots go back to the Twelve Tribes of Israel. Then there's the Nubian culture, one of the most ancient and brilliant cultures the world has ever known. A black culture. A deep culture. A culture you need to learn about."

Malcolm spoke with authority. Because I'd never really known a dad, I latched on to him. I liked how he took an interest in me. I liked reading the books on African history that he gave me because it wasn't part of school. It was part of life. Malcolm would preach and teach on street corners. One day he'd talk about Israel, the next day Egypt. He could break it all down to where you understood. Mom was impressed that for the first time in my life I was actually sitting down and reading books.

I learned that black culture is old as history itself. In fact, it's the original culture. Malcolm talked about how, without knowing it, white American culture made us feel inferior. The slavery mentality continued long after emancipation. The slavery mentality gave us a complex that, if we didn't recognize it and work to eliminate it, would impoverish our lives and kill our spirit. Malcolm taught black pride, and I was his best student. I liked him because, even though he was a Christian who'd talk your ear off about Jesus all day long, he didn't disregard the militant cats angry at racist America. Like Dr. King, Malcolm was definitely a minister for nonviolence, but he understood what was happening in the minds of young black men. We were free to openly express our feelings without judgment.

I started wearing wild-colored dashikis and African jewelry. I studied Swahili. Had me one of the first Afros in Buffalo. And when Malcolm said he wanted to start an Afro center right in the middle of the hood, I was down.

An African drummer from Senegal came in and showed me some grooves on conga. I couldn't convince the cat that I didn't have Senegalese relatives. Hell, maybe I did. Amopuza Enza, a dance teacher from the Ivory Coast, showed up with her son Ty. Without a place to stay, I invited them to my house, where Mom gave them Carmen's old room. I was madly in love with Amopuza, the most exotic woman I'd ever seen. She was tall and elegant in her flowing robes. Her bone structure looked like it had been created by a great sculptor. She was in her thirties, so I gave her respect. But I still dreamed that one day she'd walk into my bedroom and introduce me to the ancient rituals of making love African-style.

Ty was a percussionist and taught me more than Mr. Hillard ever could. Ty was a motherfucker. Never have seen anyone negotiate rhythms like him. He came over with a *djembe,* a West African hand drum that he'd mastered as a little boy. I learned to play it nearly as good as he did. We'd jam for hours on end. The rhythms of the motherland poured out of me like I was a native.

The Afro Center pointed me in a positive direction. I liked the alternative feel of a culture that was both foreign and familiar. It was like learning about myself. And when Malcolm asked me if I'd help with a picnic, I pitched in, organizing the music and recruiting the girls to cook the food. We were going to start out at noon and stay till midnight. We went to a state park with a beach on Lake Erie not far from Niagara Falls.

The day was beautiful—blues skies, mild temp, the water warm enough for swimming. Must have been forty of us having the time of our lives. Malcolm led a discussion of a book he'd given us to read—*The Fire Next Time* by James Baldwin. I loved Baldwin's passion and position—that white society had done everything to make the black man feel weak and inferior.

"You're right," said Malcolm, after hearing my synopsis of Baldwin, "but he still professes a Christian love. He still calls for forgiveness. Without forgiveness, we turn bitter. While others attack us from the outside, we turn on ourselves from the inside. We self-destruct."

I didn't know it at the time, but Malcolm was describing that force that Brotha Guru would later call the Me Monster. At that same picnic, I also didn't know that this would be my last day as an active participant in the Afro Center.

By nightfall, we'd had a great time. We swam and ate and built bonfires. We played music, danced, and discussed our pasts and our futures. It was beautiful. Until everything went crazy . . .

We heard a distant scream that sounded like someone was being murdered. We jumped to our feet and looked around. Out of the bushes ran one of dancers, blood all over her face. She'd been beaten. Then came the shouts: "Get the niggers!" Men holding torches were advancing on our campfire. Me, Ty, and the other boys picked up rocks. We were ready to rumble.

"Put those rocks down," ordered Malcolm, "and get to the bus."

I wanted to stand our ground and show these crackers what we were made of. I wanted to do to them what they'd done to our sista.

"To the bus!" Malcolm yelled.

Reluctantly, I did what I was told. We made it to the bus and locked the doors. We got on the floor and covered ourselves with blankets because the crackers were smashing the windows. They were rocking the bus. We thought they were going to turn it over and set it on fire. We thought we'd be burned to death. I wasn't as scared as I was frustrated. I was dying to fight these assholes. If Mom were there, she'd have led the charge. Yet here we were, crouched down like cowards.

After a while the crackers got bored with their taunting and left. Malcolm saw this as a victory. He found a pay phone and called the police, who escorted our bus home. There was no more singing, no more lessons on black pride. Nearly all our women were crying.

I felt like I'd let them down. And I told that to Malcolm.

"I can understand how you feel," he said. "You're a young buck and you got fight in you. But fighting would have gained us nothing."

"How about our dignity?" I asked.

"Dignity don't come from winning fights. It comes from respecting yourself."

"How we gonna respect ourselves if we run from a fight?" I asked.

"The key is not to respect the fight. Animals fight. The one with the sharper teeth wins. What does that prove?"

I didn't have an answer—but I didn't need an answer. I just knew that my disposition didn't go with nonviolence. After the bus incident, I stayed away from Malcolm and the Afro Center. That's when I started getting deeper into dope.

A month after the picnic, I was on the streets and happened to see Malcolm in his Dodge Dart. He was waiting for a light on the corner of Jefferson and Genesee when he spotted me.

"Brother James! Get in. I'm buying you lunch."

I didn't really want to talk to Malcolm. I felt guilty that I'd abandoned the Afro Center. At the same time, I couldn't refuse his invitation. He'd never done anything but try to help me.

"You in the mood for Wings and Things?" he asked.

"Always."

The spicy chicken wing was invented in Buffalo. This joint made them super-hot with something they called Mambo Sauce. We sat in the back and started munching.

"Ain't been around much, have you?" asked Malcolm.

"Been busy."

"At what?"

"This and that."

"I see. Look, I know how you feel about what happened at the picnic. But I hate for that to get in the way of your cultural education. I hate to see you give up the books for the streets."

"I haven't," I lied.

"I say that because you have a glow."

"A glow?"

"Yes, sir. You have an inner glow. A light that comes from within. Everyone has a light but yours is bright, James. Yours is special. You have a mind that connects to people and ideas. You have a brain that catches on instantly to what's being said. You have sensitivity to what others are feeling. When people see your glow, they want to follow it. Your glow can illuminate others."

Malcolm Erni was a beautiful cat with a beautiful heart. At that point, though, my heart was closed. I didn't wanna know about no glow. I wanted to keep running the streets with my boys—Danny, Moses, Truly, and Bubbles. They were daredevils; they were slick; they had the hottest chicks and the best times. They were also into smack.

Heroin was said to be the king of drugs, the highest of all highs. I wasn't about to mainline the shit—I was too cautious for that—but I wasn't against chipping. I wasn't against skin-poppin'. Wasn't long before I had a scab and found myself hooked as a motherfucker.

Smack takes money. We needed funds to feed our habit and

didn't think twice about having our girlfriends break into houses, where they would steal shit to pawn. Our girlfriends bought our fixes. When one chick got caught, though, the others got scared and stopped. That meant we had to do the dirty work ourselves. That's when I got popped by the police when a home robbery went bad. I couldn't call Mom for the bail money. I knew that would anger her, so I called Malcolm. True Christian that he was, he stood up for me and got me out.

"You're on that dope, aren't you, James?"

I couldn't lie to the brother. I confessed that I had a scag jones.

"You got to go cold turkey," he said, "or you're back to stealing and thieving. Go cold turkey now before it's too late."

I knew I had to heed Malcolm's advice. I told Mom I was going to New York to visit Aunt Louella, her older sister, who lived in the Bronx. Louella lived with a trombone player and was hip to the world of drugs. Turned out she had the same approach as Malcolm.

"You strung out, James," she said. "I see it in your eyes. If you came to me for help, I'm willing, but you ain't gonna like the treatment."

"Can't I get off gradually?"

"There ain't no 'gradually' when it comes to H. You either on or off. If you want off, I'm putting you in the back bedroom and locking the door for a week."

"I'll starve to death," I said.

"I'll bring you water and soup and enough bread to keep you going, but that's it. I ain't fucking around with you, boy. I don't got the time. Only reason I'm doing this is 'cause you're my sister's son. You hear me?"

"Yes, Aunt Lou. But you won't tell Mom, will you?"

"All I'm telling your mother is that you're in New York to hear some music. She knows how much you love music."

"Thank you."

"When I lock the door to that back bedroom, you ain't gonna be thanking me no more."

Aunt Lou was right. Before long, I was cursing her and her cold-turkey cure tactics. I was going out of my head. The withdrawals were worse than I had ever imagined. Never knew pain could be so extreme. But God bless Louella, 'cause she knew what to do. Water, soup, and bread—that was it. She didn't hold my hand and she didn't wipe my brow.

"It'll pass," she said, "and then you'll be all right."

Five days of hell did pass. Aunt Lou was true to her word and didn't tell Mom what I'd been through. I took the bus back to Buffalo. I felt like a new man. The good feeling, though, didn't last long.

MICKEY MOUSE

'm glad you went to New York," said Malcolm. "Glad you got clean. You look a million times better."

"I feel better."

"You been reading about this war in Vietnam?"

"Who hasn't?"

"They sending over poor people. They sending over blacks. You don't wanna be sent over. You wanna do everything you can to keep from going. Ain't no place for a black man. Ain't our war. There's no reason to die for something we don't even understand."

"How do I get out of it?"

"Navy Reserve. That lets you finish high school, get paid, stay home, and stay outta Vietnam. It's the smart thing to do."

"Is that what you told Danny and my boys? Is that what they're doing?"

"Danny's strung out on smack so heavy until he ain't doing nothing. And Moses, well, he's even worse. He's both selling it and shooting it. Those boys ain't long for this world. Is that what you want, James? You gonna let your glow fade out like that?"

"Don't feel like I'm ready to die."

"Then don't. Play the game but avoid the war. Do the minimum and get Uncle Sam off your back."

Malcolm's advice about kicking heroin had been right on time. The man saved my life. So I had no reason to doubt the wisdom of this new course of action. A week later, I signed up for the reserve. I exaggerated my age. I said I was eighteen when I don't think I was even fifteen.

I thought I had it all together. I always thought I had it all together.

The cats who really had it all together, though, were the singing groups, the Chimes and the Chi-Lites, the Delfonics and the Dells. In Buffalo I joined the Duprees and, believe me, we had us a bad blend. We covered all the great doo-wop hits of the fifties—"Earth Angel" and "Ten Commandments of Love"—in addition to whatever the Impressions were doing in Chicago and the Contours were doing in Detroit. Beyond helping the Duprees spin out sweet harmonies, I was also an in-demand drummer for the small jazz groups popping up on the local scene. I had an Elvin Jones/Max Roach/Art Blakey attitude that gave the boppers the fiery push they needed. Doo-wop and hard bop were my twin passions.

Those passions were so all-consuming that I sometimes forgot to attend the twice-monthly reserve training sessions. The first time I went was a disaster. I was scolded because I'd sewed my stripe upside down on my uniform. I didn't give a shit. That scolding made me not want to come back—and so I didn't. Until I had to.

"You got another letter from the navy," said Mom. "I've prayed to God that it's not telling you to go to Vietnam."

"Don't worry about that," I said. "They can't make me go to no Vietnam."

What they could make me do, though, was report for active duty at the Great Lakes naval base. In punishment for missing so many reserve training sessions, I had to spend forty-five days away from home. Didn't see it as any big deal. Except that it was.

Great Lakes was no-nonsense discipline, and I hated it. I hated getting my hair shaved off. My Afro was my pride and to have the fuckin' navy cut it down was humiliating. I hated the calisthenics, the marching, the loading and unloading the M1s and M16s, the whole military attitude that said the officer was God and you were a piece of shit.

I had my own attitude. When I was instructed to do sentry duty, which meant watching the barracks all night with an empty gun, I said fuck it. After an hour of whistling in the dark, I fell asleep. In the morning the commanding officer woke me up with a swift kick and ordered me into the brig they called Mickey Mouse.

Mickey Mouse was where I had to scrub the toilets with a tooth-brush. They had me mopping floors, washing windows, and scraping bird shit off the roof. I did this for a week. At the end of my sentence, the commanding officer came to see me.

"You understand now?" he asked.

"Understand what, sir?"

"Understand the importance of sentry duty."

"I understand the importance of not getting caught sleeping on sentry duty."

"The job itself is vital."

"If it's so vital," I said, slipping into my street attitude, "why was I holding an empty gun?"

"That's not the point."

"Exactly, sir. That's my point—that there is no point."

"Maybe you'll get the point after another week in Mickey Mouse."

After my second week, I knew there was no point to any of this military crap. The only point was to keep my mouth shut. And I did. Miraculously, I got out of Great Lakes in one piece.

Buffalo never looked so good. I looked for my boys Danny and Moses. Danny had been busted and was serving time in Attica. Moses had been shot to death on a dope deal gone bad. It was Malcolm who told me the news.

"They were good cats," said Malcolm. "They had brains and a future until smack made them stupid. In those forty-five days you were gone, they lost everything—Danny lost his freedom and Moses lost his life. What are you gonna do, James? You gonna go back on that smack and get stupid like them?"

"I'm staying straight," I promised Malcolm. I could feel fear moving up and down my spine. What happened to Danny and Moses could have easily happened to me.

"Stay with your music," said Malcolm. "Your music is your protection. Let music surround you and you'll be all right."

I hooked back up with the Duprees. I played drums for practically every jazz trio and quartet in the city. I even entered a talent contest at WUFO radio and won first place singing Ben E. King's "Stand By Me." Malcolm was right. Long as I stayed with music, music would keep me from harm.

As the cats returned from Vietnam, I could see the harm that the war had done to them. Many returned junkies. It looked like they'd lost their souls. Their eyes were blank. I witnessed a couple of robberies and holdups pulled off by Vietnam vets who acted like killing machines. I didn't blame them. I blamed the fucked-up war and how it turned them into monsters. I didn't want that happening to me.

The more I thought about the military, the more I stayed away from the reserve. I couldn't get myself to go to any more training sessions. Even twice a month was too much for me. I no longer gave a shit. The pro-war government of Lyndon fuckin' Johnson, the racist policies of a country where discrimination ran rampant, a fighting force where blacks, too poor to buy their way out of service, were the first to go and first to die—the hell with it all.

I'd sing, I'd play drums, I'd make my music all night long, but I'd be damned if I was going to show up for the reserve.

"Be careful," said Malcolm. "You might not show up for the navy, but the navy is sure going to show up for you."

Once again, Malcolm was right on the money.

After a night of sitting in with the great Thelonious Monk at the Royal Arms, a night when I thought I had died and gone to jazz heaven, a night when all my skills as a drummer had been validated by a simple nod from Monk, I woke up late the next day. I wanted to tell Mom all about how I kept up with the ultra-modern Monk, whose riffing and sense of rhythm were completely his own. Amazingly, I was able to read him right. It was one thing to be able to sing like Ben E. King; it was another, at least for fifteen or twenty minutes, to play "Round Midnight" and "Ruby, My Dear" with Thelonious Monk.

"Here's another one of those letters from the navy," she said. "It came yesterday but I was too scared to open it for you."

She handed it to me with a terrible look in her eyes. Remember—Mom was a warrior and it took a lot to make her scared. When I tore open the envelope and read it, I saw she was right to be scared.

"They calling you over to Vietnam this time, ain't they?" she said. "They calling you for real."

The letter was for real—I was to report to the naval base in Rochester and wait for the *Enterprise* aircraft carrier to take me to Vietnam.

Mom started crying. For all my macho posturing, I started crying too. She took me in her arms and we cried together.

✦

"Cried last night," the bluesman sang on the record Mom played the night before I left for Rochester, "and cried the night before. Cried so hard I don't know what I'm crying for."

That was my song and my story. I was crying on the outside and hurting on the inside. I was numb with worry and fear. I had me some blues I had never known before. I felt like I was walking through motions without any real notion of what I was doing. I felt like I was walking to my death.

Walking to the Greyhound station where once upon a time I'd run off to New York to hear Sonny Rollins and Junior Walker. Now I was headed to Rochester and the end of my life.

Walking from the Rochester bus station to a scuzzy hotel near the base.

With my sea bag over my shoulder, walking from the hotel to the base.

Walking down the hotel hallway to a little nasty room with a single bed.

Walking through my dreams of sinking ships and falling bombs, dreams of my own destruction.

Waking up late and walking to the commander's office at the base.

"You were due at six A.M.! It's now ten!"

Walking through my lame excuse that the commander didn't buy. Instead he had me chipping paint off the walls of the bathroom shower for hours on end. He told me if I was late again, he'd have me chipping paint for the next five days until the ship arrived that would take me to Vietnam.

Walking to a pay phone and calling Mom.

"You all right?" she asked.

"Fine," I lied.

"What do you need, son?"

"Just a little money till my ship arrives."

Walking back to the hotel, where, exhausted, I fell asleep.

Walking through some nightmares where men were slitting my throat and piercing my heart with bayonets.

Waking to see the clock, which said eleven A.M. Overslept again. Five hours later. This time the commanding officer would have my ass. The commanding officer would make my life hell until it was time to sail to my death.

Walking to the bathroom to take a shower.

Walking to the closet to put on my uniform.

Seeing something being slipped under my door.

A money order from Mom.

Fifty bucks.

Thank you, Jesus.

Walking out the door.

Walking to get the money order cashed.

Walking back to the bus station.

"Where to?" asked the clerk behind the counter.

"Toronto."

"Round trip or one-way?"

"One-way."

Walking on the bus.

Walking out of one world into another.

RICKY JAMES MATTHEWS,
A.K.A. LITTLE RICKY

Malcolm had planted the seed some months before. He had taken me to lunch at a little Chinese restaurant just over the Peace Bridge in Fort Erie, Canada.

"Canada's different," Malcolm told me. "Canada doesn't have the heavy racist history of America. Canada doesn't have the military ambition or arrogance of America. Canada's laid-back."

"Canada's dull," I said. I'd been going over to Canada for years, sometimes to play music, sometimes to score dope. When the Canadians want action, they come over here.

"That's changing. Montreal's gotten hip. So has Toronto. If push comes to shove, don't overlook Canada. You can go to Canada and be cool."

The thought of ducking out of the navy had been on my mind ever since I went to the base in the Great Lakes. I knew, though, that would turn me into a criminal and have the law on my tail. I also knew that if I became a deserter it might break my mother's heart. Once it became clear that I was being shipped overseas, I figured I'd just grin and bear it—except I couldn't. Everything in me screamed in protest. I was not going off to this fuckin' stupid war.

So Canada became the escape and close-by Toronto, a mere twenty-five-dollar bus ride from Rochester, became the destination. For the umpteenth time, Brother Malcolm pushed me in the right direction.

During the three-hour bus ride, paranoia started to build. I started imagining that the navy had already sent their police force after me. I knew they had no jurisdiction in Canada, but what if there was some new treaty that let them pick AWOL cats off the street anywhere in the world? I was getting myself crazy. I had to calm the fuck down or I'd have a nervous breakdown.

By the time the bus arrived in Toronto, I had talked myself into a reasonable state of mind. It was the spring of 1964, I was sixteen years old, and even though the city stood only a hundred miles from Buffalo, it might have been a million. I felt like I was on another planet. Canada was way more chilled out than the uptight USA. Folks were friendlier. Whites seemed less leery of blacks. My shoulders and neck, shot through with tension during the ride north, began to relax. I took a deep breath and sighed. No one was looking for me. I didn't need to stress. I wasn't totally broke. I did have a little money in my pocket. I passed by a newsstand that displayed a paper that said the World's Fair was opening in New York.

That reminded me that Malcolm had told me that Yorkville was the Greenwich Village of Toronto. "If you get to Canada," he said, "head straight for Yorkville. It's where the crazy artists hang out. You'll feel right at home."

I found my way to Yorkville, my little sailor bag still over my shoulder, and liked what I saw—coffeehouses, record shops, jazz clubs, strip bars. Just when I felt how great it was to be out of racist Western New York, three men came up to me with thick Buffalo accents. They were in civilian clothes and obviously drunk.

"You ain't one of them AWOL niggers, are you?"

I was about to slug him when his friends came right at me. I wasn't sure I could handle all three, but then again, I didn't have to. A trio of three other white guys saw what was happening and came running to my aid. Just like that, it was on—and the drunk assholes went down down down.

I thanked my saviors. "I'm James Johnson," I said.

"I'm Pat McGraw," said the cat who threw the best punches. "These are my friends Garth Hudson and Levon Helm. They're musicians."

"I'm a musician," I said.

"We play with Ronnie Hawkins. Ever hear of him?" asked Garth. I hadn't.

"We're his backup band," said Levon. "We're the Hawks. You oughta come by and hear us."

I wanted to. Later I'd remember this encounter when Garth, Levon, and their colleagues Robbie Robertson, Rick Danko, and Richard Manuel backed up Bob Dylan and later got famous as the Band.

We went for coffee. Garth and Levon were beautiful cats, deep into music. We talked about Muddy Waters and Cannonball Adderley. Their taste was as wide as mine. When they left for rehearsal, they scribbled down their numbers on the back of a matchbook. Meanwhile, Pat McGraw was eager to keep hanging.

"Look, man," he said, "if you're AWOL, that raises my respect. Anyone who tells the army to fuck off is cool with me."

"How 'bout the navy?"

"Fuck 'em all," said Pat McGraw. "Let's go get fucked-up."

He took me to an underground coffeehouse called El Patio, where, in the back room, we smoked. It felt great, like a weight lifted off my shoulders.

"Band's coming on," said Pat. "Let's stay and listen."

I was ready. I was glad the band played R & B. The musicians weren't bad, but the singer really couldn't hack it. Pat saw the look on my face and asked, "Think you can do better?"

"Know I can," I said.

"Well, get your ass up there and try."

Nick St. Nicholas, the bandleader, was willing.

"You know 'Stand By Me'?" I asked.

"What key?"

"E."

"Hit it!"

I hit it hard, and four minutes later everyone was up and screaming for me.

"You can sing," said Nick. He was a bass player, a blond cat with high cheekbones and kind eyes. "Here's my number. Call me."

Everyone was handing out numbers. Aside from the nigger haters who tried to punch me out, everyone in Toronto was looking out for me.

"You better crash at my pad," said Pat, "until you get some paying gigs. The way you wailing, it won't be long."

Turned out that Pat was a rounder—the Canadian term for hustler—so we spoke the same language. On the street, everyone knew Pat. At his crib, his chick Shirley, a sista, was waiting for him. She was a singer herself, foxy and sweet.

"Who you, honey?" she asked when I walked through the door with Pat.

"James."

"James is AWOL," said Pat, "and he's a singing motherfucker."

"If you AWOL," said Shirley, "you best change your name."

"That's right," Pat chimed in.

"We'll call you Rick—Ricky James Mathews. That's my cousin's name. He's dead, so he won't mind."

I didn't mind. New town. New identity.

First night I slept on Pat's couch. Next morning I called Nick.

"You serious about me singing with you?" I asked.

"Serious as sin. Come on over now."

A week later the Sailor Boys were born out of deep irony. We used my navy-issued clothes, all I had, as uniforms. We switched them up and made 'em funky, but the look was unmistakably navy. Our sound was unmistakably R & B. We covered everyone from the Isleys to Smokey and his Miracles. My voice was big enough where I could sing Walter Jackson, Bobby Blue Bland, or Ray Charles. Not only that, but I'd picked up the harmonica and had a one-man act I called Little Ricky.

Soon fans of the Sailor Boys would show up wearing bell-bottoms and sailor caps—we started a fad!—to hear us sing harmony tight as the Beach Boys. Then on one night a week, at that same club, different fans would come to see Little Ricky blow harp like Little Walter or Sonny Boy Williamson. Toronto was a music-loving town.

Toronto also turned out to be a place where I did some careful studying and listening. For the first time I found myself smack in the middle of a community of white artists who were deadly serious about making music true to their souls. I saw Joni Mitchell in little clubs, playing her guitar and singing her life-experience songs. She'd come to hear me as well and was always encouraging. Same thing was true of Kenny Rogers, David Clayton-Thomas, Gordon Lightfoot, and Neil Young. Every one of these cats respected the African-American musical tradition. They drew from it. And they let me know I was a part of it. At the same time, they taught me about the white folk tradition—Pete Seeger and Woody Guthrie and Bob Dylan. I loved it all and felt like I was in the hippest college in the world. They played me Laura Nyro records while I played them Ornette Coleman. They introduced me to Elmore James and Robert Johnson while I introduced them to Joe Tex and Pharoah Sanders. The all-night jams had my brain working overtime.

The other music we were listening to, of course, was the stuff from England. In the middle of the sixties' British Invasion, Canada, a part of the British Commonwealth, was crazy over the Beatles, the Stones, the Kinks, and the Dave Clark Five. The only thing saving American music was Motown. In fact, the English groups even covered Motown songs.

Far as I was concerned, I could do it all and it was all good. Turned out, though, that Nick was something of a slippery cat. He started gigging behind our back with a group called Jack London and the Sparrows. Dave Marden—known as Jack—was from Liverpool but the other guys weren't English at all. They faked the accent and the look and, lo and behold, got a record deal on Capitol and a pop hit, "If You Don't Want My Love." People around me were starting to make serious money.

When Nick left us for greener pastures, we recruited a superbad bass player named Bruce Palmer. Bruce brought the funk. Later in life he went big-time with Buffalo Springfield. Goldy McJohn was on organ. We were feeling big-time ourselves, selling out clubs all over town and making four hundred bucks a night. The hash was plentiful and so was the amyl nitrate. We were smoking and sniffing nearly every night.

I was stoked. I'd come to Toronto with twenty-five dollars in my pocket. Now I had hundreds, a place of my own, and a name known all around Yorkville. I'd proven that my talent was all I needed. The Me Monster was growing strong.

✦

"Your band's strong, but it can be a lot stronger," said Colin Kerr, a cat from England who wanted to be Brian Epstein. "You can explode out of Toronto the way the Beatles exploded out of Liverpool."

I was impressed by this kind of big-time talk.

"How you gonna pull it off?" I asked Colin.

"Come down to my shop and you'll see."

Colin had a coffeehouse called the Mynah Bird at Yorkville and Hazelton. That was his inspiration for the band name.

Before Colin, we dressed like regulation hippies—bell-bottoms, psychedelic-patterned shirts, wild hair, little round purple glasses. Colin changed all that.

"You need a different look," he said. "You need your own look."

So we put together outfits with yellow turtleneck sweaters, tight black leather pants, leather jackets, and yellow boots. Colin didn't change our music all that much—we were basically still an R & B band—but he did change the way we got attention.

"Gentlemen," said Colin, "it'll take more than music to get the press we need. We're going to take a page out of Sinatra's playbook."

Colin explained how in the forties Sinatra's press agent hired teenage girls to scream at his appearances. The commotion made news.

"You're going to take a shopping trip through Eaton's, the biggest department store in town, that's going to make news."

Which is just what happened. Colin had girls chasing after us as we tried to shop at Eaton's. They screamed our name and tore off our clothes as we ran to the safety of our rented limo. The next day the Mynah Birds were all over the papers. *Rock group causes riot! Girls go nuts!* And all this without a record.

We'd gone to see *A Hard Day's Night*, the Beatles movie, and suddenly I was living it. For a while I was loving it. Who didn't wanna be chased down by a gang of girls? For the most part, the girls were white and none of them seemed prejudiced. Actually, the opposite was true. As the black lead singer of the white Mynah Birds, I stood out. Ever since I'd been in Toronto—going on two years now—I'd stood out. I was an authentic R & B singer living in a city where white musicians were striving to play authentic R & B. That added to my status. It also got me laid. I'd be lying if I said I wasn't curious to taste pussy in all its wonderful flavors. White pussy was a new treat for me, and I gorged myself as much as I could.

Reflecting back, I got to say that before Toronto I hadn't thought much about sex outside my race. It just wasn't an issue. I was a product of black Buffalo and had no complaints about black women. Still don't. But most brothas of my generation were curious about white pussy, just as I'd guess many white guys wanted a taste of chocolate. The grass is always greener. When I first scored white women in Canada, it was a novelty. Stretched out in bed after a hot fuck, seeing my dark skin next to the whiteness of a beautiful lady was a novelty and a kick. After a while, though, the novelty wore off and I stopped discriminating. I quickly learned that good pussy, like true love, isn't restricted to one group or another.

The Mynah Birds was a group definitely geared to white girls. In that sense, I dug the fantasy of being John Lennon, Paul McCartney, or Mick Jagger. I dug how my musical flexibility allowed me to be part of a Canadian-concocted British Invasion group. I also dug the possibility of the group taking off and making millions.

Jagger was my man. The Stones had a harder edge than the Beatles, and with the Mynah Birds I sang a lot of the Stones' early hits, like "Get Off of My Cloud" and "Satisfaction." Much as I admired Jagger for his swagger, he was a white cat trying to sing black. I didn't have to try. I am black, and so when people started saying they liked my versions of the Stones' songs better than the originals, I wasn't surprised.

As my life went through these amazing changes, I thought back to what Brother Malcolm Erni said about the glow that he saw shining inside me. When I got to Canada, that glow got me through. It came out in my music. People saw it and liked it. The glow got all over them, and they told others about it. Word got out that Little Ricky could blow harmonica and wail some mean blues. Word got out that Ricky James Mathews was fronting the Sailor Boys and singing up a storm. Then this same guy was causing a commotion with the Mynah Birds.

I wrote Mom that all my dreams were coming true—that my musical talent was real and getting realer every day. I wanted to visit her as soon as possible. She wrote back saying that the FBI was looking for me—and to stay where I was. The cats I was playing with didn't know I was AWOL—and I was careful to keep it that way.

I wasn't much for future planning. I was, am, and will always be an improviser. I made up my life the same way I was making up my songs—on the spot. If I thought too far ahead, I'd get worried, and worry wasn't conducive to creativity. I was all about creativity. Now, with the creation of the Mynah Birds, I felt myself on the brink of a breakthrough.

I wanted fortune and fame, and I just knew that they were right around the corner. No mistake about it. I couldn't be wrong.

Or could I?

MY TIME

In my time in prison, Brotha Guru and I continue to have some deep talks. The other day he was accusing me of being cocky. Only a man like Brotha Guru, who I respect so much, could get away with saying something like that.

"If I wasn't cocky, I wouldn't have gotten where I am," I said.

"And where are you, Brotha Rick? You're in jail!"

"I mean my music career wouldn't have happened if I wasn't a confident motherfucker."

"Big difference," said Brotha Guru, "between confident and cocky."

"I don't see the difference."

"That's why you landed in prison. Confidence is moving ahead with a calm conviction that your God-given talent will see you through. Cockiness is when you start believing that nothing and no one can stop you."

✦

In 1965, a seventeen-year-old wrapped up in the explosive music scene in Toronto, I couldn't help but be cocky. I was moving up so fast and furiously that I really didn't think that anything could hold me back. That's the attitude that led me to break away from Colin Kerr, my first real manager.

Colin had the Mynah Birds practicing for months before he took us to the studio. I was impatient. I was ready to rock. I was writing songs that I thought were smash hits. But Colin's brother had songs of his own. Those were the songs that Colin insisted we record—"The Mynah Bird Hop" and "The Mynah Bird Song." To me, they were jive. But 'cause Colin was paying the bills, he got his way.

After we cut the tunes, Colin sent us to do a teeny-bopper TV show in Hamilton, Ontario. I was excited. The studio was filled with screaming girls—all hired by Colin—and, as a gimmick, I was supposed to sing to a blind mynah bird.

I went along with the program. I let them put the bird in my hand as I sang this dumb-ass song. The girls loved it, but I didn't, especially when the bird started shitting in my hand. When I tried to push him off, he dug his claws into my skin. With shit and blood all over me, I nearly bolted. Somehow I got through the song. Somehow I also got through four Mynah Bird shows at the Colonnade Theater. The girls were screaming so loud I couldn't even hear myself sing.

"This is bullshit," I told the guys in the band. "The music is bullshit, the act is bullshit, and the little money we're getting is bullshit. I say we burn these jive-ass costumes and tell Colin to fuck himself."

The guys agreed. We left Colin and kept the name Mynah Birds but changed our look. We went back to the far-out hippie image that was closer to our true character. We also changed our music, the result of something that happened when I went down to New York City and heard what was happening in the folk scene of Greenwich Village.

I was reluctant to leave Canada because of my AWOL situation, but a new friend of mine, Morley Schelman, told me not to worry. He was rich enough to buy me out of any legal hassle. Morley was gay but, knowing that I wasn't, felt uncomfortable mentioning it. I couldn't have cared less. I have prejudices, but homophobia is not one of them.

When we got to New York, a limo was waiting for us. Seated inside was Sal Mineo, Morley's best friend and obvious lover. Mineo had some killer grass and we got blasted immediately. I was buzzed, not only on the weed but on the fact that I was meeting my first movie star. I'd seen Mineo with James Dean in *Rebel Without a Cause* at least three times. It was one of my favorite flicks. I'd also seen him in *The Gene Krupa Story*, where he played the great swing drummer. In that movie, Krupa gets busted for pot, and there we were in the limo, talking about that while getting blasted on fat joints. Sal had also learned to play drums for that film. So we could talk drummer-to-drummer. I was surprised that he was familiar with bebop drummers like Kenny "Klook" Clarke and Connie Kay of the Modern Jazz Quartet. Sal Mineo was one hip cat.

We settled into the apartment of Morley's parents on Park Avenue. They had one whole floor of the building. When the elevator opened, you weren't in a hallway, you were in their crib. Never had seen that before. Also never had seen so much cocaine. In those days it was pure. One line could take off the back of your head. Morley had a small attaché case filled with blow that went with us as we hit the clubs in the Village.

"You like this coke?" he asked as the three of us—Morley, me, and Mineo—rode in the back of the limo heading down to the Night Owl Café on MacDougal Street.

"It's good," I said, "but I'm mainly a weed man. Coke really isn't my thing."

At that point I should have added "at least not yet," but I couldn't see the future. All I could see was a line of hard-core hippies waiting to get in to see the Lovin' Spoonful. Morley knew the club owner and got us right in. I dug everything I heard. Later in life when I told writers that the Lovin' Spoonful was one of the groups that influenced me most, they thought I was kidding. I wasn't. John Sebastian was a great harp player. He knew the black masters and became a master himself. John and his cats—Joe Butler on drums, Zal Yanovsky on guitar, and Steve Boone on bass—had this acoustic/electric mix of folk, blues, and rock that knocked me out. It felt fresh. I loved songs like "Do You Believe in Magic" and "Summer in the City." After their first set, we hung out for a long time and exchanged ideas. My ego got pumped when they said people coming back from Toronto were talking about me. I dug the Spoonful so much that I went to see them two more times before Morley and I said good-bye to Sal Mineo and flew back to Canada.

Couldn't wait to tell Bruce Palmer about the Lovin' Spoonful and the new direction I envisioned for the Mynah Birds. Bruce was already hip to blues-based folk rock and he suggested we get this guitarist who could help us with that sound—his friend Neil Young.

"He's staying over at Joni Mitchell's place," said Bruce. "I'll take you to meet him."

Joni was famous for letting musicians crash at her pad directly over the Purple Onion coffeehouse. She and I had a great relationship. It wasn't sexual but musical as a motherfucker. Joni was a brilliant lyricist and also a student of jazz. You could talk to her about Monk and Mingus. She and I sat up all night listening to

Miles's *Sketches of Spain*. On another night we were digging Mahler and Mozart. Joni was the first one to play me Mose Allison and I remember teaching her Horace Silver's "Juicy Lucy." Joni had killer taste, so if she recommended a musician—the way she and Bruce were recommending Neil Young—that was all the assurance I needed.

Neil was cool. He had a quirky sense of humor and a quick mind. Like most of the other white musicians in Toronto, he was into black music. His singing was a little strange, but his facility on the guitar was crazy. He got all over those strings and showed me some shit I'd never seen before. Neil helped reshape the Mynah Birds into the band I'd been hearing inside my head. Like John Sebastian, Neil bridged folk, blues, and rock in a format that didn't sound artificial. It sounded real. He was the missing ingredient. Like most bands, the personnel of the Mynah Birds kept changing, but the basic group—me, Nick St. Nicholas, Bruce Palmer, Neil Young, and Goldy McJohn—came together at the right time. And on the right night the right man came to hear us.

That man was John Craig Eaton. His family owned Eaton's department store. Morley Schelman brought him to the club. Morley and John were two rich kids in love with music. A product of his upbringing, John was a conservative, but after a few weeks of partying with the Mynah Birds, he loosened up. I could see he was toying with the idea of walking on the wild side. Morley saw the same thing. I was surprised when the two of them came to me with an idea.

"I want to manage the Mynah Birds," said Morley.

"And I want to produce you," said John.

"If by 'produce,'" I said, "you mean you'll put up the money, I'm cool with that."

That's just what happened. Within a few days John had bought us thousands of dollars' worth of new instruments and equipment and invited us to rehearse in his mansion. It was like a European palace. I was operating in a different sphere—musically and romantically as well. I'd met this chick named Elke who had me loving on her so hard I found myself doing something the boys back in my Buffalo hood swore they'd never do. I gave her head.

Don't know why, but my generation of black men had an attitude that it was the woman who did the sucking, not the man. Elke didn't see it that way. She was gonna get good as she gave. And, believe me, man, she gave plenty good. At first I wasn't sure. The experience of actually tasting pussy was new and strange. But when I saw her wild reaction and realized the power of the pleasure I was giving her, I gave even more. Elke taught me pleasing a woman is as pleasurable as getting pleased yourself.

Meanwhile, on the business front, our rich backers were eager to please us. They'd been coming to our rehearsals and watching our shows. They were sure we were ready for the big time and wanted to land us a deal. I thought we needed a bit more time. Neil and I had just started writing together, and while our songs were good, I was sure that in a few more weeks they'd be great. Neil had this machine-gun style on the guitar that inspired melodies and lyrics out of me. Sometimes he'd be so into his solos he wouldn't even realize that his guitar had come unplugged.

When I finally felt we had it together, I told John and Morley to bring the record company execs to hear us in Toronto.

"We're going one better than that," said Morley. "We're taking you to Detroit. Motown wants to hear you."

"Is Motown right for me?" I asked. "Motown's all black. Motown's crossover soul music and we're in the middle of the white rock mix."

"Motown's all about money," said John. "I've talked to Berry

Gordy and he's dying to get into rock. He loves the idea of a white rock band with a black lead. I got us an audition for next week."

I was game. I was ready to meet the cats who made Marvin Gaye. I was ready to meet Marvin himself. Bring on Smokey and the Miracles. The Mynah Birds would be Motown's next major miracle.

◆

On the way to Detroit, when crossing over from Windsor, Canada, I got nervous. Morley was reassuring.

"If they ask," he said, "I got papers here that will see us through. Just remember, though, I'm the only one who knows that you're AWOL. No one else needs to."

I agreed. By then I figured I'd beaten the odds and that, as far as the navy was concerned, I was a lost ball in the high weeds.

As far as Motown was concerned, the Mynah Birds were complete oddballs. When we arrived—sometime in 1966—it was culture shock. Detroit still looked like a city out of the fifties—the cats wearing slicked-down process do's, sharkskin jackets, iridescent pants, shiny gators, stingy-brim Stetsons. Everyone looked like a pimp. We looked like the hippies we were. My hair was out to there, my purple-and-black corduroy jeans had bell bottoms that covered my sandals. I was wore a peace-sign necklace and little oval John Lennon sunglasses. My two favorite words were "far out."

Morley and John took us to meet Gordy and his boys. Our audition took place in an office building. Berry, a little guy, seemed to be in a hurry. He reminded me of a pug, a compact dog with a sweet face. I knew he'd been a boxer and had also written songs for Jackie Wilson. Given the number of stars he'd created, he had major cred. But he also had this high-pitched childlike voice that made it hard to take him seriously. He spoke in a whiny singsong manner, and when he spoke all his minions kept quiet.

"Let's see what you got," he said.

We played "It's My Time," a song I'd written. I thought it was the best thing we'd ever done. I heard it as the Four Tops meets the Lovin' Spoonful, a combination of soul and folk rock. I was worried, though, that Berry wouldn't get it.

"I got it," he said. "And I love it. I think it'll sell. You guys just need production help. Meet my man Mickey Stevenson."

Mickey Stevenson was Gordy's head of A & R (artists and repertoire). I saw right away that he, like Berry's boys, was a Berry Gordy wannabe. They all dressed and talked like the boss. It was a company of conformists. I also knew, though, that Mickey had cowritten "Dancing in the Street" with Marvin Gaye and produced it for Martha and the Vandellas. I knew he'd worked with all the big Motown acts. If he wanted to work with us, fine. Long as there was a contract.

The contract was for six years. That's all I needed to hear. I didn't bother looking at the fine print. I was too excited about having my first record deal and an actual cash advance. It wasn't much, but it was something. We were on Motown.

Mickey took us to the two-story house on West Grand Boulevard that held the original Motown studios, the ones where all the hits had been cut. I was expecting something lavish. What I saw was something sparse. I couldn't have been less impressed. But I couldn't have been more impressed when I saw who was sitting in the control room: Marvin Gaye.

When Marvin saw me standing there, he got up and reached out his hand for me to shake.

"Marvin Gaye," he said.

"I know," I said. "I'm Ricky James Mathews."

After we chatted for a while, I asked Marvin how the company decided who got to produce who.

"It's survival of the fittest, brother," said Marvin.

"What does that mean?"

"It means it's a throat-cutting contest up in here."

"It ain't one big happy family?"

Marvin just laughed. His wasn't a harsh laugh, but an easy laugh. He was a gentle guy with a sweet smile and a soft disposition that made you feel like you were talking to a prince about to inherit his father's kingdom. There was something aristocratic about Marvin. In those days he dressed Ivy League—white V-neck tennis sweaters and Brooks Brothers slacks—and liked to talk about Perry Como and Tony Bennett. He sang R & B, but he really wanted to be Frank Sinatra. I didn't see any reason why he couldn't be.

As I hung around the studio and began to record under Mickey's supervision, I saw everyone. The great David Ruffin, lead singer of the Temptations, walked in one day with Tammi Terrell on his arm. Those duets between Marvin and Tammi were just getting started. I always thought Tammi was Marvin's girl, but Mickey set me straight: Marvin was married to Anna Gordy, Berry's sister, a woman eighteen years older than Marvin.

"Marvin married his mama," said Mickey. "Anna leads him around like a dog on a chain."

I saw Smokey Robinson, another easygoing superstar with a beautiful sunshine personality; the Isley Brothers, who had a smash with "This Old Heart of Mine"; and Norman Whitfield, a dark, brooding light-skinned producer who'd done "I Heard it Through the Grapevine" for Gladys Knight and Marvin. He was an angry cat with a big chip on his shoulder.

I got to meet all the Temptations—the bass singer, Melvin Franklin, was a distant relative of my mom's—as well as a guy who later became a close friend, Bobby Taylor, one of the singing-est motherfuckers on the planet. I related to Bobby because he grew up in the black hood of DC only to move to Vancouver, Canada, where, with a mixed-race band called the Vancouvers, he made his move to Motown. Not long after we met, Bobby scored on two fronts—he'd have a hit about a black/white romance called "Does Your Mama Know About Me?" written by Tommy Chong (later to become half of Cheech and Chong) and he'd discover the Jackson 5 (only to have Gordy falsely credit Diana Ross for the discovery). Unlike the folk-rock-edged Mynah Birds, though, Bobby Taylor and the Vancouvers were straight-up soul.

It was Bobby who pointed out a singer named Chris Clark. "That's Berry's white bitch," said Bobby. "Stay away from her. Matter of fact, you best stay away from all the bitches up in here, 'cause you don't know who's fucking who. Fuck the wrong one and you'll get fucked."

I took Bobby's advice. I didn't hit on any of the women, although all of them—especially Tammi Terrell—looked good to me. The truth is, I was practically too starstruck to do anything but stare at Diana Ross or Martha Reeves, remembering that only a few years ago I was dancing on the streets of Buffalo to their songs. When Bobby introduced me to Clarence Paul, a friend of Mickey Stevenson's and the guy who worked with Stevie Wonder, I asked if I could meet Stevie. The next day there he was—the sixteen-year-old blind kid who was tearing up the charts with "Uptight (Everything's Alright)."

"Stevie," I said, "I won a talent contest in high school singing 'Fingertips.'"

"Let me hear it," said Stevie.

"Oh, man, I couldn't, not with you looking at me."

"I can't see, remember."

"Sorry, Stevie, I didn't mean—"

"I was just fooling with you. Go on and sing."

"I'm too nervous to sing in front of you."

"You got to."

I did, and Stevie nearly fell out laughing. "Love it," he said. "What's your name?"

"Ricky James Mathews."

"That's too long. Ricky James sounds more like it. Gonna remember you, Ricky James. Next time I see you I'll be singing your hit."

Mickey Stevenson took us into the little eight-track studio, where he began to analyze our songs. I didn't like that at first. Who the fuck was he to tell me to change up my compositions? Well, he was a man with some big hits under his belt. So in spite of my resistance, I shut up and listened. He had some decent ideas about song structure and voicings. The cat actually taught me something. We were in there for days and cut a bunch of material with the help of a Canadian white dude, R. Dean Taylor. Neil was especially impressive, wailing on the twelve-string guitar, an axe I hadn't ever used before. The song everyone liked most was "It's My Time," the unanimous choice for our first single. I loved the message of that song—it was my time.

I was at fuckin' Motown records! I was hanging with Marvin and Stevie! I was chatting up Levi Stubbs and Gladys Knight! It didn't matter that a lot of the cats, like Harvey Fuqua and even Berry himself, were laughing at my hippie look. With their showbiz "Copacabana" mentality, I knew they were a little behind the times, while I was on the cutting edge. I had me an import version of Jimi Hendrix's *Are You Experienced* from England before the album ever hit America. I was all over Sly Stone before any of those Motown execs realized that the music world was in the middle of a revolution. As 1966 moved toward 1967, I had both my feet in the future.

I'm not saying that Motown didn't help me hone my craft. But they knew I was advanced. Even mean-ass Norman Whitfield, a cat as bullheaded as me, had to give me my props. He asked me questions about where I got my grooves. Not much later, it was Whitfield who watched George Clinton's Parliament, an old-school doo-wop-style group, morph into Funkadelic. Whitfield flat-out copied their shit and reinvented the Temptations with a Clinton–meets–Sly Stone sound on hits like "Psychedelic Shack," "Cloud Nine," "Papa Was a Rollin' Stone," and "Runaway Child, Running Wild." Norman had the help of Dennis Edwards, the ferocious new lead singer for the Temptations who replaced David Ruffin, but it was really Funkadelic's futuristic thinking that inspired those songs.

◆

High on my Motown sessions, convinced that the Mynah Birds were gonna be the Next Big Thing, I flew from Detroit to Buffalo to see Mom. It had been three years. I loved this woman more than life itself. So, after we embraced and I saw the fear in her eyes, I was alarmed.

"What could be wrong, Mom?" I asked. "This Motown thing is gonna make me rich. I'm gonna buy you a big house in the burbs so you'll never have to run no numbers again."

"It's the FBI, son. They still calling. They still looking for you."

"I got me a new name, a new ID. They ain't gonna find me."

"I don't think you should stay around here, James. I think it's best that you go back to Toronto."

"Only if you go with me, Mom. I want you to see how I've become a star up there. I want you to meet my friends. It's a beautiful scene."

"I'd love to, but I won't be able to stay for more than a week. I believe you when you say that one day you'll be rich, but until that day arrives, I still have to work those numbers to buy the groceries."

"Motown's given us an advance. My share's only a few thousand, but you take as much as you like."

"I'm not taking a dime. You earned it. You enjoy it."

That was Mom—always putting her children ahead of herself.

We drove from Buffalo to Toronto. Crossing the border, especially with Mom in the car, was a breeze. I loved showing her off to my friends and taking her to the clubs, where, after my Motown score, I was treated like a conquering hero. She was proud and the first to say how she loved basking in my glory. She also liked Elke, the German chick who had turned me out.

My energy was high, not only because the Mynah Birds had a soon-to-be-released record, but also because I had fallen in love with speed. That wasn't anything I was ready to tell Mom. She thought I was excited from the music I was making and the recognition coming my way. But I was popping pills that had me racing even faster than my normally racy speed.

I was in a hurry to see, do, and feel everything. I especially wanted to see that up-front Motown money. I kept asking Morley Schelman when our checks would be coming through, and he kept saying to ask John Craig, who, in turn, referred me back to Morley. I was getting sick of this shit but didn't want to start anything while Mom was in town. The minute she went back to Buffalo, though, I called Morley demanding my bread. That's when he told me to come out to his new house. When I did, I saw he also had a new motorcycle. As you can imagine, none of this went down well with me. In my imagination, I saw him spending our advance.

"I want the fuckin' money now," I said.

"It should be here next week."

"Next week's not good enough."

"I can't do anything about that."

"Well, I can."

"What?"

"I can kick your ass."

And I did.

I didn't know it then, but kicking Morley's ass was tantamount to kicking my own ass.

For a week, I was glad to have put Morley and also John out of our lives. The Mynah Birds didn't need them. The Mynah Birds had a contract with Motown. Until the call came . . .

Motown wasn't going to put out our record.

"Why?" I asked their lawyer, who was calling from Detroit.

"Because you're a fugitive. You're wanted by the FBI."

It didn't take Einstein to figure out what had happened. Morley ratted me out. I figure it had to be him because, outside my family, he was the only one who knew.

I was sunk. Not only was the Motown contract gone, but so was the possibility of signing with any major American label. The FBI had blanketed the music industry, waiting for me to make my next move. They had alerted every record company to contact them the minute I approached. I was cornered. I couldn't get signed anywhere. All I could do was stay in Toronto. The other Mynah Birds were understandably pissed that I had ruined our deal. I hadn't been straight with them about my military status. Yet Neil Young and Bruce Palmer, both great guys, stayed loyal. They didn't kick me out of the band. But how could I stay in when my very presence would keep them from getting a deal?

What the hell was I supposed to do?

"Come home," said Mom. "You're going to have to face this sooner or later. Better to give yourself up, do your time, and come out free. Then you'll be able to pursue your career. If you don't serve your time, you'll never be free."

Mom was right. I was out of options. I hated like hell to give myself up to the Man. It was against everything in my nature. But because Motown had validated my talent, I knew I could break through to the big-time. If that meant spending some time in the brig, well, I'd do what I had to do.

It all happened quickly. Still on speed, I raced back to Buffalo, called the FBI, and told them on a Friday to pick me up at Mom's Saturday morning. One last night with Mom, family, and friends.

"Got a treat for you," said Mom. "I wanna give you a memory to ease the pain of prison."

"What's that?" I asked.

"Miles Davis is playing at the Royal Arms. I got us a table up front."

Mom understood more than anyone. More than scoring some high-powered drug or some hot woman, I'd rather go see Miles than do anything else. I'd just bought his new record, *Miles Smiles,* which was the first time I heard his group with Herbie Hancock, Wayne Shorter, Ron Carter, and Tony Williams. In my mind, Tony was the most talented drummer since Art Blakey. The cat could play polyrhythms and cross-rhythms like no one else. He was light as a feather but strong as a raging river. Much as I dug Miles, I considered Tony the star of this group—and to see him live was the treat of a lifetime.

True, I had fucked up big-time.

True, I had cost myself and the Mynah Birds a chance at Motown stardom.

True, I had worked myself into this winless position where the FBI was coming to put my black ass in prison—and all this before I'd turned nineteen.

But to sit there in the club and watch Tony work his magic, to hear Herbie's beautiful chordings, Wayne's gorgeous sound, Ron's warm heartbeat, and Miles's moaning low on his muted horn, I felt that God was in the room. God was with me. Mom had brought God with her.

Next morning Mom cried when the FBI men put me in cuffs and escorted me to the their car. I was sad to leave my mother and uneasy about what the future held, but I'll be damned if I wasn't still hearing Miles in my head. I was carrying his joyful noise into whatever awaited me in the next chapter of my life.

PART TWO

BREAKING IN

IN AND OUT

What was it like?" asks Brotha Guru, wondering about the time when the FBI came and got me in Buffalo.

"It was hell."

"Where'd they take you?"

"They threw me in a brig at the Brooklyn Navy Yard. It was a lockdown on the top floor of one of the dorms on the base guarded by marines. The marines would rather beat you than look at you. They called me 'faggot' and a 'sissy hippie' because of my long hair. They cut my hair and took turns kicking the shit out of me for no reason. They threw me in with the angriest cats, the ones in for assault or murder. Some of them had actually shot themselves as a way to leave Vietnam. Every one of those motherfuckers had a story that could fill a book. But once they learned I could sing, they left me alone. The brothas would have me singing their favorite Otis Redding and Wilson Pickett songs. I told them that I had a deal with Motown, but most of them thought I was bullshitting."

"I bet you got in shape, though," says Brotha Guru.

"Great shape. Went from a beanpole to one hundred sixty pounds of solid muscle."

"How long before your trial?"

"Court martial came after seven or eight months."

"Were you scared?"

"Scared shitless. If they convicted me for desertion I could spend the rest of my life in military prison. But I had a good naval lawyer. He had me testify how, in good conscience, I had turned myself in. He had me apologize and explain how my passion for music had gotten in the way of good judgment. I was contrite."

"Did you mean it?"

"Fuck no, but I sold it. I can act, and when it came to saving my skin, I put on an Academy Award–winning performance."

"And it worked?"

"Like a charm. I was charged with AWOL, not desertion. That meant I could get out in another six or seven months."

"And the Me Monster was back in charge."

"Why you always gotta be talking about the Me Monster?"

"You the one doing the talking. You the one telling me how you fooled the system."

"I did more than that," I say. "I broke out of that motherfucker."

"How'd you do that?"

"With the help of two friends—Doc, a brotha, and Eddie, who was half black, half Puerto Rican. Doc said he'd pulled a big job before he was put in the brig and had thirty-five large ones stashed at his mom's crib, right there in Brooklyn. By then we were in a looser part of the lock-in because the three of us had been perfect prisoners. Doc had also gotten close to one of the guards, who got sick and had to go home early. He asked Doc to close down the mess hall. Doc alerted us. After the other prisoners had left, Doc showed us the one door that led to the emergency exit. Beyond that door was a staircase that went all the way down to the street—and freedom. Our only choice was to kick in the door, and that would make a racket. Doc found a couple of clothing carts that made even more of a racket when they rolled around the mess hall. So while Eddie and Doc were rolling the carts, I was kicking in the door. It finally broke open, an alarm went off, but we were down the six flights and out on the street before the guards had time to react. Sunlight! We put on our regulation navy hats and calmly walked off the base. Doc, the Brooklyn native, led the way to Flatbush Avenue, where we caught a cab. We'd done it! We'd flown the fuckin' coop."

"Congratulations," says Brotha Guru.

"You don't believe me?" I ask.

"Sure, I believe you. You were Steve McQueen in *The Great Escape*."

"Right on! That's just how I felt."

"It's a beautiful story, Rick, except for one thing."

"What's that?"

"You're in jail telling the story."

Brotha Guru is always busting my chops. I don't mind, though, because he's a good listener and someone who's helping me remember all the crazy shit that happened to me.

I remember that first week of freedom. Turned out Doc wasn't bullshitting. He did have a wad of cash stashed at his mother's. He picked it up, gave us each a nice taste, and the three of us were on our way to a three-bedroom penthouse suite in midtown Manhattan. Ray Charles had a hit out called "Let's Go Get Stoned." They were playing it on the radio every five minutes. And sure enough, an hour after we checked into the hotel there was a knock on the door. Doc's dope man had arrived with something for everyone. Doc was deep into scag. Eddie and I weren't into heroin, but we gorged ourselves on smoke and coke. That night Doc's lady came by with two super-fine bitches. There's nothing like your first fuck after being locked up for nearly a year. Pussy never tasted so sweet.

Except that Elke's pussy tasted even sweeter. By the end of that week we'd flown to Toronto, where I thought we'd be safer. Elke and I fucked for three straight days. I fixed up Doc and Eddie with some of Elke's friends and things were mellow until word got round that the FBI was after me. We hightailed it to Montreal, where we hung for a month. We were still high on the excitement of being fugitives, not to mention the high of the coke, smoke, and smack.

I was sitting in at a club singing Billy Stewart's stuttering version of "Summertime"—Billy was Doc's favorite—when afterward this smokin'-hot long-legged bitch came up and said she was an acrobat at the circus and loved her some soul singing. For the rest of the trip she had my nuts in knots—not that I'm complaining. I loved how she contorted her body to where she could lick her own clit. Her hire-wire act was something I'll never forget. Meanwhile, I was forgetting all reality—until I called home to check on Mom.

"What do you think you're doing, son?" she asked.

"Just avoiding jail, that's all."

"Not for long, James. They back on your tail. They calling every day. I don't even wanna know where you are 'cause they probably got this phone tapped. You got to come on in."

"Not yet, Mom. Not now."

"Longer you stay out, worse it's gonna get. I've been in touch with my cousin Louis Stokes. He's been elected a United States congressman."

"Cousin Louis from Cleveland?"

"The same. I told him all about your situation. He checked with the navy. He says they're as anxious to get rid of you as you are to get rid of them."

"What does that mean?"

"It means if you turn yourself in now, Louis can help. But you gotta turn yourself in."

"Again?"

"Hell, yes, again," said Mom.

So here we go again. I packed my bag, bought a plane ticket to Buffalo, and found myself flying home when I picked up a magazine someone had left on my seat. Mindlessly, I leafed through the pages—Vietnam was still tearing the country apart. Counterculture leaders were calling for be-ins. The Black Panthers, who I dug for their gutsy fuck-you attitude, were making noise in Oakland. All this was interesting, but the article that stopped me cold concerned music. It mentioned two groups—Buffalo Springfield, featuring Neil Young and Bruce Palmer, and Steppenwolf, featuring Goldy McJohn. Both groups had major record deals and were the talk of L.A. Those were my boys.

While I was running in and out of prison, my boys had carried on with the music and gotten somewhere. The article talked about the new soulful folk-rock sound they had cultivated up in Canada. I was part of that cultivation. I might even have been the major part of that cultivation. Now all I was cultivating was the thought of being thrown back in the brig to face another trial. Right then and there, I pledged that if cousin Congressman Stokes could help me put this navy thing behind me, I'd make my way straight to L.A. Like so many other teenagers in the country, I was California dreaming.

Back to Buffalo.

Another beautiful reunion with Mom, who, no matter how I messed up, never stopped believing that I'd eventually straighten up and fly right. Another call to the FBI. Another pair of agents who came to cuff me. Another trip back to Brooklyn.

What was new, though, was the reception I got when I returned to that top-floor brig in the dorm. I got a standing O. I was greeted like a hero. I was the cat who escaped. I tried to give credit where credit was due—Doc was the mastermind. But since Doc was still at large, I got the respect.

I also got lucky. During my second court martial, the court was lenient. I was given a general discharge. I was told I'd only have to serve six more months. That's because I'd enlisted when I was under-age at sixteen and also because they were tired of me. My escape had embarrassed them and they feared I'd do it again. Now I just had to get through another half a year.

Knowing that I had somehow beat the system, the supervisors and guards put me through my paces those last months. I was back to scraping shit off toilet bowls, washing dishes in burning-hot water, and mopping the kitchen floor. One of the guards, a racist asshole named Leo, had it out for me. One morning when he saw me on my knees cleaning tile, he kicked my ass so hard I fell on my face and busted my nose. I went for his throat, but before I could do anything he had a gun to my head. I was determined to get him back, but I had to wait. Two months later when they gave me potato-peeling duty, I managed to slip a mashed-up dead cockroach into the bowl of bean soup he was being served. The next day he didn't report for duty because they said he was sick as a dog. I only wish the cockroach had been poisonous.

On the bright side of my final time in the brig was a young brotha from Seattle called Fire Ride. His first year in the service he got caught stealing navy cars and selling them on the black market. He said he was named after the horse that won his daddy ten thou-sand dollars the day he was born. He also said he knew Jimi Hendrix and came loaded with not only with Hendrix's records but all kinds of great music. There was a little phonograph in the rec room that we could use on certain nights. That's where me and Fire Ride got tight. At the same time, Doc was back in the brig—they'd caught him in Montreal—and he had a connection in Brooklyn where we got the freshest records off the street. So me, Doc, and Fire Ride would have these listening sessions that opened up my ears to everything happening on the outside.

The first side that came in was *Two for the Price of One*, an album that blew my mind. The artists were Larry Williams and Johnny "Guitar" Watson. The cover flipped me out—Larry and Johnny each standing on the hoods of Cadillacs while holding leather reins like cowboys riding their steeds. The music was cold-blooded. Mom had Larry's old R & B hits in her collection—"Bony Moronie" and "Short Fat Fanny"—and I remember hearing Johnny's "Space Guitar" when I was a little kid.

"Hendrix memorized 'Space Guitar,'" said Fire Ride. "That's where he got the idea of all that feedback and distortion. He stole the shit from Johnny."

In *Two for the Price of One*, I heard how Johnny was putting a new kind of hurting on the funk. He was edgier than just about anyone else out there. He pushed the envelope in the same direction I would have pushed it had I not been locked up. He even had the balls to call a song "Coke." Like me, Johnny knew how to blend R & B and jazz. On that record, he put lyrics to a song Joe Zawinul had written for Cannonball Adderley—"Mercy Mercy Mercy," a combination jazz/R & B/soul hit. Meanwhile, rumors were coming in from the street that Miles was going electric and using Zawinul, Chick Corea, and guitarist John McLaughlin.

We were also jamming to Sly, the master blaster of the sixties. His bass player Larry Graham had a thumb-poppin' attitude that made all of us take note. There were other super-funky bass players—a bad white boy named Duck Dunn and of course Paul McCartney—but Graham came on with some shit we'd never heard before.

Fire Ride and Doc weren't crazy about the Beatles' *White Album*, but I was. I loved it almost as much as *Sgt. Pepper's Lonely Hearts Club Band*, one of the most creative records I'd ever heard. On *The White Album*, I loved how the Beatles spoofed Chuck Berry on "Back in the USSR," loved the funky "Rocky Raccoon," loved the ballads like "Blackbird" and "While My Guitar Gently Weeps." The Beatles were also pushing the envelope, writing killer songs like "Happiness Is a Warm Gun" where their slight-of-hand humor made a mockery of cornball pop music. The Beatles were out there.

I couldn't wait to get out there so I could do what the Beatles, Johnny "Guitar" Watson, and Miles Davis were doing. I knew goddamn well I was hearing everything they heard. I could make righteous musical combinations of my own. I could bend and blend genres slick as anyone.

"Once you get out," said Fire Ride, "I'm gonna hook you up with Hendrix. Jimi's gonna love you. He might even put you in his band."

"Hey," I said, "he'd be lucky if I put him in my band!"

"Don't forget us when you get out there," said Doc, taking off this gorgeous record by Rahsaan Roland Kirk, *The Inflated Tear*, and putting on Big Brother and the Holding Company's *Cheap Thrills*. The album had a live cut, "Ball and Chain," sung by this bad bitch Janis Joplin. If Hendrix was gonna be my guitarist, Janis was gonna be my chick singer.

"It's all gonna happen," said Doc, "just make sure I get to see you do it."

"You'll be road manager," I told him. "And my man Fire Ride, he'll be my musical consultant."

The three of us had beautiful times listening to sounds. Those nights got me through the abuse I was taking from Leo and the other redneck crackers.

One morning Leo came to me while I was scrubbing the pots and pans. The big smile on his face worried me. I'd never seen that motherfucker smile—not once.

"Too bad you won't be able to get any more of that jungle music snuck in here," he said.

"What are you talking about?"

"Doc, the guy who gets you all your records. He won't be getting 'em no more."

"How do you know that?"

"Because he's dead."

I nearly stopped breathing.

"Who killed him?"

"No one. The dumb bastard killed himself. Doctor says he OD'd. The dope got him so crazy that he jimmied up a window and jumped out."

"That don't make no sense."

"Neither does taking dope or listening to jungle music. Both things make you wanna kill yourself."

I wanted to kill Leo but was too shocked to do anything.

Losing Doc was rough. He was a good cat. He was one of my main supporters. He saw my talent and never tired of telling people that I was gonna make it.

The only relief came when was I transferred to another naval and marine prison, this one in Portsmouth, New Hampshire. I was glad to get away from Leo and the asshole guards in Brooklyn. Portsmouth was more chilled. I got to sing for the prisoners in the mess hall, one of the most appreciative audiences I've ever encountered. Otis Redding had died the year before and once, after I sang

"The Dock of the Bay," one of the brothas yelled, "Otis has come back from the grave! Sing on, Otis!" They made me sing the song six straight times.

✦

When I finally got out I went to Buffalo to be with Mom.

"You're free now, son," she said. "You've finally put all that navy stuff behind you. So what are you going to do?"

"I'm not sure, but it's got to have to do with music."

"Can you do it here?" Mom asked.

"I'd love to stay with you, Mom, but nothing's happening in Buffalo. You can't launch a career from Buffalo."

"Will you go back to Toronto? Toronto's not that far. And I saw for myself how you're already a star in Toronto."

That weekend I went to Toronto, thinking that it'd be cool to stay in a city only a hundred miles from home. But when I got there, I realized that the entire gang was gone. I knew that Joni Mitchell, Bruce Palmer, Neil Young, and Goldy McJohn had left, but I didn't know that Elke had gone back to Europe.

Toronto was always cool and Yorkville always hip, but it felt like its time had passed. I found some good musicians who I knew from before and worked up a little band. I figured some of the old club owners would be glad to see me fronting my group. Wrong. The old club owners didn't give a shit and I couldn't find a single gig. Pissed and discouraged, I spent my money on speed and coke.

When the dope ran out, the dealer told me he'd give me a free resupply if I helped him break into this super-hip boutique. He knew where we could fence the mod clothes for good bread. My man promised there wouldn't any problems—the back window would be easy to unlock and there were no alarms. All that proved true. I did the job, copped the clothes—keeping some choice items for myself—and stayed stoned for another week. After the high wore off, I hit a new low. I wanted to play music but it seemed like the city that had once been in love with Little Ricky, the Sailor Boys, and the Mynah Birds no longer gave a rat's ass about me.

"Home so soon?" said Mom when I returned from Canada after just a month.

"It ain't happening there," I told my mother.

"Then where is it happening?"

"L.A."

"Oh, baby, California is such a long way off. How about New York?"

"Well, maybe I'll try Florida first. Maybe I'll take a run down to Miami."

"What's down there?"

"A buddy from high school—you remember Big Red—he's living down there and says he can hook me up at Criteria Studios. Aretha's been recording there. So has James Brown. It's a hot spot."

"Just be careful."

"I always am."

I never was. Big Red, an albino brotha, was a major coke dealer who supplied the superstars in Miami. He had the run of all the studios and the minute I got off the Greyhound he took me to Criteria. First cat I met was Sam Moore, who was doing a solo album. When his bass player didn't show up, I asked the producer if he had an extra axe. He did, Sam liked my playing, and suddenly I was gainfully employed. Criteria became my hang.

I crashed at Big Red's oceanfront crib. I liked the beach scene. Big Red had all sorts of hot bitches, righteous blow, and mellow weed. He was convinced that his homeboy from Buffalo was gonna be bigger than Sly Stone. I loved his support. He'd never let me pay for a thing. Big Red was proud that his childhood pal could hang in the studio with the big dogs. At Criteria I got to play with Duane Allman and Steve Cropper, two superbad white-boy guitarists who showed me a slew of new licks. They were both brilliant. So was Cornell Dupree, maybe the slickest R & B guitarist ever. I spent days in the studio studying Cornell's style.

Looked like Miami might work out. My chops were getting sharper, producers started calling me on a regular basis, and I figured soon I'd be able to bust out with my own material. Being a sideman was cool—but it wasn't me.

Just when I thought I'd found a home in Miami, Big Red got popped. It happened on a Saturday. I'd been at Criteria and didn't get back to the crib till midnight, when I saw four or five cop cars parked out front, their lights flashing. Man, that was a scary sight. I figured it was best not to go in. I figured right. That night I went to stay with another friend of Red's, who told me it was a bad bust and that the police, who had the place under surveillance, were looking for anyone associated with Big Red. Since I'd been living with him for over a month, that meant me.

"What do you think I should do?" I asked.

"Get out of Dodge."

Next day I was back on the bus to Buffalo.

"What now?" Mom asked when I got home.

"Not sure."

"You're still thinking California, aren't you, baby?"

"You know me."

"Well, if you gotta go, you gotta go. Just wish it wasn't so far."

Much to Mom's credit, she didn't try to hold me back. She cared more about my career than keeping me close to her.

"I'll send for you soon as I get settled and get me serious money," I promised.

"I know you will."

"You're just going to have to be a little patient."

"I'm not worried about my patience, son. I got lots. I don't mean this harshly, James, because you know how much I love you—but you've got the patience of a butterfly. The second you land on one flower, you off looking for another."

CALI

Even though it was the end of the sixties when I got there, L.A. felt like the beginning—the beginning of something new and wonderful in my life. The hippie vibe had spread to L.A., where it took a different form than I'd seen in Buffalo, Toronto, and New York. To me, L.A. was Hippie Land. Hippies gave the city its flavor. There wasn't the tension I'd felt back east between the hippies and the squares. Here the hippies blended. Maybe because L.A. was laid-back, everyone left the hippies alone. They were part of the landscape—like the palm trees and the hills, like the beaches and the valleys—man, the hippies were everywhere, especially on the Sunset Strip and along Hollywood Boulevard. Laurel Canyon looked like a camp for hippies. The cats had longer hair than the chicks; hardly any of the chicks were wearing bras under their tie-dyed tops; stoned-eyed guys were offering up free joints; stoned-eyed gals were offering up free love. Free joints and free love, not to mention the warm Cali sunshine, had me believing that the world was really changing. I was in a better place. All the bitterness I'd felt in prison, all that resentment built up during my days as a half-ass hardened criminal—it all lifted. L.A. was taking me to another place where it was all about peace and love.

My first day in L.A. was one mellow surprise after another. Bruce Palmer picked me up at the airport in a red Mustang convertible. The joints were rolled and ready to light.

"You need to meet Stephen Stills," said Bruce. "Stills is the magic ingredient in our new band."

I didn't know whether I was included in the "our" or not. But the weed had me kicked back until I didn't need to ask. Time would tell. It was just cool to be floating through the L.A. afternoon, feeling the mild ocean breeze and sweet sunshine in my face. I felt at peace.

"Peace, brother," Stephen Stills said to me when he greeted me at the door of his house. "Heard good things about you."

"Same here," I said.

Another band member called Richie Furay approached me.

"You're the famous Little Ricky from Toronto," he said.

I said, "Not so famous and not so little."

He laughed and offered me more killer weed. He talked much shit and we got along great. I liked Richie a lot, a happy-go-lucky cat with no attitude.

Couldn't say the same for Stills. He didn't engage me in conversation and wasn't the least bit interested in learning anything about me. Underneath his silence, I felt the presence of a big ego.

"We need to see Neil," said Bruce. "He's been asking for you."

We all hightailed it to Neil Young's log cabin in the hills. He greeted us in full Indian regalia. We hugged like long-lost brothers and shot the shit for hours. He wanted to hear my war stories and I was eager to tell 'em. Neil and I had a great rapport—two wild artists who understood each other on the deepest level. As we spoke, I saw

Stills watching us out of the corner of his eye. Instincts told me that all was not cool between Neil and Stephen.

All was completely cool when we arrived at David Crosby's. David had the kind of smoke that melted tension and turned antagonists into allies. This smoke had me loving on the world. Like me, David was a storyteller who liked to entertain his guests. "Got some clear acid for you," he offered.

"Thanks," I said, "but I just got here. Gonna wait a minute or two to get my bearings before I start tripping."

"Can't wait no longer or we gonna miss the Daily Flash," said Bruce. "They're playing the Whisky."

More joints, more cruisin' down the canyons, more cruisin' up the Strip. Got to the Whisky A Go Go and I realized I didn't have the bread to get in.

"Don't even think twice about it," said David Crosby. "This is your welcome-to-L.A. night. The champagne's on me."

The first act, the Daily Flash, sounded like a second-rate Jefferson Airplane. The next act, though, took me by surprise. They were a mixed group—leader singer Arthur Lee and guitarist Johnny Echols were black, and the other cats were white. They played in an acid folk-rock style that had the place jumping, but I wasn't impressed. I was thinking, *If these L.A. hippies are going nuts over this shit, wait till they hear me. I'm gonna tear this town apart.*

Maybe Arthur and Johnny sensed my attitude when Bruce introduced me to them, 'cause they were a little standoffish. They were like gunslingers looking over the new kid in town.

That night I crashed at Bruce's. I closed my eyes and thought back about why it had taken me so long to get to Cali. This was the state of my mind; L.A. was the city of my soul. I felt right at home here. Musically, I knew just what was happenin'. I wasn't in the least intimidated, just frustrated that I had gotten a late start.

In spite of our initial standoff, Johnny Echols of Love became a good friend and took me to some slammin' Hollywood parties. At one of them I met a sista named Jade. She told me that she'd been living with Donovan. Naturally I knew Donovan's "Sunshine Superman" and "Mellow Yellow." Cute stuff, but not my thing. I told Jade that I considered Donovan the poor man's Bob Dylan.

"You always so opinionated?" she asked.

"Always—at least when it comes music and women."

"What kind of opinions do you have about women?"

"That you are by far the most beautiful I've ever met."

"That's an opinion I like."

We loved that night and for three nights after.

Bruce was good to me, and so was Stephen, although neither one invited me to join their band. No matter, I was still happy to be invited to Stills's house, where I'd go to jam. Sometimes I'd crash on his couch. Stills's place was a great spot for meeting musicians and chicks. It was at Stills's that I met Donovan, Jade's ex. Naturally I didn't say a word. Stills's crib was a strange but fascinating scene.

The start of the extreme strangeness happened the night I awoke to see a young dude sitting on the floor in the lotus position, stoned as a motherfucker. Nothing unusual about that except for the blood dripping from his wrist. He seemed hypnotized by the flow of his blood, saying things like, "Isn't the blood beautiful? Isn't that the deepest red you've ever seen?"

I got scared he was gonna bleed to death and ran to get Stephen out of the bed he was sharing with his girlfriend, whom I'll call Perfect.

"Oh, fuck," said Stephen, "he's doing it again." Stephen gathered up bandages and gauze and took care of the guy, who remained passive through the ordeal. When Stephen was through, he said to me, "Ricky, meet Jim Morrison."

Morrison was one far-out cat. He was the first sure-enough poet

I'd ever met. He didn't speak or act like the rest of us. He spoke and acted poetry. He started reading me something he'd written about the dead angels of history returning as groupies. He started singing a song about love among the ancient Indians who worshipped the sun. I didn't think he could sing worth a shit, but his lyrics were enchanting. You had to listen to this guy. When he asked about my past and I mentioned my stopover at Motown, he bombarded me with questions about Smokey Robinson and Marvin Gaye. He called them great poets—and he was right.

Next day, his wounds healed, Jim joined the rest of us on a trip to Disneyland. I was excited to see the place. We ran down the freeway in Stephen's wooden station wagon but were turned away 'cause our hippie threads were too far-out for white-bread Disney. Fuck Disney. We went to some dumpy bumper-car place and had a ball. The more I hung, the more I was digging L.A.

The big night was when the Doors, the house band at the Whisky, opened for Buffalo Springfield. I know that the Doors became one of the biggest bands in history and Morrison, like Dylan, influenced the world. I also know Jim was sincere, and that he was one of the inventors of theatrical rock. Until Jim, I always thought a singer had to be a guy with a great voice. Jim showed me that attitude was as important as voice. In years to come, David Bowie and Lou Reed would also get by on attitude and theatrics. All that's fine, but, far as Morrison went, I got a little bored. I needed more fire in my rock and more funk in my folk. The Doors were weak tea.

After the Doors' set I was hanging with Morrison in his dressing room. We were sharing a joint and shooting the shit when he asked me if I wanted a mint. "Sure," I said. He popped this little blue mint into my mouth. I didn't think anything of it. As I picked up one of his acoustic guitars and started to strum, the mint tasted sour, but then turned sweet.

"What is this?" I asked Jim.

"Happy sailing," he said.

Acid. Oh well, it was going to happen sooner or later. Now was as good a time as any. Soon I started feeling a little strange. My fingers numbed out and the world turned extra bright. That's when Jade appeared.

"You look fucked-up, Ricky," she said.

"Morrison slipped me acid."

"I'm tripping myself. Mind if I join you?"

"Let's take off together."

I'm an uninhibited guy, but I usually don't start balling a chick in a dressing room with the door unlocked. But that's the first thing that happened on my maiden acid voyage. Jade and I melted into each other. We went down to the bottom of the mystical sea. God knows how long we were down there. Later Morrison told me that people were passing through the room while we were fucking, but damned if I knew. I was swimming through a sea of love I had never seen before. If LSD opened the floodgates of this kind of loving, I wanted more. I officially became a love child.

Because I was too busy tripping-fucking, I missed hearing Buffalo Springfield that night. I did, though, get a chance to hear them many times after that. I heard them as good, not great, but I'm sure my opinion was prejudiced by the fact that they still hadn't asked me to join them. With me as their lead singer, I was convinced the band would improve by at least 50 percent.

After several months in L.A., I saw that I could hang with the heavyweights. The only thing they had that I lacked was money. And I knew it was only a question of time before I'd get mine. Meanwhile, I was honing my music hustling skills, an essential for success in the record biz. I was meeting all the right people. I got lucky when Stephen Stills didn't wanna take Perfect to a fancy party thrown by Jay Sebring, a cat who'd made millions selling hair products.

"You take Perfect," said Stephen. "You get along with everyone. I'm fed up with that Hollywood crowd."

Well, I was just getting started with the Hollywood crowd and jumped at the opportunity. It felt a little strange to be trusted with Perfect, who was super hot, but she was game and so was I.

Sebring was cool. He turned out to be one of the era's slickest movers and shakers. He took a liking to me and I saw he took an extra-special liking to Perfect. Everyone was blowing cocaine and dancing to Marvin's "I Heard It Through the Grapevine." Jay saw that me and Perfect were the ideal party people and a week later invited us back. Naturally I asked Stills if it was okay. He had no objections and we went back over to Sebring's place several times. That's where I met Sammy Davis and Steve McQueen. It's also where I saw Sebring making a move on Perfect. The truth was that Perfect had the hots for me, not Jay, and, man, I had the hots for her. Yet I restrained myself. I didn't want to betray Stephen. I also didn't want to hurt her budding friendship with Sebring because I saw how much he respected her. Perfect had a brilliant business mind and was starting to give him advice about his products. That's when I got an idea.

Before we walked into one of Sebring's high-time parties, I said to Perfect, "Get him to back a band for me. Tell him I'm the next Sly Stone."

"You are," said Perfect.

"Get him to believe that. Get him to give me some bread. I know the musicians I need. They're in Toronto. I could fly there and within a few weeks get a band together that would tear up this town. Will you talk to him?"

"I will."

She did—and guess what? Jay Sebring sprang for the bread—with one condition: that Perfect accompany me to Toronto and supervise the operation.

How lucky can one man be? My glow was getting brighter by the day.

BACK TO THE FUTURE

The future was staring me in the face—and her name was Perfect. Perfect was perfect in all ways—luscious lips, big tits, long legs, sculpted booty, smiling eyes, high cheekbones, bubbly personality, and super-sharp mind. Our relationship began in honest friendship. I thought she was cool and vice versa. When she started balling Jay Sebring behind Stills's back, we'd laugh about it. She trusted me with her most intimate secrets. The hottest secret, though, was that we were falling for each other. Because she was juggling two powerful men at once—both of whom could help my career—I had good reasons to keep my hands off Perfect. And because Perfect hardly needed to contend with another lover, she had also decided to keep our thing platonic.

Yet the second the plane took off from Los Angeles and we found ourselves alone on the flight to Toronto, something shifted. A restraint lifted. We felt free. After the jet leveled off, she glanced over to the bathroom and then glanced back at me. She got up and began walking to the back. I waited a few minutes and followed. She'd left the door ajar. I walked in and locked the door behind me. She laid out two thick lines of blow. We snorted them up in a second. She lifted up her skirt. Nothing underneath, just her fluffy moist bush. I crunched myself up on the floor so she could crouch down over my face. I tongued her until she came. Then I lifted her onto the sink and fucked her until she came again. I exploded seconds after that. We cleaned ourselves off, went back to our seats, and, halfway through the trip, returned to the bathroom to repeat the operation. She came another four or five times. I'd never been with a bitch this hot.

When we checked into our hotel suite in Toronto, the bellhop was barely out the door before we tore off our clothes and were at it again. In contrast to the tiny airplane bathroom, the king-sized bed gave us a feeling of incredible freedom. We fucked our brains out. We added our own chapter to the Kama Sutra.

"What am I gonna say to Jay?" asked Perfect after we both admitted that it was more than lust between us; it was love.

"The same thing you're gonna say to Stephen," I said. "Nothing."

"They'll know."

"They probably already know. Besides, they've got all kinds of other bitches. I wouldn't worry about it."

"I won't."

And she didn't. She slipped into a pair of tight denim bell-bottoms and put on a sheer T-shirt. No bra. Perfect didn't need a bra. Her breasts had a natural uplift. Seeing her dressed that way made me wanna undress her all over again, but we had to start finding me a band. It was ten P.M. when we hit the clubs in Yorkville. I still had a lot of fans in Toronto, and it was good being recognized. It was important for me to show Perfect that in Canada I was a star. She thought it was funny that everyone called me "Little Ricky"—back in Cali I'd started switching over to Rick James—but she liked how the club owners treated us like royalty. It was well after midnight in the third club we visited when I heard what I'd been looking for. The group was called Ooppicks. They had a groove. They had a look. They had a funky edge that had me and Perfect hand clapping and finger popping. Watch out, Sly Stone! Watch out, George Clinton! With these cats at my back, I knew I'd blow up in no time. Ooppicks was the bomb.

"They're it, aren't they, baby?" asked Perfect.

"My dream's coming true," I said. "With you and this band, my life's complete."

Just as I was about to approach the guys, the owner tapped me on the shoulder and said someone wanted to see me.

"Be right back, sugar," I told Perfect. I figured it was a fan.

Went outside, where two guys in suits grabbed my arms, snapped handcuffs on my wrists, and threw me in the back of a sedan.

"What the fuck's happening?" I asked.

"You're under arrest."

"For what?"

"Breaking and entering."

"You got the wrong guy. I just got to town."

"It happened before you left. It was a clothing store. Your fingerprints were all over the place. We've been waiting for you to get back. Welcome to Canada, nigger."

Came to find out that not only was I too dumb to wear gloves during that break-in with the drug dealer, I'd also brought with me a couple of the outfits that I'd stolen that night to Toronto. The cops went to my suite and found them hanging in the closet. Man, I was double dumb.

They say life turns on a dime. I don't know if someone dropped a dime on me or whether it was my pure stupidity that did me in. Either way, in less than a minute I'd gone from heaven to hell. A few seconds ago, my life was perfect—the perfect bitch, the perfect financier, the perfect backup band, the perfect connections to the perfect music scene in L.A. Now perfection had turned to pure shit. Now I was at the police station, put in a room, told to strip, and, for no good reason, beaten by the same two assholes who picked me up. I tried to fight back but got nowhere. As they slugged me, careful to avoid my face so the judge wouldn't know, they couldn't stop talking about niggers who came to Canada to fuck their women. It was an old American story—fear of the black man's sexual prowess—with a Canadian twist.

I was determined to bust their dicks for assaulting a defenseless prisoner. I got a lawyer and was going to take it to the highest court in the country. They had me on the break-in charge, but I had them on my jail beating. Long story short, my legal complaint got me nowhere except nine long months in prison. Far as Perfect goes—the super-passionate lady I loved so deeply and who said she felt the same about me—well, I never saw the bitch again.

Nine months is enough time to have a baby. Nine months in a nasty Canadian prison is enough time to have a nervous breakdown. Nine months is enough time to permanently put out my glow. Nine months of hearing records like the Temptations' "I Wish It Would Rain" that had me crying my eyes out. I remember hearing the Dells singing "Stay in My Corner" and wondering if anyone was in my corner. Jail was a helluva place to celebrate my twentieth birthday—February 1, 1968.

"I love you, baby," said Mom when they allowed me to call her that day.

"I feel like I've let you down," I said.

"Why do you say that?"

"I made promises I haven't kept. I told you I'd buy you a house and a car and fix it so you wouldn't have to work."

"I like working, and besides, you're still a young man with plans. Soon as you get out, I know you're gonna get on the right track. You've learned from your mistakes and you'll put this past behind you."

"You sound like you still believe in me, Mom."

"More than I believe in anything in this world. You'll be, fine, I know you will. This isn't your best birthday but it's still a milestone. Just keep your mind and soul together, and time will pass."

Time was a burden. It moved slower than at any time in my life. I watched the second hand go around, I watched the minute hand, the calendar. Out of my little window I got a postage-stamp view of the sun coming up in the morning and the sky turning dark at night. A fellow prisoner, a brotha who'd been to college, asked if I wanted to learn bridge. Why not? What else did I have to do? Within a few weeks I was playing and winning like a champ.

"You got a great mind," said the brotha. "You always been this brilliant with cards?"

"Never played before and when I get outta here I'll never play again."

I didn't give a shit about bridge. It was music that haunted me. Hearing James Brown sing "Say It Loud—I'm Black and I'm Proud" went right to my soul. I wish I had written that song. The Beatles' "Hey Jude" was magnificent. It's another tune I wish I'd done. I was, in fact, writing songs, but without a guitar or piano they were lyrics without melodies. I had a million ideas—a million grooves were moving through my mind—yet the more creative I got, the more frustrated I became because the prison wouldn't give me an instrument. They didn't even have a piano.

I harbored hope that Perfect might get in touch and say how much she missed me. That hope died hard. Perfect never sent as much as a postcard. It was Mom and Mom alone who got me through those nine months in Canadian prison. Her letters came every week and every two weeks I got to call her.

On the day of my release Mom was at the border when the immigration officials dropped me off.

"It's over, baby," she said, taking me in her arms. "From now on, it's all gonna be good."

I wanted to believe her but somehow being free brought me down. Made me realize how much time I had wasted running afoul of the law.

"Why don't you call your friends Neil and Stephen in California?" Mom asked.

But what was I gonna tell them? I was the guy who messed up the Mynah Birds. I was the guy who fucked Stephen Stills's girlfriend and ran through Jay Sebring's money. The Cali cats saw me as a loser. I couldn't call them.

"What about Motown?" Mom asked. "You said that they saw your talent."

"They got so many stars up there, they don't need another one."

"You have your writing talent, James, as well as your singing talent. I know Motown is always looking for good writers. Maybe you could call Mr. Gordy."

Seemed a far-fetched idea, but what the hell. God bless Mom for pushing me. The chances of Gordy calling me back were a hundred to one. In fact, he didn't return my call, but I was shocked when one of his underlings, Ralph Seltzer, did.

"Of course we remember you in Detroit," said Seltzer. "You made quite an impression. Have you taken care of your legal obligations?"

"I have. And I've also written dozens of new songs. I can play 'em for your producers."

"No harm in that."

"If I came to Detroit, could I come by the office?"

"Call me when you get here."

I was stunned. Motown was still open to my ideas. A week later I was walking up to the famous house/headquarters on West Grand Boulevard.

The first guy I ran into was Norman Whitfield. He was riding high on his Temptations hits, not to mention the Marvin Gaye smashes, like "Chained" and "Too Busy Thinking About My Baby."

"Look who's back," he said. "The wonder boy. Heard you got your ass kicked a couple of times."

"More than a couple," I admitted.

"That's good for you. So you've come back to be a star."

"You guys have enough stars. I've come back to sell some songs."

"You have demos?"

"Need a studio to work up a few."

"I'll arrange it."

Whitfield was a strange cat. He'd go from belligerent to friendly in an instant. He helped me get my demos together and liked what he heard. In less than a week, he talked to Gordy, who hired me as a staff writer. The money wasn't big but I was thrilled to be back in the game. It was also great to have Whitfield as a mentor. During my first go-round at Motown, he had made fun of my hippie threads. Now he said I was the coolest dresser in Detroit. Not only did he let me watch his sessions but he got the other great producers, like Clarence Paul and Harvey Fuqua, to show me their producing techniques as well.

"You're smart to want to be a producer," Whit said. "You'll soon see that the artists aren't the stars at Motown—the producers are. We run the show. Except for Smokey, who's an artist and a producer— not to mention Berry's best friend—the artists are always kissing our ass, hoping we'll take them into the studio and give them hit songs. Because Berry started out as a writer and producer, this company is controlled by the cats behind the scenes—us."

I liked the way that sounded and went from being a cocky lead singer/artist to a conscientious student writer-producer. I wouldn't say I was altogether humble—humility has never come easy to me—but I was surely respectful of these men whose track records were astonishing. In a period of six or seven months, I earned the equivalent of a PhD in record production. The Motown producers were not only the best in the business, but they worked nonstop and were fiercely competitive. I liked that vibe. Only the strong survived.

My staff-writing stint in Detroit happened during a transitional period in Motown history. When I was there back in '66 with the Mynah Birds, the great production/writing team of Holland-Dozier-Holland was still cranking out monster hits for all the acts. But then HDH thought they were getting a raw royalty deal, so they sued Berry and quit. He countersued and the legal warfare was on. By the winter of '68 when I was back in Detroit, HDH had left Motown to form their own label. Berry was also spending most of his time in L.A.

The general notion was that Detroit was past and present and L.A. was the future. Berry wanted to go Hollywood. Certain artists, like Marvin Gaye, who was not a follower, stayed in Detroit. This was when Marvin went through his big rebellion against conventional R & B and started getting political. Even though he was having huge duet hits with Tammi Terrell, he kept telling me how pop music was bullshit and how he was gonna write about the fucked-up Vietnam War. In his mind, he was already planning *What's Going On.*

Bobby Taylor, the cat I met my first time in Detroit, was also a rebel. He wouldn't take shit off any of the producers 'cause he was sure he could produce himself. He'd just gotten back from Chicago, where these five kids had opened for him at the Regal. They called themselves the Jackson 5, and Bobby swore that the littlest one, named Michael, was the best singer he'd heard since Clyde McPhatter. He put all five in his car and drove them to Detroit, where they auditioned for Berry, who signed them on the spot. Bobby took them in the studio and had little Michael cover Smokey's "Who's Lovin' You." None of us could believe it. Smokey himself couldn't believe it. The kid burned down the building. When Bobby had him singing Sly's "Stand!," he sounded better than Sly.

"BG's taking the kids to Hollywood," said Bobby Taylor, referring to Berry Gordy. "He thinks I'm producing them too black. He wants to present them as a pop act."

"What did you tell BG?"

"I told him to fuck himself—no one could be doing a better job with those kids than me."

Turned out that Bobby was both right and wrong. His initial Jackson 5 productions were beautiful—pure R & B. But when the L.A. productions came out—"I Want You Back" and "ABC"—I understood what BG was going for. They were about the best pop records I'd ever heard. Plus he packaged them like psychedelic Disney characters so they'd appeal to everyone.

Being around other writers, my own writing was improving by leaps and bounds. I wrote a song called "Out in the Country" that everyone liked. It was in the style of "I Wish It Would Rain," the hit Whit had written for the Tempts.

When Norman heard it he said, "Sounds like you've been going to school on my shit."

"You don't like it?" I asked.

"I think it's strong, but keep it away from the Tempts. They're my group."

"Produce it on me, motherfucker," said Bobby Taylor when he heard it.

"Why? You're a producer yourself."

"Yeah, but sometimes a producer needs a producer. You'll put a hurting on it that I won't. It's your baby. I'll make sure the right cats do the session."

By that he meant the Funk Brothers, the most legendary rhythm section in the history of R & B. When I walked in the studio and saw Earl Van Dyke, James Jamerson, Richard "Pistol" Allen, and Dennis Coffey, I froze. I could hardly talk. Finally, I managed to say, "Y'all don't know me from Adam. And here I am about to tell y'all, the baddest motherfuckers on the planet, what to play and how to play it. So if I say or do something stupid, just ignore me and follow your gut. In other words, help me, fellas!"

Jamerson, the best bass player ever, led the way. He set up the groove and sculpted the sound. The guys could not have been more cooperative. They could have made me feel like a rank amateur, but instead they respected me. They helped me fulfill the song's potential. Bobby sang it tough. I knew I had the next single on the Vancouvers. Unfortunately, the quality control board that governed what got released didn't agree. "Out in the Country" made the album but was never issued as a single. I still think it's a Motown masterpiece.

When it came to sex, there was a lot of sleeping around at Motown. The intrigue was intense. I was living at the Lee Plaza apartments, where I saw a lot of the artists running in and out with lovers who were not their spouses. Jimmy Ruffin, who'd hit big with "What Becomes of the Brokenhearted," was one of them. He had a white girlfriend at the time and so did I, an ambitious chick from Toronto who dug me so hard she wanted to bring me money. Jimmy's gal wanted to do the same for him.

"I'm not sure," I told Jimmy.

"I am," he told me.

The idea of pimping was not all that appealing—but the idea of extra money was. Besides, so many of the big-name men at Motown had worked as pimps that it was practically the norm.

I tried, and I failed. Jimmy and I took the girls to Canada, where they worked the clubs and brought in bread. At one point I had three or four bitches selling pussy. But I lacked the hard-edged discipline and cold-blooded attitude a good pimp requires. I was lax. If my bitch said she was too tired to work, I said go home. If she said some john had beat her, I'd find the john and beat his ass. I loaned them money and, within a few weeks, saw the whole operation as heartless. Pimping was too inhuman for me. I let the girls go and went back to my music.

Calvin Hardaway, Stevie Wonder's brother, was another superb writer and producer who became a mentor. He got me to study Burt Bacharach and Hal David's songs. They had written a slew of hits for Dionne Warwick, like "Alfie" and "I Say a Little Prayer." Calvin also pointed me in the direction of José Feliciano, who had reinvented two songs in a Latin soul vein that intrigued me—the Doors' "Light My Fire" and, even better, "The Star-Spangled Banner." His funked-up version of the national anthem sung before the World Series in Detroit in '68 was the kind of scandal I loved. During those days when the dirty war in Vietnam was still raging, José was revealing the dark side of that milquetoast patriotic song.

For all that I learned in Detroit, for all that I loved about working at the city's famous record company, I was still restless, especially since Motown wasn't exactly making me rich. It all became clear to me the night I got wiped out by Norman Whitfield at an east side pool hall. He won a thousand dollars off me in thirty minutes.

"Why didn't you tell me you were a shark?" I asked.

"You didn't ask. Besides, I wanted your money. I've been hustling cocky motherfuckers like you since I was a kid in Harlem."

"Rub it in, Norman."

"It's a hard way to learn a lesson, but the truth is that you ain't as good as you think you are."

"In pool maybe, but I can write songs."

"And you can sing. I've heard you sing. Fact is, you can do it all—write, produce, and even be a star. But it ain't gonna happen in Detroit."

"Why?"

"Because Detroit is done."

"The studio's still here. Marvin's still here. And so are—"

"Name whoever you want, Rick, but in a couple of years they'll all be out in L.A."

"Including you?"

"Especially me. Don't you see—Motown's all about crossover. You cross over from R & B to pop, you cross over from the black market to the wider white audience, and you sure as shit cross over from an old down-in-the-dumps city like Detroit to a modern space-age glamour city like L.A."

"Maybe Berry would put me on staff in the L.A. office."

"Are you kidding? If BG hasn't given you any play in Detroit, do you really think he'd pay any attention to you in Hollywood?"

"I guess not."

"You don't have to guess."

"Then what do I have to do?"

"Go west, young nigga."

"With what money? You just hustled me out of mine."

"I'll give back enough for bus fare."

"I'd rather fly."

"Tough shit," he said.

With that, Whit handed me fifty bucks and left me sitting alone in the pool hall.

SPICE

Summer of '69 was all about Blood, Sweat & Tears' "Spinning Wheel." That song had me spinning. I was back in L.A., giving the wheel another spin while remembering that only a couple of years ago David Clayton-Thomas—the Blood, Sweat & Tears singer—had been playing the same club circuit as me in Toronto. If David could do it, why not me?

I arrived back in California with Greg Reeves, a bass player who'd been mentored by the great James Jamerson. My notion was that I could front a group with Greg, a white boy who could bring the funk, and call it Salt 'n Pepper, corralling that crossover audience Norman Whitfield had talked about.

My first move was to approach Motown. But Whit's warning proved accurate. Not only couldn't I get to Berry, I couldn't get to the assistant of Berry's assistant. Ironically, the first connection I made was a Berry Gordy nemesis, Eddie Singleton. According to Eddie, who had spotted my talent back in Detroit, his career as a music producer had been stymied ever since he married BG's former wife Raynoma.

"You can stay in my place in the Hollywood Hills," said Eddie.

"Cool."

Turned out Eddie's brother booked the talent for *The Dating Game,* so you can imagine the beautiful bitches running through there. I found myself back in the showbiz circuit, where I met two wonderful women, Pam Louise, a tall black model, and Nancy Leviska, a fun and foxy white chick. Pam considered herself a witch and Nancy saw herself as a free spirit. I loved them both. They became my tripping partners and lovers. I ran back and forth between the two of them. If they minded sharing my love, their protests were mild. I would have not minded a ménage à trois but unfortunately that never happened. It was a period when free love was flowing in many directions. Another irony was that while Berry Gordy gave me no attention, he wound up lavishing attention on Nancy, a lovely lady, and together they had a son.

Pam was deep into tarot cards and astrological projections. I was deep into acid and orgies. In the midst of the sexual madness, Salt 'n Pepper was born. We found a manager, a gay boy from Beverly Hills with taste and money, and we found a groove but never an audience or a big-label deal. The excitement of sex and drugs overwhelmed my career ambition—at least for the moment. Then something else happened that, in this world of multiple partners, I hadn't expected—I fell in love.

It happened at a wild party where I was looking for lust, not love. Romance was the last thing on my mind, and yet there she was, seated in a chair, a portrait in quiet femininity, her eyes catching the moonlight shining down from the skylight above her. Our eyes locked for a long, long time. When we spoke it was brief, just a few words. It was one of those moments when words were beside the point. Our hearts did the speaking. Later that night we made love in the literal sense—the act itself created a deep loving feeling. We went way beyond lust to something mystical. Her name was Seville Morgan and she became my first live-in lover. We set up house in an apartment on Alta Loma with high wooden beams and a heated pool. I was living the life.

But the life costs money, and because Greg Reeves had moved in with us and slept on the couch, the food bill alone was considerable. Salt 'n Pepper was gone. For a minute I had a group called Heaven and Earth that RCA Canada thought might work. They put a single out but the single flopped. My musical income was zilch. I was living on love and the generosity of my white rock-and-roll friends. Understandably, that generosity had run its course. And then another friend appeared.

"What's happening, Rick?"

I looked up from my stool at Duke's coffee shop on Sunset and saw Jay Sebring standing over me. My first reaction was that he'd be pissed. I'd taken his money and blew it in Canada, where I wound up in jail. I'd also fucked his girl Perfect.

"Hey, Jay," I said.

"Where you been hiding?" There wasn't anger in his voice, just genuine curiosity.

"I've been back for a while."

"I never knew what happened to you in Toronto."

"Perfect didn't tell you?"

"Perfect disappeared. Tell me the story."

I told him, and amazingly, he wasn't at all pissed. He was understanding. Jay was a jewel. You had to love the guy.

"What a lousy break," he said. "I hope things have gotten better for you since you've been back."

"Got a cool apartment with a cool chick, but right now I'm tapped out."

"Right now I'm flush. Let me give you a couple of grand to get you back on your feet."

"Wow. What can I say?"

"You don't have to say a thing. When you blow up, just get me front-row seats to all your concerts."

"Every single one."

With a big smile on his face, Jay handed me the bread. What a guy! His faith in me was a beautiful reminder that the glow was still there.

Friends who'd become stars were all around me. I figured that it was a matter of time. Meanwhile, I had a little bread to buy a little weed and chill with my woman Seville, who turned out to have chops in the kitchen that rivaled her skills in bed.

Greg and I spent lots of time figuring out a new musical direction that combined white rock and black funk. Two new albums really got to us—Poco's *Pickin' Up the Pieces* and *Crosby, Stills & Nash*. I knew all those cats—Richie Furay had helped start Poco after Buffalo Springfield got unsprung. His country/rock thing was hip. Stephen Stills had also busted a hip move with those thick harmonies. When "Marrakesh Express" hit, I felt happy for the guys. Before I knew it, they'd become one of the biggest bands in the world.

I was buzzed when Furay called to invite me to a Poco gig at the Troubadour. Backstage I ran into Stephen Stills. Big hugs.

"Hey, Ricky, you gotta come up to my new crib. I bought it from Tork."

Our mutual friend Peter Tork was one of the Monkees. Naturally I'd never pass up a chance to hang with Stills and see his new pad. So Seville, Greg, and Greg's old lady went up there with me. Good vibes, good smoke, good times. Good to be back in touch with Stills.

"You could do me a favor," said Stephen.

"Name it, man, and you got it."

"Bruce is in bad shape."

"Palmer?" I asked.

"Yeah."

"He sounds great on your record," I said.

"Since then it's been downhill. I think it's hard drugs. Bruce Palmer is one of the best bass players ever, and I hate to see him that way—especially since we got this huge Woodstock gig coming. Before that we're doing the Greek with Joni opening for us. Bruce has gotta get himself together before all this happens."

"What can I do?" I asked.

"Talk to him, Ricky. He loves you. He respects you. You're his man."

"Where's he living these days?"

"Up in Topanga."

"I'll do what I can," I told Stephen, feeling funny about talking to a cat about drugs when I wasn't exactly abstaining myself. On the other hand, I didn't consider myself addicted. I was mainly smoking as opposed to coking.

Topanga was a hippie haven. It was only a few miles from the smoggy Sunset Strip, but it seemed like another world. The counterculture musicians were there in droves. Bruce's place was a log cabin. I went up there with Greg Reeves, who wanted to meet the great bassist.

The reunion was sweet. Bruce called me his brother and said how much he missed me. He talked about how beautiful it was to be in a famous rock group. His eyes told me that he was definitely fucked-up, but somehow I didn't have the heart to get into his drug problem. We were having too much fun reminiscing about Toronto. Later that night we went over to Stills's, where we all jammed for hours. Out of respect to Bruce, Greg played guitar, not his normal instrument. Bruce's bass licks were off, but hell, it was only a jam.

Next morning I was awoken by a knock on the door. Standing there were Stills and Graham Nash.

"Why don't we get a little lunch?"

"Great."

We went to the Source, a health food restaurant on Sunset. I wasn't sure what to expect. I halfway wondered if they were going to ask me to join the group. Crosby, Stills, Nash & James didn't sound bad.

We ordered carrot juice and soy burgers topped with sprouts.

"What's on your minds?" I asked Stephen and Graham.

"Music," said Stephen. "Always music."

"I hear you, man."

"Always thinking of ways to make the band better."

Maybe I was right. Maybe Stills and Nash had invited me to lunch to make me an offer.

"I've heard you and Greg jamming," said Graham. "You guys are great."

"Thanks, man," I said.

"We wouldn't want to do anything to break up your duo thing," said Stephen, "but we were thinking . . ."

He hesitated.

"Thinking what?" I asked, convinced he was about to pop the question.

"Thinking whether you'd be bummed out if we asked Greg to audition to replace Bruce."

What! They wanted Greg, not me!

"You look surprised," said Nash.

"I am," I said without telling them why.

"I can understand," said Stephen. "You guys are so tight."

The burgers arrived. Seeing the sprouts didn't make me happy. The Stills/Nash offer didn't make me happy. Going with their group would have meant big money. And if they'd put me in the starting lineup, it would have meant fame. It would also have meant stretching their musical boundaries, but why not? Like me, these cats were experimenters. They needed a brotha like me. On the other hand, I could see why they didn't want a brotha like me. They already had their thing together. They were afraid Bruce would mess up their upcoming big gigs and had to make sure the bass parts were covered. Bruce had been my man. Now Greg was my man. I had love for both these guys. But I also had some jealousy. Sitting there, staring at the sprouts, I made a quick decision—I wouldn't let my jealousy get in the way of helping a friend.

"Sure," I said. "Audition Greg. Greg's the bomb."

When I gave Greg the news that night, he couldn't have been cooler.

"I want to keep our thing together, Rick," he said.

"Our thing ain't going nowhere, Greg."

"It will in time."

"But right now it's Crosby, Stills & Nash's time. Those motherfuckers are huge. You'd be crazy not to jump on this."

Greg knew I was right, and a few days later we were at Stephen's house for Greg's big moment. We went to the rehearsal room, where Dallas Taylor, the group's badass drummer, had set up his traps. Stephen sat down at the organ and Graham grabbed his guitar. Then David Crosby arrived. It had been a while since I'd seen him, and he greeted me with a big bear hug. I introduced him to Greg. They shook hands before David took out his guitar and began to tune.

"I'm nervous, man," Greg whispered to me as he broke out his bass. "These guys are serious."

"You gonna kill it, bro," I said. "You're the fuckin' star student of James Jamerson, the king of 'em all."

They started kickin' it and Greg fell into a nice groove. At first

Greg was mainly supporting. Nothing fancy. He laid down a solid bottom that felt good. But after a few minutes, he started breaking out his artillery. From Jamerson he learned that the bass could be melodic as well as percussive. Jamerson was a very free player, not restricted to any written line. He knew how to make the funk fly. Greg had that same gift. It didn't take him long to lay some shit on their ass they'd never heard before. Greg was bad. There was no doubt—not for a second—that he could cut it. Besides, he had memorized that first Crosby, Stills & Nash album and knew all the changes better than they did. In the middle of the jam, Stills broke into a broad smile and threw me a vial of pure pharmaceutical cocaine.

"Thanks, man," was what he said, indicating that Greg had the gig.

The blow felt fantastic. Things couldn't possibly get any better—except they did. The door opened and Neil Young walked in.

"Ricky!" he said. "Great to see you, man."

We shot the shit for a few minutes before Neil took his guitar out of his case and joined the jam. I didn't realize it then, but this was the birth of Crosby, Stills, Nash & Young—with Greg Reeves on bass.

When I went home to Seville, she asked how it went.

"It was beautiful," I said. "Greg killed 'em. He's in."

"And you're okay with that?"

"Sure."

Except I wasn't that sure. I had done my brother a solid, but I have to admit that I also felt left out—plus I had lost my bass player. There was no compensation, either monetary or emotional. But, on reflection, maybe there was. I had learned that I could be selfless. That was something new. I could help someone without demanding anything for myself. Even in the cutthroat music biz, there was room for kindness.

Norman Whitfield, thought to be a killer competitor himself, had taken the time to school me. So why couldn't I take the time to help a good guy like Greg? I could and did, and although I was still broke, I felt better about myself. When I called Mom—the only person in the world with whom I could be completely honest—and told her the story she said, "I couldn't be prouder of you, son. Didn't I say that you have a heart of gold?"

I felt the glow washing all over me.

FEAR

The long summer of '69 seemed like it would never end. Greg moved out to go off with the group to be known as Crosby, Stills, Nash & Young. The first album he'd record with the group, *Déjà Vu*, was a brilliant classic. Poco continued to gain popularity. Rumors were going around that Billy Preston, who I knew from the R & B circuit, was cutting tracks with the Beatles in London. The Stones were working on *Let It Bleed.* It was all cool, it was all interesting, was all something I felt connected to. And yet the connection never really worked.

My plan to break into the big time through the world of white rock and roll hadn't happened. I'd always thought that if Hendrix, who went from straight-up R & B to white rock, could do it, why not me? We were both black hippies. Naturally I wasn't a guitar genius like Hendrix, but like Jimi, I was an innovator. I felt like I could lead the world in new musical directions. And yet there I was, living on Alta Loma with my thumb up my ass.

Maybe it was my anger or resentment of my exclusion from white rock that got me to fall in so easily with a light-skinned black cat I'll call Mike the Mack. Mike was a mack daddy from Chicago, a serious gangsta who lived in a mansion on Mulholland with a bevy of gorgeous white women. He wore a black leather cowboy hat, red leather pants, and rhinestone-encrusted high platform shoes. He wore gold chains around his neck and diamond rings on both hands. He reminded me of the baddest cats I knew back in Buffalo, the brothas with the balls to compete with the Mafia dons who had employed Mom as a numbers runner.

Mike the Mack liked me and I liked the fuck-you-white-world attitude he represented. He'd built his own empire on his own terms. Sometimes he'd have me up to his palatial pad, just to hear me sing. He bought me a guitar, bass, and electric piano just 'cause he got a kick outta watching me play all the instruments. His instruments were coke, smack, and counterfeit money. Knowing that my money was funny, he'd throw me a grand now and then to keep me and Seville in groceries. While in Mike's company, I also had free access to anything in the drugstore. At this point in my life, my thing was mainly weed. I dug coke but not to the point of excess. And heroin was off my menu completely.

I was Mike the Mack's music man, the entertainment at his all crazy parties. He trusted me completely. When he went off on a three-week business trip, he asked me to hold a large quantity of blow and heroin. "Don't sample any," he said. "It's all promised to a customer who'll be in L.A. when I return." Being a fool, I sampled some of the coke and sold some of the H to musician friends. I knew that was wrong but needed the money. Mike got back and saw that I chiseled some of his drugs but didn't say anything. I was relieved. I thought we were still cool.

With that thought in mind, I called Mike when my weed dealer

Junior said there was a pot drought in L.A. and he desperately needed ten keys. Mike, with his access to major suppliers, said ten keys was no problem but he needed a G a key. Junior agreed to the ten thousand dollars. I was at Junior's house when Mike came over with the ten keys neatly wrapped up in cellophane. He gave us sample joints and, man, after one hit I knew the shit was the sure-enough bomb. Junior forked over the ten Gs; Mike thanked us and left.

Turned out that five of those keys contained grass—not get-you-high grass but mow-the-lawn grass. Mike had ripped off Junior for five thousand dollars, approximately the dollar amount of the coke and heroin I'd chiseled from Mike. Drug lord justice. Junior wanted to go after Mike, but I convinced him that this was one drug lord he didn't want to fuck with.

With Mike out of the picture, I had to shift gears. Fortunately there were other party scenes where I was still welcome. The most welcoming of all was Jay Sebring's. In my early California adventures, Jay was probably my most loyal and supportive friend. He loved Seville's home cooking and would often come over for dinner. He never needed an invitation and never failed to leave us with a little weed or cash to cover that month's rent. He was a cat you could talk to—a big-time music lover and a super-hip patron of the arts.

One early afternoon, Jay came over. I was still asleep. Seville woke me. I was glad to see Jay but was nursing a wicked hangover. Jay was in a great mood and wanted to take me and Seville to Roman Polanski's crib, where the actress Sharon Tate was living. There was gonna be a big party and Jay didn't want us to miss it. Sharon had once been Jay's girl. Even after Sharon married Polanski, who'd just done *Rosemary's Baby*, she and Jay stayed friends. Polanski had rented a huge house on Cielo Drive in Benedict Canyon that Jay said was incredible.

"You and Seville will love it," he said. "There's a pool and a guesthouse and lofts and fireplaces made of stone. It's at the end of a cul-de-sac and completely private. Cary Grant used to live there."

I'd gotten wasted the night before and couldn't think about partying—at least not at that moment.

"I can't move, Jay," I said.

"You gotta come, Rick. You'll have a ball."

"I know I will. But let me catch up with you later. Just leave the address."

On a piece of paper Jay wrote down "10050 Cielo Drive." He also made me a little map showing how to get there. I immediately fell back to sleep. When I woke up, Seville mentioned Jay's party. She really wanted to make the scene. I did too, but my temples were throbbing. Usually a couple of aspirins are all I need. In this case, though, the headache wouldn't go away. In those days it took a lot for me to pass up a party—especially one with Jay Sebring involved—but hard as I tried, I couldn't get myself to make the trek.

"Come on, Rick," Seville kept urging, "Jay always hangs out with the grooviest people."

Seville was right. It would be a cool scene and a mellow time. I started to put on some party clothes when, out of nowhere, the headache returned with a vengeance and knocked me on my ass. I could hardly move.

"Sorry, baby," I told Seville. "Something weird's happening. Maybe this is what they call a migraine. Whatever it is, I need to lie down."

I fell into bed and closed my eyes, and when I woke up it was morning. Here my memory gets fuzzy. I can't remember whether it was the next morning or the morning after that when I went out to the grocery store to pick up some coffee and milk. I happened to glance down at a vending machine selling the *Los Angeles Times*. The headline read, SHARON TATE, FOUR OTHERS MURDERED. My heart stopped. I fumbled around and finally found the right change to buy the paper. My eyes read the words but my brain couldn't comprehend what it said—five people had been killed in what was being called a "ritualistic slaying." They were Sharon Tate, who was eight and a half months pregnant; Abigail Folger, heiress to the coffee fortune; Voytek Frykowski, a filmmaker friend of Roman Polanski; Steven Parent; and Jay Sebring, former fiancé to Sharon Tate and Hollywood hair product mogul. I stood there and read it again, and then again, hoping that somehow if I kept reading it the words would change, the names would change, and the story would disappear. But it didn't. Later that day more details came in over the television. The one that hit me hardest was that Jay had been found dead with a rope around his neck. He was stabbed seven times. On the door of the house the murderers had written "Pig" in blood.

I was freaked the fuck out. I was devastated that my good friend had been killed in cold blood. I also couldn't help but think how it could have been me and Seville. We were supposed to be there. Jay had come by to get us. Normally, I would have gone in a split second. I loved Hollywood parties. I loved Jay. It was only the headache that stopped me. Why? Why would I get a headache at that moment? Why was I spared when a good guy like Jay wasn't? I couldn't think of what I had done to deserve this kind of break. I couldn't think of what Jay had done to die this kind of brutal death. None of it made sense.

The whole Hollywood community, me included, was scared shitless. It got even worse when the next night two other people, Leno and Rosemary LaBianca, were slaughtered in their home in Los Feliz, a neighborhood right next to Hollywood. The killer carved "War" on Leno's stomach. The words "Death to Pigs" were written in blood on the wall.

Because this was a time when everyone was smoking tons of

weed—a substance that sure as hell feeds paranoia—we were out of our minds with fear. Who the fuck knew who these killers were? We ran out and got heavier locks for our doors and barred the windows, and in my case, I got me a piece. I wasn't taking no chances. If some crazed killer showed up at our crib, I'd blow his fuckin' brains out.

I resorted to calling my mother every night. She was the most comforting thing in my life. When I told her the story of how I was almost with Jay that night, she was quick to say, "God spared your life for a reason."

"Maybe so, Mom, but I gotta say I'm scared."

"Who wouldn't be, James? It was a horrible, frightening thing that happened."

"I wanna come home."

"I'm not sure this is the time."

"Why not?"

"Well, you haven't done what you set out to do. You were gonna start a band, weren't you?"

"I was, but I got sidetracked. Stephen Stills hired Greg Reeves away from me. Greg and I were gonna be Salt 'n Pepper."

"I'm sure Greg's great," said Mom, "but I know there are a lot of other musicians you can work with."

"There are, but right now I'm not too hip on running the streets to look for musicians. The streets out here are full of killers gone crazy."

"Killers are everywhere, James. You grew up in a city where there were killings all the time."

"It's different here, Mom. The crazies are crazier. They cut up people and use their blood to write secret messages. They got messages on the walls and on the sidewalks. They're looking for their next victim. I think they've targeted musicians."

"You sound like you been smoking too much."

Mom knew me, and I loved her too much to lie.

"I'm trying to cut back," I said.

"Try to get yourself together, son. You owe it to yourself to develop your talent. Stop smoking them funny cigarettes and start making music."

Mom always had the last and best word. I knew she was right. As scary as it was to stay in L.A. that summer of slaughter, I remained where I was.

A week after the bloody murders, Woodstock went down in upstate New York. I watched the TV reports saying that a half million hippies had made the scene. Crosby, Stills, Nash & Young were on the bill. The biggest act of all, Jimi Hendrix, closed the festival. Watching the news clips, I asked myself why I wasn't up there. These were my peers. I heard what they were doing and knew I could do it as well or better. I saw how they were dressing and knew I had just as much style—if not more. I'm not taking anything away from Janis Joplin or Sly Stone or the Who or the Grateful Dead. They were all bad. They had their own sound and their original songs. But so did I. Yet they had found a way to get themselves out there in front of the hippie nation while I was still farting around in my little apartment.

I hadn't become a hippie act like Santana or Country Joe and the Fish, and I hadn't become a soul music act like Aretha Franklin or Wilson Pickett. I had fallen in the cracks of the two worlds of pop music—black and white—knowing that I could do both those styles with originality and skill.

Why hadn't I done what I'd set out to do?

Mom had the answer. I was stoned all the time. I was too fucked-up to take care of business. I had to throw out the weed, flush the blow down the toilet, pour out the wine and the whiskey, and concentrate on what God had saved me to do—write songs, sing songs, be an artist. The only thing that was getting in my way was fear. I had to defeat the fear.

Fear's defeat happened in a strange way. I was eating a hot dog at Orange Julius on Santa Monica Boulevard when these fine chicks came and handed me a piece of paper about chanting. It talked about how chanting relieves stress and lifts fear. I'd never heard that before. If the chicks hadn't been so fine, I might not have paid that much attention to their solicitation, but I did. I kept the paper and the next day drove to the address on it in Beverly Hills to see what chanting was all about.

I learned it was a Buddhist thing. Cool. Buddhism was a peaceful religion. Buddhism might help me cut back on the stimulants that had been exciting my fears. In that room, the vibe was not fearful. Everyone sat on Persian rugs. The leader faced the rest of us in lotus position. We were told to close our eyes and become conscious of our breath. We were told to let our thoughts go, let them pass through us. We were told not to hold on to anything but simply follow our breath. And then we were told to chant. The chant was more of a sound than a word. The sound had a resonance that I liked. It helped me move from my thoughts and stay in my body. After a while I felt myself leaving my body. I looked back at my body from a place I'd never experienced before. I felt outside time and space. I just was. The chanting went on and on. Can't say how long—maybe an hour, maybe two. When the session was over, the leader looked at me and put his hands together, as if in prayer. He nodded and smiled. I felt changed.

I felt motivated. My relationship with Seville, which had been rocky because of all my drugs, got better. I got more focused on music. I started writing and singing. My lyrics got deeper and my voice got stronger. I went into the clubs and looked for talent. I couldn't get Greg Reeves, who was married to Crosby, Stills, Nash & Young—but I was gonna resurrect Salt 'n Pepper anyway.

First cat I found was Eddie Roth, who played the shit outta the Hammond B3. Wasn't nothing Eddie couldn't play—any groove, any genre. Plus he blew flute good as Herbie Mann.

Second cat was David Burk on guitar. Think John McLaughlin and Al Di Meola, then multiply times two and the result is Burk. Rock and jazz were coming together back then, and Burk was the guy who blended them to perfection.

My drummer was Coffey Hall. Because I'm a drummer, I'm a hard critic on any percussionist. But there was nothing to criticize about Coffey. He could backstick on a bottle cap and do fancy rolls with one finger. Amazing chops.

Fourth member was Chris Sarnes on bass, who was simpler than Jamerson and Reeves but just as earthy. He provided that big rock bottom every group needs. His forte was simplicity. Sarnes's thing was to keep it hot, funky, and anchored to the earth.

It was all about musical virtuosity. These boys could blow as bad as anyone on either coast. Tapering off drugs—not entirely but doing way less than before—I got my voice in great shape. The chanting helped. I was writing all kinds of original material on all sorts of subjects. I had a song called "Alice in Ghettoland" where, instead of falling down the rabbit hole, Alice falls into a trash can and winds up on the chocolate side of town dealing with gangstas and pimps. Another, called "Train Song," had elements of Curtis Mayfield's "People Get Ready," a song about racial harmony. I was open to all the musical currents flowing through the country. Taj Mahal was making a splash with his hip retro country blues. It was Taj who inspired me to do Willie Dixon's "I Just Want to Make Love to You" through a heavy psychedelic filter.

Yes, along with Led Zeppelin, was being called the next big thing in rock coming over from England. Yes had made a big splash with their debut Atlantic album, and when Salt 'n Pepper were booked to open for them at the Whisky it was a big fuckin' deal. We were pumped. Yes was a progressive rock band, but we knew no one was more progressive than us.

We rehearsed like madmen. On opening night, in spite of all the anticipation for Yes, the audience wouldn't let us go. We did four encores. We blew off the roof and made Yes work like motherfuckers to come up to our level. During that week, Yes guitarist Steve Howe was asking my guitarist, David Burk, for pointers. Yes drummer Bill Bruford was taking lessons from my drummer, Coffey Hall.

When Norman Whitfield came by to see us, he said, "Rick, I'm glad I chased you outta Detroit. This band is serious. This band is gonna worry Hendrix. It's gonna worry everyone."

Neil Young dropped by and heard me play his "Cinnamon Girl." I twisted that song into a shape Neil had never imagined. He loved it. "You gotta meet my manager," he said.

Enter Elliot Roberts. At the time Elliot was a super-manager, flying high with Joni Mitchell and Crosby, Stills, Nash & Young. Roberts heard us and signed us. I knew this was the break I'd been waiting for. I had a killer band and now a killer manager. Everything was in place. Except it wasn't.

We couldn't get Elliot's attention. He had bigger fish to fry. Later I learned he was chasing after the Eagles. Whatever it was, we were neglected. When I confronted him, though, he was cool. "I think Salt 'n Pepper is fantastic," he said, "but I just don't have the time. Let me get Bill Graham to help you."

Roberts came through. Enter the great Bill Graham. He heard us, loved us, and booked us in his club the Fillmore West, where we opened for Jethro Tull. We were finally in the middle of the mix. This was the big time.

The start of a new decade—the seventies—and the start of a new career for me. I was fronting what I knew had to be the next big thing in rock, soul, and funk. I had it all together. When Bill had us open for Chicago, the Allman Brothers, and Boz Scaggs, all those cats gave us props. Even though we didn't have a record deal, it couldn't be long.

It wasn't. Enter Phil Walden, the guy who'd made Otis Redding and then managed the Allman Brothers. Walden said he'd put us on Atlantic Records—and that's what he did. The label of Ray Charles, Solomon Burke, Wilson Pickett, Sam & Dave, Aretha Franklin—not to mention Yes and Led Zeppelin. Atlantic was just where I wanted to be. Soon I saw myself crossing and busting up England the way I was about to bust up America.

Contracts came through and next thing I knew Tom Dowd, the famous Atlantic engineer who'd become a producer, came to check us out. He wanted to assess our sound. The world looked at Dowd as a genius, but I didn't. He made a few suggestions that I thought were bullshit. He talked about dynamics, but, hell, Salt 'n Pepper was the most dynamic band going. Not wanting to fuck up the deal, I pretended to take him seriously. Atlantic sent us plane tickets to fly to Miami and cut our first record, which Dowd would produce. I wanted Mom to be there.

"Can't come in for it, son," she said. "Too busy here."

"You can stop running those numbers now," I told her. "This record we're about to make is gonna be the bomb. You can kiss your money problems good-bye."

"Ain't got no money problems, James. That's because I keep on working. Anyway, I'm proud of what you're doing and I know this thing is gonna be a success."

It wasn't. I was happy to go back to Criteria Studios, where I had freelanced before, but Miami was the pits. Atlantic was the pits.

They rented us a house with no air-conditioning in the middle of a blistering summer heat wave. They didn't get us the equipment we needed for the studio, and when I called to complain they said that the boss, Jerry Wexler, had to approve it all and couldn't be reached. He was on his yacht. Our manager, Phil Walden, was suddenly hard to get. We were told our advance was sent to him and yet we hadn't seen a dime. Phil kept ducking my calls. The studio still wasn't ready and the scorching heat got hotter.

Whoever I tried reaching—Dowd, Wexler, or Walden—was in meetings or had gone fishing. When I finally got a midlevel executive at Atlantic, I said, "Does the label want us to make a goddamn record or not?"

"Can I get back to you on that?" the guy asked.

I hung up in his ear.

I looked out on the ocean. I thought of the expression "Water, water, everywhere, nor any drop to drink."

The ocean was the music business. Everyone I knew was in a ship that had left port. Everyone was sailing over a smooth sea. Meanwhile, I was drowning on dry land. I was out of patience and out of ideas.

I was back in L.A. without a nickel to my name.

MOTHER EARTH

Seville was an earth mother. We fought like couples fight—we even broke up several times—but our bond was tight. She was a beautiful person, beautiful lover, and beautiful homemaker. When she told me she was pregnant with our child, my first thought was that I'd wanted to be rich and famous before having kids. I was neither. My second thought was that new life was always a blessing. I was thrilled. I knew Seville would make a great mom. I wasn't sure what kind of dad I'd be, but I was determined to give it a try. I didn't take the responsibility lightly. I thanked God for the gift of life.

I needed that piece of good news to offset the blues that came with the dissolution of Salt 'n Pepper. My hopes were dashed. I'd convinced myself that Salt 'n Pepper was gonna captivate the nation. Instead, the deal collapsed and I was staring into space. I had to gear up all over again. That takes effort. How many times can you strike out before you start believing you've lost your stroke?

Well, I was goddamn certain that I did have my stroke. My

friends were on teams that were winning the World Series. They didn't have anything that I didn't have. All I was missing was a break. And yet having missed that break time and again, I couldn't help but get down. Fortunately, Seville's pregnancy gave me something positive to focus on—her health and the health of our child. I kept drugs out of our house and found the occasional gig to keep us in groceries. Good friends like Stephen Stills threw me some money now and then. We got by.

When our angel girl, Ty, was born, I was over the moon. I danced with joy. The first thing I wanted to do was show Mom her grand-daughter. So we went to Buffalo. I can still see the joy in my mother's eyes as she saw Ty for the first time. Mom and Seville got along like mother and daughter, and I felt safe back in a city I knew better than any other. Then came the bad news from Toronto.

Morley Schelman was dead, killed in a fiery motorcycle ac-cident. Even though Morley and I had fought bitterly and even violently, his death hit me hard. He was a guy who had believed in my talent. At the same time, I learned that Elke had returned from Europe and was in a Toronto hospital, where she was dying from lung cancer. Another huge blow. I decided to visit her. I wanted to tell her good-bye.

I drove across the border and rushed to her side. I her told that she looked fine and would be out of the hospital in a matter of days. She wanted to believe me. She needed support. But I knew she'd never leave the hospital. She was down to skin and bones. The doctors told me that her cancer was spreading everywhere. Yet even in her frail condition, she was encouraging me. When I told her the hard time I'd had getting a deal, she said it was only a matter of time.

"You'll be one of the biggest stars in the world," she said, putting her hand to my cheek.

"I love you, baby," I said.

"I love you too."

Those were her last words to me. When I returned the next day with another bouquet of flowers, they told me she was gone.

Sickness was everywhere. Seville's mother was seriously ill in L.A.

"I've got to get out to California to see her," said Seville. "Ty and I will come back to Buffalo as soon as my mother gets well."

I stayed in Toronto. The scene was dead except for a couple of clubs. I sat in with some groups and made some loose change. My heart was heavy. Elke was gone and so were Seville and Ty. One night at a club I was singing the straight-ahead Bobby Bland/B. B. King twelve-bar blues when I locked eyes with a chick named Kelly. Kelly was prettier than pretty. The girl was gorgeous—big brown eyes, full lips, crazy body. She waved me over to her table. Turned out to be Canadian English with an enchanting accent. She was deep into brothas and black music. She was deep into me. That night the heavens came down as we loved until daylight. We loved all that week. By then I knew good pussy, but this was another category altogether. Kelly and I went beyond the physical. Our shit was metaphysical. It took us all the way to Mars and back.

I was torn. I loved Seville and our baby, but damned if I didn't love Kelly. I stayed in Toronto for nearly four months while Seville was caring for her mom. All that while the thing with me and Kelly was getting deeper.

I was getting guilty. I told Kelly about Seville. Because Kelly was such a cool chick, she said, "We need to stop. We need to do what's right."

I agreed. It was tough but necessary. When Seville's mom improved, Seville and Ty came to Toronto. I decided to stop the lying and confess. I told Seville about me and Kelly. Then Seville told me that she also had had an affair. We were both hurt and pissed.

"This isn't working," said Seville.

I agreed.

We tried for a couple of weeks but the tension was too much. Our relationship was crashing all around us. We were fighting like alley cats.

"This isn't good for the baby," said Seville.

"It isn't good for anyone," I said.

"I'm going," said Seville, "and I'm taking the baby with me."

I had no arguments. I had no alternative plans. Seville left with Ty. More regrets, more confusion.

One thing was clear, though. I still wanted Kelly and Kelly wanted me. We fixed up an old Victorian house and moved in together. Kelly got my motor going. She motivated me to get back on my hustle. I started writing songs again. We went out to clubs. I identified different musicians I thought might be able to bring off my ideas. Most importantly, I found a rich, party-loving, music-loving lawyer who spotted my talent and was willing to back me in a band. This time I was gonna flip the script and do something different—and bigger.

As I planned my next move, two musicians had a big impact on me—Marvin Gaye and Miles Davis. Marvin and Miles were both experimenters. They were bold pioneers willing to go places no one else had gone before.

Marvin had come out with "What's Going On," a radical departure from the singles he'd been doing with Whitfield. First of all, he put himself in the pilot's seat. He produced the thing himself. He cowrote all the songs. And he also created a concept album rather than a bunch of disconnected singles. He told a long story of a cat who comes back from the fucked-up war in Vietnam and tries to adjust to the fucked-up big-city black ghetto. Marvin laid it all out—politics, drugs, religion, even ecology. Later he told me Berry Gordy didn't want to put it out 'cause it was too controversial. Marvin told Gordy to get fucked; if it wasn't released, he'd never record for Motown again. Gordy backed down and—just like that—the producer-driven era was over. Soon Stevie Wonder, taking Marvin's lead, would be producing his own albums. The whole thing—Marvin's gutsiness, Marvin's vision, and Marvin's sweet funky music—was an inspiration.

✦

Miles had started fooling with electronic instruments in *In a Silent Way.* For a straight-ahead jazz cat working in the purist jazz world, that was a brave move. But with *Bitches Brew* he kicked in the doors. He introduced serious funk and rock into the mix. The shit was free-form as a motherfucker, and I loved it. Miles also had the taste to include virtuoso cats like Wayne Shorter, Joe Zawinul, Chick Corea, John McLaughlin, Jack DeJohnette, and Lenny White. The riffin' over those polyrhythms blew my mind. I felt like Miles was saying to us artists—musicians trying to figure out our next move—"Go for it."

I went for it. I told my party-loving lawyer that I wanted to do something big. I wanted a big band. I wanted to paint on a large canvas. To realize the sounds in my head I needed lots of players. I'd loved big bands in every era, starting with the first time I heard Benny Goodman play "Sing, Sing, Sing" with Gene Krupa on drums. I loved Dizzy Gillespie's big band and I loved Gil Evans's big band—especially his records *Out of the Cool* and *Sketches of Spain*, which he wrote for Miles. For a minute Monk had a serious big band. And of course I loved rock bands like Chicago and Blood, Sweat & Tears. Soul bands were also my thing, especially Tower of Power, who had just put out *East Bay Grease.* And naturally I never stopped learning from Tower of Power's main inspiration, James Brown. The Godfather was the grease, grit, and guts of groove-centric R & B.

In short, I wanted horns and reeds and a rhythm section that could burn down the barn. I needed money, and lo and behold, the lawyer coughed up the dough. He saw the fire in my eyes and was willing to bet on my talent. I started writing. I quickly hired the right cats. I quickly found my sound. Influenced by Marvin, I had songs like "Mother Earth" that concerned protecting the planet. I had a thing called "Country Girl" that rocked hard in a Blood, Sweat & Tears mode. "Don't You Worry" had a rock vibe that I knew would worry Crosby, Stills, Nash & Young. Besides the killer music we made, I'd also come up with a killer name for the band—White Cane.

Knowing that I'd never get a deal from Toronto, I convinced my backer to fly me, Kelly, and the band to L.A., where we could showcase for the music biz moguls. We hit the ground running. We smoked the city, tearing up club after club until a label boss finally came up with the mean green.

When we scored a $250,000 advance, I couldn't help but be happy, except for a funny feeling I had about the label, MGM. Mike Curb, who signed us personally, ran it. When I went to Curb's office there were all sorts of pictures with him and his other big act, the Osmonds. There were also photos of him with that asshole Richard Nixon, one motherfucker I couldn't stomach. I got the idea that Curb was a card-carrying Republican. First thing he said was, "I love your music, Rick, but you'll have to change the name of the band."

"Why?"

"It's promoting drugs," he said.

"What drugs?"

"Cocaine."

"Cocaine is spelled C-A-I-N-E. We're C-A-N-E. 'White cane' is talkin' 'bout sugarcane. We're sweet as sugar."

"I don't think so, Rick."

"Well, Mike, I know you're the boss of MGM, but I'm the boss of White Cane. So either you'll take us with our name or we'll find someone who will."

Sensing we were about to break wide and not wanting to blow an opportunity to make big bread, Mike caved.

"White Cane is okay," he said, "long as you have no songs promoting drugs."

I wanted to say I had lots of songs promoting pussy, but I decided to shut up. I'd won the battle. The next battle had to do with the producer. I didn't think we needed one. Mike did. This time I caved. Even though I knew what the band had to do in the studio better than anyone, it was Mike's dime.

Jimmy Ienner was Mike's producer. I didn't like the guy. I didn't like his toupee and I didn't like his plastered-on phony smile. I called him "the Tooth." He bragged about his big success with the Raspberries. I wasn't impressed. To my way of thinking, he had only the most superficial understanding of the three elements that made White Cane so good—jazz, funk, and rock.

I was glad when the Tooth took us to Village Recorders, one of the best studios in L.A., but I was horrified when he started producing. He massacred our music. He found a way to deconstruct what it had taken us months to construct—a full-bodied sound with layers of close harmonies over in-the-pocket grooves guaranteed to keep the party going all night. I fought with the Tooth all night. Ultimately, because I didn't have control, I lost. I was excluded from the mixing process and at one point barred from the studio. When the record came out, the trades said White Cane had potential but that the production sucked. The trades were right.

Curb tried to boost sales by having us tour with B. B. King. B was super-hot with his first crossover hit, "The Thrill Is Gone," and it was an honor to open for him. I loved B, a beautiful man who treated me like a son. One night I asked him whether if I called my mother, a big B. B. King fan, he would talk to her. He talked to her for fifteen minutes. That made me love B even more. Yet for all the goodwill between B's band and mine, for all the excitement of our live tour, the record itself bombed big-time. Not only did the production do us in, but the production costs ate up our advance. When it was over, I was left with nothing. Curb dropped us, White Cane disbanded, and I was broke.

Kelly and I hung around L.A., where I tried to keep the band together. Without the support of the label, though, I couldn't do it. I looked around and saw that soul music was all about Donny Hathaway, Roberta Flack, Al Green, and the Chi-Lites. I saw Bill Withers, who I loved, and understood his brilliant marriage of folk and soul. I could have done that. I thought of going to Philly, where the O'Jays and Harold Melvin & the Blue Notes were turning out smashes for Kenny Gamble and Leon Huff. I could have done that as well. Neil Young had a huge hit with "Heart of Gold." I could have gone with his group if he had asked me. On the rock side, the Crosby, Stills & Nash–style America had "A Horse with No Name." I could have done that. I could have done all this shit, but I didn't do any of it. I heard all the sounds that were making stars. I knew all the stars who were making money. I had what they had—musical vision, originality, stage presence, a voice, a look. Except that I had been denied—over and over again. How long could I put up with defeat? Subsisting in another crummy Hollywood apartment with a clogged toilet and peeling paint, at age twenty-four I asked myself a question for which I had no answer.

What the fuck am I gonna do now?

PASSAGE TO INDIA

So far this has been a tale of three cities—Buffalo, Toronto, and L.A. I'd been running back and forth between those places, looking for a way to get over. L.A. had always proved to be a dead end, Buffalo was always dead period, and Toronto seemed to yield the most. Toronto was the only place where my talent was really recognized.

It's no surprise, then, that Kelly and I fled to Toronto after the demise of White Cane. Kelly's parents weren't pleased that we were still together—they didn't like the idea of their girl going black—and tried to break us up, but the love was too strong. The love bonded us in all ways—even our forays into scamming the system.

I was disgusted with the music business. I didn't see how I could put together a better band than White Cane. If White Cane couldn't cut it, fuck the whole thing. There were other ways to make money, especially in Canada, where the bankers weren't all that vigilant.

Our first scheme worked for many months. Kelly would dress

up in her sexiest outfit. When she walked in the bank, every loan officer hoped that she'd come his way. Their eyes were popping and their dicks were hard. When she chose the lucky guy, she'd tell him a sob story—her mom died, her dad got cancer, her brother broke his neck. She'd tell him how she had just started a new job with a decent salary and her boss would be glad to testify for her. She'd give the loan officer our home number and I'd answer the phone in the whitest voice since Richard Nixon. I'd pretend to be the boss and sing her praises to the sky. Time and again she scored the loan. Soon we had enough bread for a car and a cool apartment. After a few months, we foolishly overdid a good thing and Kelly got popped. She avoided jail but was told she'd have to start repaying those loans.

What now?

Drugs were always a good source of income. And in Toronto in the early seventies hashish was the drug of choice—especially black hashish from Nepal. Two friends of mine—I'll call the white Tom and black Jerry—had made serious bread smuggling. They talked about the cheap price of hash and coke in India and its trouble-free accessibility. These cats weren't exactly Einstein. If they could do it, I figured I could, too. If we skipped the country, it was also a way for Kelly to get out of all those loan payments. Besides, I'd never been to that part of the world. I wanted the adventure and I wanted the money. Kelly was game, and after securing our passports, we were off.

✦

Another world. Another culture. Another look, feel, and smell. The streets of New Delhi were thick with humanity. Beggars were everywhere, while cows, considered holy, walked around like they owned the city. If you hit a cow, even by mistake, the consequences were grave. My first impression of India was fat cows, thin people, and unbelievable poverty. I'd grown up in the ghetto; I thought I knew

about poverty. But American poverty ain't shit compare
they got in India. Kids eating out of garbage, frail old la
over dead in the street, men crapping in the alleys, the t
always in your mouth.

I was amazed and also cautious. I was a black cat tra
a white chick and didn't want to fuck with Indian law
could, I kept a low profile. Being streetwise, I figured I'd f
around, long as I was patient.

I didn't have to be. No sooner had we checked into
ommended by Jerry than the bellboy who carried up o
where we were from.

"Toronto," I said.

"Do you know Jerry?"

"A black guy?"

"Black as night," said the bellboy in extremely good

"He's my man," I said.

"Mine too."

Turned out the bellboy was Jerry's connection. We
running. I gave him a bottle of Scotch and he took m
drugstore, where the druggist locked the door and bro
glass container of pharmaceutical cocaine. The shit
and only thirty U.S. dollars for two grams. I was qui
love with India.

As is often the case in the world of drugs, one th
other. Through the bellboy and druggist we met oth
hooked us up with big quantities at low prices. We we
Something about the exotic nature of that city kept
fucked like crazy. We also felt a spiritual vibe that's a
of India. We met a relative of Ravi Shankar who sold
gave me lessons. I loved the axe. We traveled to see t
saw it just as the sun was setting. We'd just had a bl

were feeling this incredible high. When we laid eyes on this other-worldly monument, both Kelly and myself had tears in our eyes.

Strange to think, but the other huge impression that stayed with me from India was the music of Barry White. His first album had come out, and believe it or not, they were playing it in a lot of the underground clubs Kelly and I discovered during our dope-buying forays. Much as I loved the sitar, I got to say that it was Barry White who haunted me throughout my travels in India. Like me, Barry was an arranger. He had a musical vision that required a big sound. Not only reeds and horns, but strings as well. He took what Isaac Hayes, Curtis Mayfield, and Marvin Gaye had started—orchestrated funk—and took it to another level. He elevated the shit. When I heard "I've Got So Much to Give" and "I'm Gonna Love You Just a Little More Baby," I knew Barry was the next big thing. He had a theatrical excitement in his music that was good for dancers and just as good for listeners. Sometimes they mix up Barry with the disco craze, but I didn't hear it that way. Disco was formulaic. Barry was original. Disco was superficial. Barry was deep. Barry had his Love Unlimited girl singers and his Love Unlimited Orchestra. He was the kind of maestro I wanted to be—a brotha capable and confident enough to do it all. It was strange to discover the magic of Barry White in the mysterious country of India.

In New Delhi, I was confident enough to hide my big-ass haul of hash in a dozen pair of boots. I cut off my hair to look like a nerdy student. The officials bought the look and, although I was sweating like a motherfucker, we eased on through customs, got on the plane, and with a couple of vials I kept in my coat, snorted all the way to New York. The situation at Kennedy airport was tense. Governor Rockefeller was passing strict antidrug laws. Get caught with more than an ounce of blow and go to jail for life. We smiled our way through customs with my stomach silently screaming all the way.

In the city, given the nervous drug vibe in New York, I sold our hash for half of what it would have brought a month earlier. No one wanted to get caught holding big quantities. I was eager to get to Buffalo and see Mom. It had been too long. Kelly stayed in Manhattan.

Reunion with Mom was warm and wonderful.

"Got a surprise for you," I said.

"Seeing you is surprise enough."

"Add five thousand dollars to that surprise."

I opened a suitcase stuffed with bills and handed Mom the cash.

"Where you'd get this?" she asked.

"You really wanna know?"

"If I didn't, I wouldn't ask."

"India was profitable."

"You said you went over to learn some new instruments."

"That's true, but I also made a connection."

"You made a drug run, son?"

"Afraid so."

"You know you're crazy, don't you?"

"I've been told."

"And I'm telling you again—bringing dope into the country when the country is on this antidope campaign is plain foolish. You get caught, you burn."

"I realize that, Mom, but I ain't getting caught."

"That's what they all said, including John Dillinger and Al Capone."

"I ain't working on that scale."

"The scale don't matter. What matters are smarts. You gotta be smart enough to know when to walk away from that stuff. I know, James. I work in that world. It's easy to get to feeling no one can touch you."

"I don't feel that way," I said.

"You sure as hell talk that way, boy."

"Mom, I'm paying you back your five thousand dollars. I'm even throwing in an extra five hundred dollars for interest."

"I don't charge my children interest."

"Well, I'm paying it. So take the money and be glad."

"Just stay outta that damn dope business, James. Soon you'll be sampling all your wares."

I already was.

It was good being back home with that stereo system set up in the living room. Miles had an album out that year—*Big Fun*—where he used Herbie Hancock and Chick Corea, not to mention Lonnie Liston Smith on piano and Michael Henderson on bass. Miles played electric trumpet with a wah-wah pedal. Fuckin' Miles was out there. So was Marvin Gaye. He'd gone from *What's Going On* to *Trouble Man* to his current thing, *Let's Get It On*. In Buffalo they were playing Marvin's shit night and day.

Two songs hit me especially hard—"Funky Stuff" by Kool and the Gang and "Ecstasy" by the Ohio Players. Both groups were funkier than White Cane, but I thought White Cane was on a higher musical level. White Cane, though, was a memory, and these groups were making a mint. The thought of making a mint led me to an idea.

With the bread I made from selling the hash, why not promote an Ohio Players/Kool and the Gang concert? Those groups had just started out, and although they each had a hit, I didn't see them getting top dollar. I was right. I got them both for three thousand dollars through the Queen Booking Agency. That was cheap. If I ever have a smash hit like them, I thought, you can bet your ass I won't be bought that cheap. Anyway, my event was a smash. I made out like a bandit, took my profit, and bought me a Mercedes that I drove out to the coast with Kelly at my side.

With my pockets full of cash, I moved into the party mode. The party went on for six months in L.A. Living in high-class hotels, we stayed high and lived large. I wasn't thinking about going back into making my own music 'cause the music scene had burned me so bad. Just wanted to party. One night I partied so hard that I totaled the Benz by driving into a car. Suddenly I was broke again.

Everyone's funny when it comes to money, but my thing is that I don't start hustling till I have to. At the start of 1974, I had to. Kelly had left to hang out with her parents and I was alone in another crummy studio apartment. The only thing that kept me from going completely bonkers was an old Fender bass that I'd taught myself to play—that and my afternoons shooting hoops at a playground at Santa Monica and Vine. It was there where I met a guitarist who said he could cop us some studio time. I figured I had nothing to else to do, so I might as well cut some tracks.

It was the first time I played bass on a session. I did two songs—"My Mama" and "Funkin' Around." I dug 'em well enough to start shopping 'em. Lo and behold, A&M Records was impressed. With Supertramp and Peter Frampton on their roster, A&M was hot. They put out my single, but when I wouldn't agree to sign an exclusive deal with them as an artist/producer until they guaranteed me an ad budget for "My Mama," they stopped all promotion and the single died. That would be the end of another fucked-up record biz story if the record hadn't sold in Europe.

When I learned that "My Mama" was going great guns in England, Germany, and France, I got my ass in gear, put together a four-piece band, and flew over. My hustle kicked in. I found a promoter who booked us on a nice tour in good-sized clubs. I was making bread. I was turning out the crowds. I was convinced all over again that, like Jimi Hendrix, I'd make it overseas and return home a conquering hero.

The only thing that stopped my momentum was Stockholm. I arrived in the dead of winter when it was colder than hell. I knew Sweden was a jazz-loving, blues-loving land. I knew the great saxist Stan Getz had lived there and was revered as a god. And I knew the hip song "Dear Old Stockholm" that Miles had recorded with Coltrane. I was ready for Stockholm to be hip, but man, it was hipper than hip. The ladies loved brothas. Musicians were especially admired, just as I admired the beautiful taste that went into their artful way of life. I'd never seen such elegant furniture, lamps, and clothing. I wandered through the museums, where I felt I was in the presence of a people who understood how to make their surroundings beautiful.

Then I met this beautiful nineteen-year-old Swedish chick. With her blond hair and blues eyes, her tall stature and her easy smile, she was freedom itself. Free sex seemed to be the thing in Sweden—they didn't have puritanical hang-ups like Americans—and so we were exploring the outer limits of physical pleasure. Much to my surprise and delight, those limits were extended when her mother walked in her room and joined us in bed. This was my real introduction to fully realized freakery.

At first I wasn't sure. Was it too crazy? Well, they didn't think so and ultimately neither did I. Mom was only in her midthirties and just as fine as her daughter. They liked sharing me and I liked sharing them. You'd think jealousy would rear its ugly head, but it never did. Their pad became my home base in Europe. I'd jump over to other countries for a gig now and then, but I was mainly with these lovely women.

Cool as Stockholm was, after nearly a year of living abroad, I was missing Kelly. We'd been writing back and forth. (Naturally I didn't say a word to her about my mother-daughter setup.) I was also eager to get home and see Mom. And besides, after a while even the freakiest scene can lose its heat.

When I told my two lovers that it was time to split, they weren't happy. They thought our little scene would go on forever. I assured them that I'd be back someday, but that wasn't good for them. So one of them—I still don't know which—hid my passport. The hassle to get a new one took nearly a month. When I finally left Sweden I saw that their free attitude about sex wasn't as simple as I first thought.

◆

Kelly and I hooked up in Toronto, where I found work in a blues band called Mainline that worked all over Canada. They had a big album at the time and paid well. I felt that I was marking time until I made another solo move. I knew that would happen because I was writing more original material than ever before. Living in Europe had given me a worldlier outlook.

Kelly and I decided to get married. We went to Buffalo and had the preacher come to Mom's house. The ceremony was small but pretty. Mom was crying. A few months later, I was crying. Seemed like marriage killed the happiness between me and Kelly. Back in Toronto, we were sniping at each so often that I moved out of her apartment and moved in with a coke dealer.

Turned out the dealer's best client was George Clinton. I was eager to meet the man. The dealer said I could bring Clinton his coke on his next stopover in Toronto.

George was cool. Seven years older than me, Clinton was one of the heaviest cats in the history of R & B. He had the balls to wear diapers onstage and dye his hair every color in the rainbow.

After I delivered his blow, he invited me to do a line with him. We started chatting and I ran down my history. He was impressed and wanted to hear some of my new songs. He had a piano in his suite and invited me to play. I did some of my newer stuff. It was all funky and George was all smiles.

"You shouldn't be running no toot," George said. "You need a major label behind your music."

"I've tried before," I said, "but it's never worked out."

"I can help you."

"Man, that'd be great. I'd really be grateful."

"No problem—just keep the good blow coming while I make some calls."

Before George left Toronto, I showed up two more times with special deliveries of high-octane cocaine. Both times he repeated his offer to hook me up with industry bigwigs. When he left town, though, he still hadn't done anything for me. Over the next several months, when I called the numbers he'd given me, no one answered. In fact, George Clinton never did one fuckin' thing to help me. I swore that one day I'd pay him back.

I found a little deal on a Canadian label called Quality that wasn't quality at all. They didn't know shit about distribution or promotion. Used two different band names (Rick James, and Hot Lips and Gorilla) and put out a couple of singles ("Hollywood Stars" and "Sweet Surrender") but they both tanked.

With music still looking like a dead end, I concentrated on drugs. I was making good money dealing coke but saw that if I could reach Canada's main connection, I'd make more. Years later when I saw Al Pacino in *Scarface,* I completely related. Just like he climbed up the ladder from dealer to dealer until he decided to meet the source himself in Latin America, I did the same. If I was going to deal, I was going to deal big-time.

Next thing I knew I was flying first class to Cartagena, Colombia.

PART THREE

BREAKING BAD

BLOW BY BLOW

looked in her eyes and said, "Baby, I wish you could understand my words when I tell you that you've got the body of life."

She said something to me in Spanish that I didn't understand. But I sure got the message when she opened her beautiful brown legs and let me in.

Bathed in moonlight, we made love on a soft blanket on the beach. Waves rolled in off the gentle Caribbean. Trade winds cooled the night. We were coked to the gills. She was the wettest, wildest lover I'd ever known. I couldn't stop balling and she couldn't stop coming. In the land of sweet pussy and prime blow, I was in heaven.

It didn't start out that way. When I arrived with my dealer pal—I'll call him Myron—we went looking for our connection, a Colombian cat we'd met in Buffalo. He was off on vacation on some island. We didn't know what the fuck to do so we checked into a hotel and cased the city. It was a big beautiful resort town, kicked back and sunny, on the country's northern coast. We were careful with our money because we wanted to use the lion's share to buy drugs. Meanwhile, there was nothing to do but wait for the return of our connection.

Weeks passed. Our main hang was a hip little bar across the street from our hotel. The owner was a friendly cat I'll call José. The clientele was affluent, dudes with expensive rides and bitches with sleek jewelry and chic clothes. One night I noticed a guitar in the corner. I picked it up and started to play and sing. José smiled. He liked what I was doing and bought me a drink. I kept singing and before long I'd captured the attention of every motherfucker in the place. Within a few days I was one of the featured attractions among the smart set of Cartagena.

José kept feeding me drinks and the fans kept feeding me tips. They dug American soul. I gave them a taste of everything from Ray Charles to Al Green. I also knew the latest Bill Withers songs, which went over great on acoustic guitar. Chicks came on to me and one of them—Maria—was the one who loved fucking on the beach. Her dad was rich and she never let me pay for anything.

All this was fine, even exciting, but after five or six weeks it seemed clear that our connection wasn't coming back to Cartagena any time soon. Me and Myron were eager to make our big score. We needed merchandise to bring home.

"I ask you something and you answer honestly," said José one night after I packed 'em into his place.

"Ask," I said.

"You are a musician, but you come to Colombia for another reason. Am I right?"

"Sure, you're right."

"I can help you with that other reason."

"You can?"

"We fly to Bogotá tomorrow. That okay?"

"That's okay, José. You lead the way."

By then I'd been in Cartagena for nearly two months and trusted this man. He paid me good money to sing. Who would have guessed that he was a major dealer himself?

Bogotá was a blast. There was political nervousness in that city, where the military guarded every corner, but José knew all the cool spots. He took me to a fence where I bought a handful of hot emeralds for a song. He took me to the best restaurants in the city. He also took me to meet the Man, where I bought five keys for twenty-five Gs. Myron and I packed it up and shipped it to Montreal, keeping two ounces for the trip. I was warned not to carry coke across the borders, but I was too bold to be told anything. I kept the toot in the body of an expensive hairbrush. Me and Myron flew into Montreal, blasted on the world's best blow.

Myron went off to sell our shit while I decided to catch up with Mom in Buffalo. She looked good and had lots of questions about Colombia. I told her all about my music gig at José's, but that didn't fool her. If she had any doubts about the real reason I went down, those doubts went away when I said I'd soon be sending her fifteen thousand dollars.

"What's this for?" she asked.

"Money you've loaned me over the years."

"So it was a good business trip," she said with a smile.

"The best," I said. "I won't have to work for a year."

"But you always have to work on your music, James. You can't neglect your music. Your music is your gift."

On the subject of music, I saw that George Clinton was playing Buffalo. Parliament had signed with Casablanca out in L.A. and had a smash album, *Up for the Down Stroke*. I can't lie and say I wasn't jealous. Clinton was funky, but his verbal shit between tunes was lame. I hated it when he talked instead of played. After the show, I had something to talk to him about.

"You were gonna hook me up with a label," I mentioned to him. "Then you fuckin' disappeared."

"I'm a working musician, man. I been traveling. I'll get to it. In the meantime, you holding any interesting merchandise?"

"I'm holding the bomb."

"Cool. As they say on TV, let's make a deal."

I sold George a few ounces at triple my normal price.

◆

It had been a few weeks since Myron had gone to Montreal to turn our Colombian supply into cash. I got word he was back in Toronto, but when I called he never answered. I decided to catch up with his ass in person. I flew to Toronto, where I ran into Kelly. Enough time had passed to let us forget all our fights. The vibe between us was good again. The sex was even better and I was feeling great—except for fuckin' Myron, who was nowhere to be found.

The shit was getting serious. Word around town was that he'd bought a new pad and a Rolls. That was my goddamn money he was using! The more he evaded me, the more enraged I became. Who did this lame motherfucker think he was! I was not about to get ripped off.

Though he kept his address a secret, I slipped a friend of his a hundred for the information. I knew better than to knock on the front door. Instead I hid out in the garbage alley. I wore a hoodie over my head and had a butcher knife in my hand. When he came out to dump his garbage, I jumped him. He was a pussy. He started crying like a baby, begging me not to hurt him.

"Where's my fuckin' money?" I asked, nicking his Adam's apple with my knife. "And why the fuck haven't you called me back? Why you been hiding?"

"The coke got confiscated by customs."

"Lying motherfucker."

"I swear."

I pressed the knife a little harder against his throat. As I drew blood, I said, "Give me what's mine or I'll kill you."

He knew I wasn't kidding, so he led me into the house, where he opened his safe and gave me fifteen Gs in cash and a pound of blow.

"Ain't enough," I said.

"All I got," said Myron.

"Sell your Rolls. Sell your crib. I don't care how you get it. Just get it. If I don't get another sixty thousand dollars, I'm coming for your ass."

A week later I had the money and me and Kelly had a badass town house in an exclusive section of Toronto. We were living high. I wanted to show her the beautiful beaches of Colombia so we flew over to Cartagena, where I hooked up with José, who kept us high and happy for a sunny two-week second honeymoon. I couldn't leave without scoring some of that serious toot. I bought several ounces. All the blow didn't fit in the body of my brush. Not wanting to leave any behind, I wrapped the remainder tightly and hid it inside the big Windsor knot of my tie. I dressed like a college-kid nerd—at twenty-seven, I looked seventeen—and with my blue blazer, khaki pants, button-down shirt, and repp tie, who would ever think to search me?

The customs cats—that's who. Happened at the Miami airport. They went through our shit and fortunately didn't open the brush. But that wasn't enough for them. They put me in a room and told me to strip. I was scared like a motherfucker. Took off my jacket, my shoes, my socks, and my pants, and carefully slid off my tie, making sure that the knot held tight. I placed my tie on the floor, took off my pants and underwear, and stood there shivering. The officials—mean-looking bastards—went through the pockets of my pants, my blazer, and my shirt. They ripped open the lining of the blazer and looked in the cuffs of the pants. They kept stepping around my tie. If they decided to open it, my ass was grass.

"Okay," said one of the customs cats, "you can get dressed."

I tried not to sigh too deeply 'cause I didn't wanna show my relief. But I dressed quickly and was about to leave when the guy said, "Wait a second. Let me take a look at that tie."

Oh fuck! It was all over. As I waited for him to tell me to take it off, I wondered about the length of my prison sentence. But instead of having me take it off, he just came over and felt the lining. He ran his hand all the way to the knot, and then—miracle of fuckin' miracles—he stopped.

"You're clear," he said.

Silently I said, Thank you, Jesus.

◆

Back in Toronto, Kelly and I settled down at our cool town house. That close call with customs gave me a feeling of invincibility. I could pretty much get away with anything. I had some bread, I had some new ideas for songs, and I had my wife back. What could go wrong?

◆

Sexual loyalty was not my strong suit. One morning I arrived home at eight A.M. after a wild night. I had found me a pair of bitches who were flying their freak flag high. I was willing to fly high myself, and the ménage à trois was something I wouldn't soon forget.

Kelly wasn't in her bed so I figured she'd gone shopping. To get the pussy juice off me, I took a long shower and then fell into bed. When I woke up it was four P.M. and Kelly wasn't back. I made some calls but still couldn't find her. Slept alone that night and next morning woke up alone. Still no Kelly.

Her call came two days later.

"Where the fuck you been?" I asked.

"You got no right to ask me that," said Kelly. "You wander off when you wanna and never think twice about calling me."

I couldn't respond because Kelly was right. What she didn't know was that I had even screwed a couple of her girlfriends—or maybe she did know. In this conversation I decided the best thing was to keep quiet.

"I've had it," Kelly said. "I've gone back to my ex."

She'd gone back to him before. One of those times I'd gone over to his place and kicked his ass. But I didn't see myself doing that again. Even though I loved Kelly, I couldn't help but realize that I'd been too heartless with her for too long.

"I'm sorry, baby," was all I could say.

"Sorry won't do it, Rick. This time I'm gone for good."

I knew she meant it. I knew she wasn't coming back. And for reasons I can't entirely explain, I felt myself falling apart. When I tried to write songs, I couldn't. I thought I'd compose a sad song about losing Kelly, but the blues were too strong to let me work. I wouldn't even call it the blues. I'd call it hard-core depression. I thought I'd use dope to kill the pain, but the dope got me even more down. I thought some wild pussy would change my mood, but I couldn't fuck. My dick wouldn't get hard. That had never happened to me before. Talk about depression!

I moped around the house. I stared into space. I thought back on my life and all I saw was failure. Marvin Gaye had done the soundtrack for a film called *Trouble Man* that should have been my movie. He had a hit, "I Want You," that was burning up the charts. My friend—you could even say my mentor—Norman Whitfield was producing Rose Royce, who'd broken through with "Car Wash," an across-the-board smash. Neil Young was a big solo artist. David

Crosby, Stephen Stills, and Graham Nash were touring the world. All these people were making monster progress and I was still on my ass.

Aside from buying and selling Colombian cocaine, I hadn't done shit. My music had gone nowhere. I felt like it never would. I felt like I should call Mom, but I knew that Mom would say what all moms say: that it'd get better, that I had to have faith, that God had given me this talent for a reason. I didn't want to hear those words because those words would only make me feel worse.

I didn't want to do anything except sit around and sleep all day. When I woke up, I put Bobby Blue Bland on the box singing about "Stormy Monday but Tuesday's just as bad." I smoked hash until I couldn't see straight. Then I'd go out and stuff myself with some greased-up funk food and go back to sleep.

If I picked up a bitch to try to raise my spirits, she got pissed when I couldn't raise my cock. I went through all my blow. I went through all my money except for enough to buy me a pistol. I wanted to end the agony. If music couldn't bring me out of this, if dope couldn't do it, if sex no longer excited me, what was the point of living?

There was none.

I loaded the pistol and put it on the kitchen table.

I stared at it for hours.

I took it in my hand and put it against my temple.

I felt the cold steel against my skin.

All I had to was pull the trigger.

I wanted to. I wanted out.

YOU AND I

Brotha Guru is all caught up in my story.

"Why didn't you do it?" he asks me. "Why didn't you kill yourself?"

"I was chicken shit."

"Are you saying, Rick, that a braver man would have shot his brains out?"

"I'm saying that I didn't have the guts."

"What do you think takes more guts—to face death or to face life?"

"Both take guts."

"I agree. So you had the guts to go on living."

"If that's how you see it, Brotha Guru."

"I see you as a classic narcissist who couldn't imagine a world without you in the middle."

"Is a narcissist someone who's just egotistical?"

"More than that. It's someone who can't view the world from any point of view other than his own."

"Then aren't we all narcissists?" I ask.

"Some are more extreme than others."

"I wouldn't argue that I'm extreme."

"Narcissism can drive you to do things other people can't."

"So it's not a bad thing?" I ask.

"I'm not judging it and I'm not judging you," says Brotha Guru. "I'm saying that narcissists have their own strategies for survival. They have their own way of breaking through crises."

"That night when I put the gun to my head, I wasn't breaking through," I say. "I was about to break down."

"There's a thin line between a breakdown and a breakthrough, Rick. A very thin line."

◆

In Toronto in 1977 at age twenty-nine, I walked that line. I did put the gun down, and I did manage to climb my way out of the depression. In fact, in the aftermath of my almost-suicide I did experience a major breakthrough. Funny, how you can go from near self-destruction to self-confidence in just a few weeks. In my case the medicine was music and Mom.

I went to Buffalo, where I knew my mother's company would do me good. She was all positive energy, and positivity was just what I needed. I also needed my friend Tony, the drummer. He also helped me out of the Dumpster. He had a happy-go-lucky personality and a key contact with a cat named Aiden Mow from South Africa who played great George Benson–style guitar. We started writing together and suddenly I was alive again. The grooves brought back joy. The songs had a spirit that made me feel that there was something good inside me, something I needed to share. I just needed to get up and dance.

"Get Up and Dance" was the name of the tune Aiden and I

wrote. When Tony heard it, he flipped and said we'd have to go in a studio and do it right. I went back into the dope-selling business long enough to get the dough to make the record. Amazingly, Tony got Randy and Michael Brecker. Randy played trumpet and Michael tenor. They were brilliant jazz cats who wrote R & B horn charts better than anyone in the world. With the Brecker brothers both blowing and arranging, we went into a twenty-four-track studio and killed it. I sang the shit outta the song. We knew we had something hot that the world had to hear. Rather than go the usual route, we had enough bread to put it out on our own.

That's when I started Mood Records. I put a moon on the label because I dig astrology. We opened an office and found a distributor, and suddenly we had a hit. It went number one in Buffalo, Rochester, and Syracuse. The record stores in Western New York couldn't keep it in stock. On WUFO and WBLK in my hometown, it was all you heard. Finally! A fuckin' smash!

Only one problem: the distributor wouldn't pay us until we delivered a whole album. I wanted to argue with the distributor but Mom, who knew her way around that world, was quick to say, "The distributor is hooked up with the same guys who run the numbers." The distributor was mobbed up as a motherfucker. We had a red-hot hit but no bread coming in.

I didn't know what to do, but Tony did.

"We're naïve to think we can do this without a major," he said. "So why don't we cut a whole album and then sell it to a national label? That's the only way."

I agreed. I also knew that the way I was writing, it wouldn't be long before I had enough songs for an entire album. That's because I was composing at Mom's. Her home cooking did me wonders—not to mention her supreme confidence in me. When I got a dozen songs, we rented a studio in the countryside outside Buffalo that had been built in a barn by Spyro Gyra, the jazz fusion band, who had yet to release a record. Spyro Gyra's career and mine would take off at roughly the same time.

Disco had taken over the market, and for any artist who wanted to do dance music, disco couldn't be ignored. If you call Barry White, Peter Brown, or B. T. Express disco, then disco was cool. But the truth is that most disco was derivative dribble. It was the same shit over and over. Van McCoy, with his "Hustle," was something else; Van was creative. "Disco Duck" was not creative. I never wanted to be a disco star. Disco artists had a short lifespan and besides, routine disco bored me. Disco lacked surprise and spontaneity. At the same time, disco was commercial. And having flopped so many times before, I was gung-ho determined to have commercial success. I knew I couldn't ignore disco if I wanted a hit.

That's why the first song I wrote for this new album, "You and I," had a disco intro. But I quickly moved off that groove to something funkier. My background arrangements were influenced by Lou Reed's "Walk on the Wild Side," when he talked about how "the colored girls go doo da-doo da-doo." When I wrote the lyrics, I was thinking about Kelly, who, although living far away, was still my wife. "You and I" are essentially Kelly and Rick. At the end, my concluding riffs were very Funkadelic, even operatic.

The other tunes came quickly—"Mary Jane" was about my love affair with pot. I wrote the song on a Fender bass. Peter Tosh was much on my mind. Once I got in the studio, I added an unfinished rock piece as an intro. Then I added flutes and, toward the end, broke it down to reggae. That rhythm guitar ain't nothing but a James Brown thang.

The third song I wrote was "Hollywood." I knew it was prophetic. Even though I had said that I hated Hollywood, and even though Hollywood had burned me more than once, I knew Hollywood was my future. I knew I'd wind up there. I saw "Hollywood" as a seminal song that described my undying dream of fortune and fame. It was written for Mom, who never stopping believing in my dream. Writing all these tunes reignited that dream. And though I needed the stability of my mother's home to anchor me, I had no doubt that the ship would soon be sailing.

Sgt. Pepper was on my mind. I studied that album. One of the cool things about the Beatles was how they emulated other groups they loved—the Beach Boys, the Everly Brothers, even the Marvelettes. I did the same thing in putting together what I saw as my funk/dance masterpiece. I had snippets of the masters I admired most—Holland-Dozier-Holland, Barry White, Marvin Gaye, the Isley Brothers, Isaac Hayes, James Brown, Norman Whitfield, even the Italian producer Giorgio Moroder, who wrote for Donna Summer. When the album was sequenced the lead-off cut was "Stone City Band, Hi!" an unapologetic nod to George Clinton. He might not have helped me find a deal, but I couldn't deny that the motherfucker was funky as Satan himself.

My songs were not simple or small. They contained a lot of elements and required a band. In that regard, my vision—beginning with Salt 'n Pepper and going through White Cane—had not changed. Sure, I saw myself as the star lead vocalist. But I wanted a star band, with its own identity. Barry White had his Love Unlimited and I'd be damned if I didn't have my Stone City Band. It wouldn't come together until my album was complete, but I was already planning it while I was still in the studio.

Half of that first album was cut in Spyro Gyra's barn in the woods and the second half at the Record Plant in New York. Once I saw how good it was going, I decided to pour even more money into the project. I hired Shelly Yakus, a famous rock engineer, and found myself recording at the same time and in the same building as Bruce Springsteen and Aerosmith, who were in adjoining studios.

There were limos lined up outside and groupies hanging in the lobby. They weren't for me but I knew soon they would be. At one point Steven Tyler poked his head in and asked if he could hear what I was doing.

"Sure thing, man," I said.

I was an Aerosmith fan. I loved "Dream On" and their version of "Walkin' the Dog." Far as I was concerned, Tyler was a black soul singer. And Joe Perry, the guitarist, was a master riffer. He created rock as raw as the Stones.

When Tyler heard "You and I" over the massive studio speakers, he started dancing like James Brown. "This is the fuckin' bomb!" he shouted over the music as he pulled out a big bag of blow and a long bowie knife. He dipped it in the blow and scooped up what looked like two grams. He tooted it up and asked me if I wanted some. Hell, yes.

I didn't snort up quite as much, but enough to wire me to where I was feeling like I could stand toe-to-toe with the great Tyler.

We kept taking hits off that knife.

"So this is what it's like to make it," I said.

"Yeah, man. And there ain't no doubt you're making it. Your shit is bulletproof."

With the cocaine dripping down my throat and my music blasting into Steven Tyler's ears, I never felt more confident.

"I'll see you up there, Rick," he said before leaving.

By "up there" I knew what he meant. Far as I was concerned, I had arrived even before I got there.

I worked like a demon in that studio for the next eight weeks. When I left, I had what I wanted—eight killer tracks that expressed exactly who I was: a singer/funkster/writer/composer/arranger who could dirty up the disco vibe without succumbing to its silliness.

I also had the perfect name for the album. It said exactly what I wanted to the public to do: *Come Get It!*

With drummer Tony by my side, I flew to L.A. to shop it. My attitude was simple—I'd go with any label except Motown. In the past, I'd gotten nowhere with Berry Gordy and his minions. Why would it be any different this time? I had my sights set on Warner Bros. or Atlantic, RCA or Columbia. Motown would not be part of my mix.

Tony and I checked into the Continental Hyatt House—called the Riot House by rockers—on Sunset. After cruising the Strip that first night, we started setting up meetings. We had a couple in a building on Sunset just east of Vine that housed several prospective buyers. We were in the elevator going up to our first meeting when a cat recognized me.

"Rick James?" he said.

"That's me."

"I'm Jeffrey Bowen. I met you during the Mynah Birds days in Detroit."

"Oh yeah, man, I remember. What's happening, Jeffrey?"

"I'm still a producer at Motown. You still singing?"

"Singing eight songs on this tape I'm holding in my hand."

"That's great," said Jeffrey. "Would love to hear it."

"Motown won't like it."

"Why not?"

"It ain't the Motown style. Besides, other than the Commodores, y'all are cold as ice."

"Can't argue with you, Rick. But that's why we'll respond sooner than anyone."

"How soon?"

"I'll play it for Berry today and have an answer for you tomorrow morning. Long as you don't play it for anyone else."

"So you want an exclusive?" I asked.

"For twenty-four hours only."

"What do you think?" I asked Tony.

"Waiting a day won't kill us."

Next day there was a knock on my door at the hotel. I was fast asleep. I fell out of bed, looked through the peephole, and saw Bowen.

"Open the fuckin' door," he said.

I let him in. He was all smiles. "I love your album. Berry loves your album. Everyone at Motown loves your album."

"Am I awake or dreaming?" I asked.

"I got something that will wake your ass up," said Jeffrey.

That first fresh hit of the day was always the best. Now both my eyes were open and my brain was working. Jeffrey Bowen started talking a mile a minute about the big plans Motown had for me. They were convinced I was the Next Big Thing.

The blow had me excited, along with the news that Motown wanted me. But I also thought that I should get a bidding war going. If my shit was so hot more than one label would want me.

"I ain't sure, Jeffrey," I said. "I think I'm going to shop this tape."

"You said we had an exclusive, and besides, your partner Tony is already meeting with Suzanne de Passe."

"Who's she?"

"Berry Gordy's chief lieutenant."

"Tony didn't tell me anything about that."

"Well, he's in her office right now."

I got dressed and went with Jeffrey to see de Passe. She was a pretty light-skinned sista with the no-nonsense manner of a high-powered exec. Jeffrey said Gordy considered her a genius. After my buddy Bobby Taylor discovered the Jackson 5, de Passe was the one who signed them—and fashioned the story that Diana Ross had discovered them. Jeffrey said that helped the Jacksons break through. De Passe was apparently brilliant at breaking acts.

No doubt she was a smart chick, and I was curious to meet her. She got down to business immediately. She told me that Tony was messing with my deal. He was trying to manipulate the situation so he could have control over me. I was shocked, but when I confronted him later on I saw that Suzanne had told the truth. I was grateful to her for having alerted me. It took a while to cut things off with Tony, but, with Suzanne's help, I did it. I hired a lawyer who negotiated the final contract with Motown and wound up with a fat bonus and a favorable ownership position on the publishing of my songs.

Suzanne said something else that at first took me aback.

"Your songs are terrific, Rick," she told me, "but you need to rework your material with a seasoned producer. They lack the right finishing touches that will turn them into surefire hits."

"I don't agree," I fired back. "They're smashes just the way they are."

"Look, Rick, this is your big chance. You have nothing to lose by going into the studio for another few weeks with someone you trust."

I'm impetuous. I'm headstrong. Lots of times I'm convinced I know it all. But when someone as savvy as Suzanne de Passe tells me to rework my material, I have to give it some thought.

About this same time I happened to drop by Marvin Gaye's studio, its own self-contained building on Sunset and Hudson, a few blocks west of the Motown offices. Marvin had to maintain his own space, separate from everyone else. I respected that. I liked going over there, not only because Marvin was so cool, but because he always had killer blow. It was there where I met Art Stewart, Marvin's engineer and the man who had produced Gaye's current hit, "Got to Give It Up."

I loved that jam. It was Marvin's sly reply to disco. Marvin didn't like to dance—he wasn't comfortable shaking his ass—so he wrote a song about the anxieties of a wallflower. The groove is so strong that it finally gives him the guts to go out there and cut a rug. Meanwhile, the feeling is loose, like a blue-light party in the basement. Art had the cats in the studio beating on juice bottles. When Don Cornelius from *Soul Train* wanders in, you can hear Marvin shout out, "Hey, Don!" In some ways it mirrors the beginning of "What's Going On," only with a lighter flavor.

Knowing that it was Art Stewart who put the production together, I was naturally interested in the brotha. He turned out to be an Aquarius like me, but unlike me, he wasn't the kind of cat who had to take charge. Art was mild-mannered and modest. Most of the producers I'd met—including Holland-Dozier-Holland and Norman Whitfield—couldn't stop talking about themselves and their hits. They had to let you know that they were the power behind the throne. Not Art. He just did his work, and he did it with a flair I'd never before seen in the studio. He was subtle—a slight suggestion for bringing up the horns here, a hint to change the bass line there. Art was just the man I needed. He saw that my ego was big enough for the two of us. Art could just kick back and be my chief adviser.

When I told Suzanne that I wanted Art to go in the studio with me and help resculpt and reengineer *Come Get It!,* she was all smiles.

"You couldn't have made a better choice," she said.

Late one night Norman Whitfield came by the studio when Art and I were at the tail end of the project.

"Hey, Rick," he said, "hear you finally got it together."

"Listen to this jam and tell me what you think."

I played him "You and I."

When the song was over, he said, "Smash."

"Thanks, man."

"You definitely got a sound. That's the first step. Now you gotta take the second step."

"What's that?"

"You gotta get a look."

A SOUND AND A LOOK

Whit was right. I had to concentrate on my image. If I had been smarter, I would have also concentrated on Kelly, since she'd come back into my life. During the period I was refining *Come Get It!* with Art Stewart, Kelly had shown up in L.A. I was thrilled to see her. Our love hadn't died, and this time I was determined to give our relationship the attention it required. She was full of forgiveness and I was full of good intentions, but in the end it turned out that I was full of shit. In the fever of preparing *Come Get It!*, I got carried away, left the studio late, and wound up with a couple of wild chicks. They sensed that I was on the verge of being a superstar and were eager to sign on as groupies. I should have known better, yet didn't. Justifiably, Kelly was disgusted and flew back to Toronto. I could have chased after her—and maybe I should have—but my mind was so focused on making this record work that no woman, not even Pam Grier, could have competed with my music.

I remember the moment that I learned I had a hit. I flew to

Washington, DC, for a promo appearance. My brother Roy, who had a high-powered job as a lawyer, was living there. We had a great reunion. I was glad to see him doing so well, and when I told him that I was on the verge of breaking out, he seemed happy but held back his excitement.

"I'm pulling for you, bro," he said, "but you've been so close so many times before I don't wanna jinx it by congratulating you too soon."

He was right. He told me that on a Monday, the day that "You and I" was being released. There was no guarantee that it would hit. That Friday, Roy and a friend took me to a party given by some straitlaced government officials. Next to them, with my long hair, earrings, black leather pants, and red boots, I looked like Freddy the Freak. I didn't give a shit. Marvin Gaye, who'd been raised in Washington, told me it was the squarest town in America. What surprised me, though, was when the party got under way, those suit-and-tie squares started snorting coke and smoking weed like fiends. I was happy to see that even the U.S. government cats liked to get down. I got my high on and was having fun when the host tapped me on the shoulder and said I was wanted on the phone.

I became a little alarmed. Who the fuck could be calling me? No one knew I was here. Might have been the drugs, but paranoia set in. I trusted my brother, but maybe someone had used him to set me up. As I went into the bedroom to take the call, my heart started hammering. A couple was on the bed making out. He had her panties off and was about to eat her pussy. My presence didn't disturb them in the least.

"Hello," I said.

"Rick James?"

"That's me."

I can't recall the guy's name, but he said he was from Motown and that "You and I" was the most added single of the week. It was number one in Atlanta and was selling like hotcakes up and down the coast. "At this rate it's gonna be number one, not just R & B, but pop."

I had no idea how in hell this Motown exec had found me at this party. I also didn't care. The chick being serviced by her boyfriend was screaming in ecstasy. No matter how good she felt, though, she could not have felt better than me. Better than pure cocaine, better than dripping-wet pussy, better than anything—the fact that I had a certified hit record was the best news I'd ever received. In this instant I knew my life was changing forever.

◆

Back in L.A., I thought about Whit's suggestion. I needed a look. I found that look when I went to a concert by Babatunde Olatunji, the incredible Nigerian drummer. I'd met him in New York but had never seen his full show. Man, I was blown away—not only by his polyrhythmic genius, but by the theatricality of his presentation. He had at least two dozen people onstage. His dancers were out of sight. They had the amazing hairstyles of the Masai. They wore animal hair woven into their own braids, creating long extensions twisted in fabulous shapes. Backstage, after greeting the master and asking him about these hairstyles, Olatunji was gracious enough to introduce me to the woman in charge. She gave me a brief history of African coiffures. The idea of the Masai was to assume the power of the animals whose hair you wove into your own. That's all I needed to know! I had the woman come to my place before the troupe left town. She spent all afternoon putting in extensions, beading, braiding, and weaving my hair with the hair of wild animals. When she was through I looked in the mirror and couldn't help but feel strong. I looked like a Masai warrior. I made no apologies to anyone for this look. I was about to walk through the American music-making money jungle, so I sure as hell better have the attitude of a warrior.

I flew to Buffalo to show Mom the new look. She loved it. She understood that, more than ever, I had to stand out.

"Baby," she said, "you finally got it all together. Can't tell you how proud I am."

"You gonna give up your job?"

"I better not, honey. Better hold on to it a little longer."

"The song's already a hit, Mom."

"I know that, James, but it'll take a while before those big checks come rolling in. Besides, my job keeps me busy. I've got to stay busy."

"I want you out in California with me. I hate for you to have to spend another winter in Buffalo."

"I'll be out there before you know it."

Before I knew it, my buddy Prez and I were at Eduardo's, an Italian nightclub in Buffalo that had a disco night every Saturday. The big dance hit was Parliament's "Flash Light." It had been on the charts for a while. When the deejay dropped it, the dancers got busy. But when he followed it with "You and I," the dancers went crazy. They started hooting and hollering. The deejay let 'em know I was in the house. The dancers came and got me and started carrying me on their shoulders like I was a football coach who had just won the Super Bowl. I had left Buffalo in handcuffs and returned as a hero. As Marvin said, "How sweet it is!"

The same week another friend, Icky, asked me if I wanted to go to a Kiss show.

"Fuck no!" I said. "Why would I wanna see a cheesy band like Kiss?"

"They say those guys put on a great show," said Icky. "You might see something you like."

Icky broke down my resistance and turned out to be right. Kiss blew me away. Their music wasn't shit, but their stage presentation was the bomb. All that black leather, those high boots, those face masks, the lighting—those cats knew how to create a dramatic look. Their look was as important as their songs, maybe even more important since to my ears they were just playing generic rock and roll.

Kiss hammered home the importance of high drama. They understood that in this arena you can't be over-the-top. Kiss's attitude was, if you fly your freak flag, fly it high. The color of that flag was black. The dominant color of the Kiss show was black—black leather, black backdrops, black everything. Kiss was all about maximum impact. If you went to a Kiss show, you'd never forget it. I decided to design my show with the same goal; I wanted my fans to remember my show for the rest of their lives.

Maximum impact meant a big band. I needed horns, reeds, rhythmic variety, and the best dancers on the planet.

I decided to build up my band in Buffalo because Buffalo was where I had originally built up my own musical strength. I needed more than a strong band behind me; I needed a strong family. I centered that family on Levi Ruffin Jr., a brotha I knew since childhood. He had married his grammar school sweetheart Jackie, who sang background with us. They had three kids, were beautiful people, and provided the stability I needed. Oscar Alston, a killer musician, gave me the bass bottom I needed. For a while I thought about playing bass myself in the band, but I decided I needed the freedom to stalk the stage. The Hughes brothers—Lanise and Nate—were whizzes on every percussive instrument you can name. My first keyboardist was Ramadon, who carried on in every style imaginable, and my first guitarist was a bad white boy named Allan Symanski. As time went on, the personnel would change. Danny LeMelle, who could blow tremendous sax as well as write his ass off, became an integral part of my operation. Tom McDermott was another monster guitarist. I loved all these guys. They knew me and could express everything I wanted to say musically. In fact, I saw the Stone City Band as an extension of myself. Some artists can tell their stories through the simplicity of their voice and voice alone. My stories, though, were never that simple. I needed the blast of a band—a cold-blooded band of brothas to help me get my message across.

That message also had to be illustrated on the cover of my album. Before the release of the single, I had been wondering about what that image should be when I ran into my buddy Calvin Hardaway, Stevie Wonder's brother, at Stevie's studio. It was a couple of years after Stevie's *Songs in the Key of Life*, probably the biggest album in his career. Steve was saying how Berry Gordy was bugging him for a new record—but no one could rush Stevie. No artist has ever been more in touch with his muse.

"What do you tell the boss when he's insisting on your next product?" I heard someone ask Stevie.

"I tell him to wait," was Stevie's simple answer.

He was fooling with some new material that would eventually wind up on *Hotter Than July.* We were both deep into Bob Marley, who influenced Stevie's "Master Blaster (Jammin')." The difference between me and Stevie, though, was that I smoked beaucoup ganja while Stevie never touched the stuff. Maybe that's what gave him the clarity to write a ballad like "Lately." Hearing him sing that song made me realize that there are other ways to tap your inner muse than resorting to chemicals.

A night in Stevie's studio was always stimulating. Adding to the excitement was Calvin's girlfriend, Valerie, a wonderful designer. When I began talking about cover art concepts with her, she had ideas of her own. Together we came up with the notion of me wearing high black boots with silver lightning bolts running down both of my legs.

"That's sexy," said Valerie. "But you also want to show your heart."

With that in mind, my top was custom-made in the form of a red rhinestone heart. We hired a gorgeous model in a provocative baby-blue outfit, her breasts barely covered. She reclined on the floor, her back arched, her eyes focused on me as I reached down to take her hand. I wanted to look like a hero. But not to grab all the glory, I also put the name "Stone City Band" on the cover right under mine.

Everything about *Come Get It!* was right—the music, the package, and the historical moment. Disco had peaked, and even though my stuff had a disco flavor, my extra layer of funk made all the difference in the world. There was an edge that I gave disco—even a danger—that was new to the game. And man, did it pay off!

Once the album was out and selling strong, my second single, "Mary Jane," was released. Industry insiders were predicting that it would outsell my first.

That's when I got an invitation to hang with the Man Himself. In the lingo of Motown, the Man was the Chairman, Berry Gordy Jr., the seat of all power and the source of all wisdom. Not only did he ask me to his home for lunch, he was gracious enough to send a car for me. Me being me, I naturally had to smoke a joint on the way up to his Bel Air mansion. As we climbed high into the hills of the most expensive neighborhood in the world, I got high myself. The gate opened and we rode another long stretch until we reached the main house. Security men stood around conspicuously, and I couldn't help but notice they were white. I was ushered into a fabulous book-lined room that looked like the private study of an Italian prince. A white butler asked if I wanted anything. I said white wine. The wine was brought and I waited another ten minutes. No problem. If anyone was entitled to make a grand entrance, it was Berry Gordy. When he finally walked into the room wearing a white linen Sergio Tacchini leisure suit, I thought of that moment in *The Wizard of Oz* when the curtain is pulled back and, expecting to see an overpowering monster of a man, you see this little-bitty bashful guy.

It had been years since Berry had signed me and the Mynah Birds in Detroit, and we spent a few minutes laughing about those days. He couldn't have been more charming.

"You're doing great things for this company, Rick," he said in his unusually high-pitched voice, "and we appreciate it. We're lucky to have you on the label."

"I'm lucky to be there . . ." I wasn't sure what to call him so I said, "Mr. Chairman."

He laughed and said, "Just call me Berry."

I knew artists who had claimed Gordy had fucked them many times over, and I knew other artists—like Smokey Robinson and Stevie—who credited him with making them stars. Any way you looked at it, though, the Chairman was a heavyweight and even a genius. Not only did he write hit songs for Jackie Wilson, he'd discovered more talent than any executive of his generation. On top of that, he was a black man who retained ownership of his empire in a white world.

When I told him that it was a pleasure seeing him again, I meant it.

"If there's anything else I can do for you, Rick," he offered, "just let me know."

"I love the promotional push Motown's giving me," I said. "But it wouldn't bother me if you could have your guys push even harder."

"Glad you brought that up that, Rick. That reminds me that I have to make a call.

"Rebecca!" Berry called out to his secretary. "Get Dick Clark on the line."

The Chairman spoke on the speakerphone so I could hear both sides of the conversation. Seemed that Clark had requested Diana Ross for his TV show. Berry was calling to say he could have Ross— if I was on the show as well.

"Anything you want, Berry," said Clark. "I know Rick James has a big hit and I've heard he's a real talent."

"A major talent," Gordy said, underscoring it.

"Consider it done."

In a two-minute phone call, Berry had secured my first national TV appearance. The next day, though, I learned that there was a stipulation—I could only bring two background singers and would have to sing to tape. In my book, that was fuckin' karaoke! I couldn't be separated from my band, especially on my national TV debut.

I called the Chairman to see if he'd call Dick again.

"Sorry, Rick," he said. "This is a funny town. You have to know when to call in favors. Call too often and you're suddenly out of favor."

I had a feeling that Berry was referring to both my call to him as well as my request that he call Dick again. In any event, there was nothing I could do. I went to the show with my two background singers. I wore a little miniature Coca-Cola bottle around my neck that held a good supply of blow. In the dressing room I dipped in and got wired. Then, after a huge fanfare intro, I performed "You and I." Between that and my next number—"Mary Jane"—Clark did a long interview with me. He was wonderful, sweet and relaxed, one of the nicest cats I'd ever met. His questions were gentle and genuine. The interview went well except for the fact that my nose started running. I started sniffing and wiping myself until it had to be obvious to Dick and a million viewers what was really going on. Dick didn't seem to mind. I'm sure he'd seen this shit a million times before. The viewers didn't care either. After all, this was the end of the seventies, when the cocaine culture still ruled Hollywood. Tooting a fat line—in a music exec's office, in the studio, or at practically any party—was as acceptable as drinking a beer. It was all part of a world in which I was being recognized as a guy with the gumption to be exactly who I was.

And who was that?

A rebel, a renegade, an artist-singer-writer-producer-bandleader intent on branding my identity in the most dramatic terms. My music was about me—a man deep into drugs, sex, and funk. The more drugs, the more sex, the more funk, the more my fame would grow.

THE BONUS

When I think back on the part of my story when I became a superstar, I can't help but be amazed by the culture that surrounded me. Not only was the music of the late seventies some of the hottest this country has ever produced, but the artists with whom I was in closest contact—Stevie Wonder and Marvin Gaye— were undisputed geniuses. And to think I could drop by their studios whenever I wanted! That access proved to be one of the great gifts of my life.

I was always into books and remember reading about the Renaissance, when Michelangelo and Leonardo da Vinci had their art studios filled with students. The students were there to watch and learn from the masters. Marvin and Stevie were my masters. Going to Marvin's studio on Sunset, for example, where he was working on his masterpiece *Here, My Dear*, was a trip and a half. Unlike Stevie, who worked in a drug-free zone, Marvin worked high. *I Want You*—his great work before *Here, My Dear*—was fueled by the fires of cocaine. This new thing was a more personal piece. Having married Berry Gordy's older sister Anna, Marvin was now divorcing her in a bitter legal hassle. He told the judge that she had taken all his money and that he had no assets. The judge ordered Marvin to give her the profits of his next album. So Marvin called it *Here, My Dear*, and wrote the story of their marriage in something that sounded like a soul opera. He combined all his styles, beginning with his training as a doo-wopper in the Moonglows, and turned out a suite that, to my ears, was nothing short of magnificent.

"I don't know if it'll sell, Rick," said Marvin his mellow voice, "and I don't care. If it doesn't sell, less money for Anna."

The irony, of course, is that despite whatever was strained about their relationship, Anna was the one who got Marvin into the studio to work. And now, even when they were divorcing, that pattern held.

Marvin fascinated me because he was such a contradiction between cool and crazy. No one was more kicked back and spiritual. In a second, he'd suspend whatever music he was working on to engage you in a two-hour discussion about God. He was a Christian who loved Jesus. But Marvin also believed in the devil and was convinced that in the war between God and the devil, the devil was winning. As he leaned down to Hoover up another line of blow, he'd tell you that blow was the devil.

When his divorce was final, Marvin married Janis Hunter, the beautiful young woman he'd met when he recorded "Let's Get It On" back in 1973. Jan was something else. She was a spiritual soul like Marvin, but Marvin had caught her up in his insane lifestyle. One day he loved Jan more than life itself; the next day he couldn't stand her and claimed she was torturing him. I never thought he appreciated Jan's beautiful spirit. But then again, I was an outside observer. I was a student in Marvin's studio.

"Hey, Rick," Marvin said one night. "How's *Come Get It!* selling?"

"Double platinum, baby," I said.

"Wow. What are you going to do with your bonus?"

"What bonus?"

"You mean you haven't gotten your bonus yet?"

"For what?"

"For a million dollars. Motown pays a half million each time you go platinum. Berry didn't explain that to you, brother?"

"No, he didn't."

"Well, you're new. I guess you gotta learn the hard way."

"The hell I do. That motherfucker ain't gonna fuck me."

I ran out of Marvin's studio over to the Motown building, where I saw Lee Young, a high-ranking exec.

"Where's my bonus?" I asked.

"What bonus?"

"The bonus for going double platinum."

"I don't know of any such bonus."

"The hell you don't. I'm going to see de Passe."

I charged into Suzanne's office and asked the same question.

"I'm not familiar with any bonus plan," she said.

"I'm telling you right now. I am not gonna be fucked over. Get Berry Gordy on the line or I swear I'll call a press conference and make such a stink it'll be in every newspaper in the country."

I was beside myself. I thought about how Suzanne and Berry had charmed me with their slick sales manner. I thought how vulnerable I had been. I saw myself as another lamb gone to slaughter. But no; I was not gonna accept this bullshit. A million bucks was a million bucks—and I wanted mine.

I finally got the Chairman on the phone.

"What is it, Rick?" he asked.

"You owe me a million."

"For what?"

"The bonus plan you give every artist that goes platinum. A half million for every million records sold. I've sold two million, so I got one million fuckin' dollars."

"There is no such plan."

"I don't believe you."

"Careful, Rick. I know you're the exuberant type, but being insolent isn't helping you any. I'll let you talk to any of my artists directly—Stevie, Smokey, the Commodores. They'll tell you that no bonus plan like the one you described has ever been in place."

"That's not what Marvin said."

"Marvin Gaye?"

"Yes, Marvin Gaye."

"Now I see."

"See what?" I asked.

"Marvin is messing with you, Rick, 'cause Marvin wants to mess with me."

"Why?"

"Because that's Marvin. Don't you remember the name of his record?"

"Which one?"

"*Trouble Man.*"

When I took the story back to Marvin, he laughed his easygoing laugh. "You didn't take me seriously, Rick, did you?"

"I sure as hell did."

"Well, once you get to know me better, you'll understand my humor."

Marvin's humor became more baffling as time went on.

It took me a long time to understand another thing about Marvin—and Stevie as well. At the very time that I came to them as a student, they were learning from me. I don't say this to brag, but only because it's obvious if you listen to their work after I came on the scene. If I had never showed up at Motown, Stevie and Marvin would have continued to turn out masterpieces. Their genius was hardly dependent upon me. But in the world of funk, where the groove comes from the street and the street is ever changing, the true funkmeisters—George Clinton, Norman Whitfield, Barry White—have to keep their ear to the street. Sometimes when you make it big, you lose contact with the street. And if someone like me comes in, fresh off the street, with a new groove that's selling like a motherfucker, you pay attention. You listen to how I'm arranging the horns; you note how I'm popping the bass; you listen to my drum fills; you hear how I place my hooks in relation to my verses. Listen to some of the songs done in the late seventies and early eighties—Stevie's "Cash in Your Face" or Marvin's "Funk Me"—and you'll hear something of my funk. I know their impact on me was greater than my impact on them. But I now understand that back then, as they came by my recording sessions to compare notes, they took something of me with them. And I'm glad, and flattered, and only wish I'd taken the time to do a full-length collaboration with those two towering masters.

✦

Royalties began pouring in. My long-held dream of getting rich was coming true. I bought a mansion in Coldwater Canyon once owned by William Randolph Hearst with a sunken living room and a dramatic fireplace that looked like it came out of *Citizen Kane*. I bought it with Mom in mind and flew her out to see it. When she walked through the door, tears were streaming down her face.

"I don't know what to say, James."

"You don't have to say anything, Mom. Without your belief in me, this would have never happened."

She gave me a huge hug. "Can't tell you how proud I am. You said you'd do it and you did."

"You're the only one who never doubted me."

"Never did and never will."

"Will you give up your job now? Will you finally stop running those numbers?"

She wiped away her tears and said, "I do admit that I'm getting a little old for that work. And now that you've hit the number, I think I am ready to retire. But the funny thing is that I think I'll miss the excitement."

I was my mother's son. Like her, I thrived on action.

The action got more intense when the band arrived from Buffalo. I could accommodate all of them in the house. Most of the cats hadn't been to L.A. before and wanted to go sightseeing before we started rehearsals, but I said there was no time. First things first—I was bringing in professional chicks to braid their hair in the Masai mode. They had to have that look.

While Mom was with me, I never did drugs in front of her. Because she knew me better than anyone in the world, she could tell when I was high on weed or blow—which was most of the time— but she was cool enough not to say anything. Even though her work in Buffalo had been restricted to running numbers, she knew the drug culture. Her Mafia bosses were the main suppliers in Buffalo. Far as entertainers went, she knew that smoking and coking were a normal part of the lifestyle and made no judgments.

Mom also knew that music, in addition to being art, was also commerce. Music was a commodity that had to be packaged and sold. It was about image. And with all the references to drugs and freaky sex in my songs, my image was rooted in outrageousness. In developing my second album, *Bustin' Out of L Seven,* I was aware of what my market wanted. They not only wanted tight-and-right dance music, they wanted a party leader—me!—who would say, as I did on the title track, "Well, all right, you squares, it's time you smoked. Fire up this funk and let's have a toke. It'll make you dance and some of everything. Everybody get high!"

Yet drugs weren't the whole story. Listen to "Love Interlude" and you'll hear a gorgeous Miles Davis–flavored trumpet solo over the subtle sounds of a couple deep in romantic dialogue. "Spacey Love" also took the music to a different place; it was a fall-on-your-knees old-fashioned ballad that I wrote and dedicated to Patti LaBelle and the Bluebelles, whose far-out costumes influenced my own sense of stage fashion and whose "Lady Marmalade" was one of the baddest dance jams in the whole fuckin' history of dance.

The always dependable and creative Art Stewart coproduced my sophomore effort. The cats who became my horn section—Danny LeMelle and Norman and John Irving—also helped me expand my sound. I called them the Punk Funk Horns.

Wasn't long before I was being called the King of Punk Funk. I came up with the label because I related to the riotous spirit of English punk groups like the Sex Pistols, who had been touring the U.S. about the same time as the release of my first records. I also just dug the sound of those two words. As a distinctive moniker I thought "Punk Funk" would stick—and it did.

Bustin' Out busted out so big that big man Berry Gordy asked me, before I went out on tour, if I'd produce Diana Ross. She'd just done the film version of *The Wiz*, which was seen as something of a flop. Fans thought she was too old to play Dorothy. They wanted Stephanie Mills, who'd originated the role on Broadway. Berry knew that Diana's career needed a restart and looked to me, the hottest writer-producer in his stable.

I was stoked. Ross had always been Berry's pet project, and the fact that he was entrusting her to me did wonders for my already overinflated ego. I quickly knocked out a song, "I'm a Sucker for Your Love," designed as duet for me and Diana. She heard and loved it. The plan was to do the album quickly. Then came the memo from the Chairman. He said he was glad I'd be doing three or four numbers for Ross. Three or four numbers? My understanding was that I'd do the entire album—written, produced, and arranged by Rick James. When I tried calling Berry to discuss it, his assistant made it clear that there was nothing to discuss. Either take it or leave it.

I left it. I figured if I was good enough to do three cuts for Diana, why not give me the whole record? When I went to Diana to recruit her help, she was, as always, extremely sweet with me.

"I love your productions, Rick," she said, "but the Chairman has a different vision for this record. He wants a variety of producers."

"Fuck the Chairman!"

After I said those words, I realized that Diana, as Berry's former lover, had done exactly that—which, no doubt, in addition to her great talent, had helped her become a superstar. But she wasn't willing to fuck him again.

The project went away. Ironically, when Ross's new album, *The Boss*, came out, it was entirely produced—not piecemeal produced—by Ashford and Simpson. At the time they had more clout than me. That was understandable since, despite my breakthrough success, I couldn't claim classics like "Ain't No Mountain High Enough" and "Reach Out and Touch (Somebody's Hand)." Besides, Ashford and Simpson were the first writers I read about who used the word "stoned" in a title. Their Ray Charles hit was called "Let's Go Get Stoned."

In truth, I wasn't all that worried about missing out on a Diana Ross record. That's because while I was cutting *Bustin' Out*, I heard a Motown singer who captivated me much more than Diana. Even though she was white, she sang blacker than Diana. She had a sound and a soul that excited my imagination. If I had a future as a producer of acts other than myself and my band, this was the kind of singer I wanted to work with.

Meet Teena Marie.

WILD AND PEACEFUL

"Before we meet Teena Marie," says Brotha Guru, "let me take a look at that *Bustin' Out* album you got over there."

One of the prison guards just gave me an original LP to autograph. I hand it to Brotha Guru, who looks over the cover, which is a cartoon drawing of me breaking through a prison wall as I lead three big-busted chicks to freedom.

"I see you got your winged leather boots."

"That was my trademark," I say.

"And this time you got a heart over your dick."

"Actually," I say, "it's right above my dick."

"They draw you like a superhero."

"It's a cartoon, man. It was meant to be cute."

"So you were happy to be a caricature of yourself?" asks Brotha Guru.

"Why not? The Jackson Five did it. After their early hits, they had their own cartoon program on TV. Since I was the biggest thing since the Jackson Five, I didn't see why I couldn't be a cartoon character like them."

"I don't see the Stone City Band name on the cover like it was on the first album. Did the Me Monster keep you from crediting them?"

"Why you bustin' my chops, brotha? The only reason I didn't put their name on the cover was that I was planning to produce their own album. It would be all them."

"I don't see the logic. By crediting them here, wouldn't that spread their fame and help their solo project?"

"You're not a record man, Brotha Guru," I say. "You don't understand these things."

"And what prison are you busting out of?"

"The prison of conformity, man. The prison that had kept me from being a star. The prison that wouldn't let me take my music to the world. Doesn't that make sense?"

"It does, Rick. You're a poet and poets employ metaphors. Prison is a powerful one. You use it well, brotha. You do everything well. God gave you a first-class imagination and talent to spare. I'm just looking for that moment in your career when the Me Monster took over."

"There wasn't no Me Monster at this point. There was young Rick James, thirty-one years old, growing as an artist, looking to do more than produce himself. What I did for Teena Marie, I did for her—not for me. And she'll be the first to tell you that."

"So when all these early hits of yours came out, your ego was under control?"

"I ain't saying that. I'd been working half my life to hit it big, and when I did, naturally I tripped. Who the fuck wouldn't? All I'm saying is that I took some people along with me. It wasn't all about me."

"Tell me all about Teena."

◆

One afternoon I was at the Jobete Music Company, the song publishing division of Motown, when I heard this soaring female voice come out of a practice room. It had to be one of those two-ton sanctified mamas from church. But when I poked in my head, I was shocked. Sitting at the piano was this itsy-bitsy white chick who couldn't have been taller than five feet. She told me she was doing demos for Diana Ross and Thelma Houston. I sat down in a chair next to her and asked what music she loved the most. She said straight-up soul.

"Sing some of that," I said.

Accompanying herself, she sang Etta James's "At Last" and Aretha's "Angel." She did a scary version of Smokey's "Ooo Baby Baby" and tore up Al Green's "Love and Happiness." The girl was more than bad; she was superbad.

Teena had the voice of an opera singer—an incredible range and power for days. She took my breath away. Personally, she was a sweetheart, shy and polite and respectful as she could be. She told me how much she loved my music and wondered if there was any way I'd ever produce her.

There was no way I wouldn't. Turned out Berry had signed her some time ago and spent hundreds of thousands of dollars experimenting with producers. I heard the tapes. None of them understood her. I did. I was also amazed that a company as shrewd as Motown could waste so much money on the wrong creative marriage. Because she was white, Motown was trying to take her pop. But Teena Marie was no more pop than Millie Jackson. She had to be produced and sold as a soul act. I had no doubt she'd soar up the R & B charts. If she crossed to pop after that, fine. But there was no way black music buyers, who know true-heart singing forged in the tradition, would pass her by. White as she looked, white as she was, Teena Marie wasn't white at all. She was a soul sista.

Teena was living with her manager, Winnie Jones, and Winnie's live-in boyfriend, Fuller Gordy, brother to Berry. Winnie's daughter Jill would later become a protégé of Prince's. Teena wound up in this household because her own parents, angry that she was hanging out with blacks, had kicked her out of their home in Venice. I loved that she was a rebel like me.

We fell into a beautiful collaboration. The songs just flowed. I already had "I'm a Sucker for Your Love," originally written for Diana. I decided to do it as a duet with Teena. Much to my delight, it became a top ten hit. Because of boss Berry's refusal to let me produce his diva's entire album, Ross lost out.

I thought Teena had the poise and chops of a true diva and started calling her Lady T, a name that stuck. She inspired me to write "Déjà Vu," a languorous ballad about reincarnation that Teena delivered with a delicately supernatural touch. Seeing that she had talent beyond singing, I also encouraged Teena to write. Her song on her debut album was "I'm Gonna Have My Cake (And Eat It Too)," which I cut with upright bass. I invited in older jazz cats so Teena could show off a whole different aspect of her vocal personality. Lady T was deep.

Al Stewart coproduced Teena with me. I called the album *Wild and Peaceful*, a perfect description of the two different moods we wanted to create. The album was a major hit that produced a major new artist. Like Berry Gordy, I was establishing my own stable of artists. The idea that I could launch a singer like Teena at the same time my own career was taking off was further proof: I could build an empire.

People have asked why I didn't put Lady T's picture on the cover, given that she was so pretty. I wanted to create mystery. *Wild and*

Peaceful was a mysterious title and now Teena's ethnicity would be a further mystery. Was she white? Was she black? Let the guessing games begin. I also knew that back in the day Berry Gordy had tried promoting one of his lovers, a white singer, Chris Clark, who didn't get over. I figured that was because fans associated Motown with black artists. I didn't want that prejudice to hurt Teena. Once her music was out there, I knew it would be accepted. I also figured that most listeners would assume she was black—and they did. She got over as a soul artist and when fans learned she was white they didn't care. They were already hooked on her music. It gave me great satisfaction to know that I'd done something the Chairman himself had not been able to do—sell a white singer to a black audience. Teena would eventually find white fans, but her core audience was always black. They accepted her, as did I, as a sista. Soon, with great love, they started calling her Vanilla Child.

◆

Time to tour.

Bustin' Out had created a massive fan base, and my new manager—Shep Gordon, who also represented Alice Cooper and Teddy Pendergrass—booked me up on a four-month coast-to-coast forty-city tour. Shep won me over not only because he was the agent to big stars but because he had gone to school in Buffalo. Both reasons were dumb. Ultimately I'd drop him like a bad habit. He didn't do anything for me that I couldn't have done myself. Slowly I came to realize that all managers are basically pimps. They kick back and count their fat commissions while their artists work their asses off.

I saw Teddy Pendergrass as a competitor whose solo career, after singing lead for Harold Melvin & the Blue Notes, took off a little earlier than mine. Obviously Teddy could sing, and his Teddy Bear image got the chicks hot. But I never liked the guy. He thought he was God's gift to the universe. I know I'm in no position to call someone arrogant. But the difference between me and Teddy was that I knew when I was being a cocky bastard. I could step back and laugh at myself. I had people who called me on my bullshit. I was aware of my ego-tripping. Teddy wasn't. You couldn't tell that motherfucker shit.

We warmed up for our tour in Fresno, a California city with more cocaine than L.A. We stayed wired for that week and, to be honest, for most of the tour. I called it the Magical Funk Tour and it sold out everywhere. Our stage show—with the Masai image, the hard-hitting Stone City Band, the super-sexy dancers—was a sensation. When I lit up an overstuffed joint onstage, the fans went nuts. The only negative was the occurrence of near riots. Our venues weren't big enough—the demand was greater than the supply—and at Boston's Orpheum Theatre I watched cops beating on fans clamoring to get in. I pledged never to play places too small to hold my fans. I've kept that pledge.

Back in L.A. I was exhausted but pleased. A royalty check—for $1,875,000—was staring me in the face. Best of all, I'd convinced Mom to leave Buffalo and come live with me in my Hollywood splendor. I bought a Rolls-Royce and a Jaguar and hired a staff of servants.

"You happy, Mom?" I asked her one night when we were dining on lobster and steak in my state-of-the-art kitchen.

"Happy for you, baby," she said.

"But not happy yourself?"

"I'd be happier if I found a connection to run some numbers. In this spread-out crazy city I can't even find a corner bar where the action is."

"The corner bars are way down in nigga town," I said. "You don't wanna be hanging out down there."

"Why not, James? Been doing that my whole life. I feel safer in those corner bars than I do in a big house like this where if someone broke in and I started screaming, no one would hear me."

"No one's breaking in, Mom. Besides, I got me a burglar alarm and a couple of security cats who ain't gonna let no one hurt you."

"I understand that, sweetheart, and I appreciate this good life. It's just a little boring for someone who's used to working the streets."

"You're just homesick. You'll get used to L.A. It'll grow on you."

It never did.

One night a serious earthquake rocked the house. In the middle of the night we were thrown out of our beds and ran out in the street. We thought that the roof might collapse. Standing there in her robe, Mom looked at me and said, "I love you, baby, but I'm outta here."

Within twenty-four hours, Mom packed her things and split.

The aftershocks did nothing to calm my own jittery nerves. With Mom gone, I felt especially insecure. I've always been impulsive, and my impulses were telling me to get the fuck out of Dodge and join my mother in Buffalo. Just like that, I sold my fancy Hollywood digs and moved home. The Stone City Band, mainly Buffaloers themselves, were thrilled.

I was rich enough to buy the baddest house in Buffalo, a place in the lily-white suburb of Orchard Park, where racists had burned crosses on the lawns of a black doctor who owned the crib before me. It was a fabulous spread, a pool, a tennis court, a separate clubhouse, the works. The *Buffalo Evening News* greeted me with a headline that said, CROWNED PRINCE RETURNS HOME. This was the moment when the blessed Linda Hunt walked into my life. She started out as our housekeeper but wound up running everything for me. She became more than an assistant. She became a life organizer and lifesaver— my most loyal and trusted employee.

At first I worried that leaving L.A. might hurt my career. After all, L.A. was Motown central and the center of all pop culture. But I realized that I was big enough to live wherever I wanted. Being back in the same house as Mom was important to my peace of mind. Far as returning to Western New York, I enjoyed the benefits of being a big fish in a small pond.

Yet I was still restless. I was eager to get in the studio and start my third record. Much as I loved Art Stewart, I figured I no longer required a coproducer. So I flew to the Record Plant in Sausalito, California, where Sly Stone had worked. My engineer, Tom Flye, had done records with both Sly and the Grateful Dead. He was just the cat I wanted behind the board.

At the same time I put together the Stone City Band's first album—*In 'n' Out*—a mix of funk, jazz, Latin, and rock. I was using all the weapons in my arsenal.

I found another weapon that I used unsparingly—the Pointer Sisters. I got them to sing on Stone City's first single, "Little Runaway," with me singing lead. They were also all over my own album. I loved those sistas, especially Ruth, who was tall and fine like an African queen. I'd be at the console snorting blow and getting a huge hard-on just watching them sing in the studio.

When my album was complete I knew I had at least one new monster hit—"Love Gun"—and I was right. That song became a permanent part of my repertoire. The cover of the album also became iconic. The poster nearly sold as many copies as the record. My idea was to switch from black to white. I was dressed in tight all-white high leather boots, a fancy white top, and a white cowboy hat. My hair fell below my shoulders, and in my right hand I held a joint. I exhaled defiantly. Naturally I had to call the thing *Fire It Up*.

The joint sold. I lost track of whether it went double or triple platinum. All I knew was that the industry was saying that I had the

Midas touch. The industry was also saying that they hadn't seen a start this explosive since James Brown—and that I was defining the sound of music for a new decade.

The eighties had arrived. I felt like I was racing a souped-up Ferrari with no one challenging my front position. But then I looked into my rearview mirror and saw this one sports car gaining on me. The driver was so small I could barely see his head above the steering wheel. Strange thing is that, on the advice of others, I had invited him into the race. He didn't catch me—and he wouldn't for a long time to come—but I never liked his fuckin' attitude.

He called himself Prince.

TWO DRUMMERS

did all of *Fire It Up* in thirteen days, a feat the studio cats are still talking about. My creative output was crazy. I was on fire. I had so many songs inside me that I put down tracks for a second Stone City Band album, *The Boys Are Back*. When that record dropped, though, programmers started complaining that the Stone lead singer, Levi Ruffin, sounded too much like me. They didn't know whether it was a Rick joint or a Stone joint. I had so many joints out there that the world was getting confused. But that was the kind of confusion I could live with.

Adding to the confusion was the introduction of this new artist called Prince. Promoters had been telling me that he wanted to open for me. They said that my music had heavily influenced his. I hadn't heard of him—this was before his "I Wanna Be Your Lover" hit big—and I asked to see him perform on tape. They were right; he did remind me of myself, only he didn't move as much onstage.

When his song came out, I loved it. Why not help a young brotha with such obvious talent?

Our first confrontation happened down south. So far Prince hadn't come to introduce himself to me, which was strange, since I was the cat giving him a shot. I was told he was shy. I didn't really care—I was just curious to see what he looked like. A couple of hours before showtime I walked in the theater and saw this tiny guy sitting behind a drum set playing a groove I considered weak. He was grinning like he'd come up with the beat of life. His entourage was gathered around him, nodding their heads to his drumming like he was Tony Williams. I decided to have a little fun. My drummer had set up his kit on the other side of the stage. I went out there and took an extended solo that incorporated about six thunderous grooves at once. If Prince wanted to fuck around on drums as my opening act, he'd better understand what was coming after him.

After watching me, he simply got up and left the stage. He still didn't introduce himself.

That night I was curious to see what his show was like, so I watched from the wings. I thought it was lame. He came out wearing a trench coat and heels. His New Wave rock and roll didn't do anything for the hard-core funk fans. He hardly moved. At the end of his set he took off the trench coat and stood there in his bloomers. The crowd booed. I felt sorry for the cat.

When I got onstage, I glanced over and saw Prince watching me. I had some trademark moves—flipping the mic and catching it backward, putting my hand to my ear as I called out my funk chants to the fans, and ending up by flashing the funk sign.

A week later one of my musicians came to me and said, "Rick, hate to say this, bro, but that Prince cat is copping all your licks."

"What do you mean?"

"He's doing your show, man."

Next night I made it a point to watch him from the wings. My guy was right. Prince was emulating my mic moves like a motherfucker. He was calling out my funk chants and even flashing my funk sign. I know imitation is the sincerest form of flattery, but because my act followed his, it looked like Rick James was copying Prince rather than vice versa.

The bad blood got worse. My band was a bunch of friendly down-home brothas loved by everyone. His band was a bunch of snobs who never bothered to acknowledge my guys. My band was ready to kick their asses—but I said no. Let's work this out like gentlemen.

We had a come-to-Jesus meeting, but even that was hard to arrange. I wanted Prince and his band to come to my suite, but he insisted I come to his. I figured I'd be the mature one; I'd cave; I'd let him have his way. I went to his suite. Prince, his manager, and his scrawny-looking band were on one side of the room. My cats, looking like Masai warriors, surrounded me.

I said, "You're stealing my shit."

He denied it, saying he had developed his style years before ever seeing me live.

I said, "Your band acts like they're too good to say hello to us."

He denied it, saying his band was preoccupied with rehearsing.

I told him I was tired of his copping my licks.

He said they were moves I'd copped from people like Jackie Wilson, James Brown, and George Clinton.

I said, "You're not entirely wrong—except some of these moves are very specific to me and you're using them minutes before I get out onstage."

He said he'd try to curtail that.

I said, "Cool."

We left without shaking hands.

My band reported that he hadn't curtailed shit and kept copping my moves during his opening act.

On February 1, 1980, I celebrated my thirty-second birthday. Prince and his crew crashed the party. I went over to his table, grabbed him by the back of his hair, and poured cognac down his throat. He spat it out and started crying like a baby. I laughed.

✦

"Can I ask you a question about Prince?" says Brotha Guru on one of those prison days when I'm discussing that famous Rick/Prince tour.

"Sure."

"Do you think you saw him the same way George Clinton saw you?"

"What do you mean?"

"Clinton saw you as the Next Big Thing so he put you off. You had the new groove. You were a threat. Maybe that's how you saw Prince."

"Prince's groove wasn't shit."

"How can you say that, Rick? After all these years he's proven to be one of the baddest brothas ever. They compare him to Michael Jackson. You can't deny the boy's talent."

I have to stop and think. Brotha Guru isn't wrong. No matter what I might have thought of Prince in the early days, he has turned out some of the funkiest shit on record.

"I resented him," I admit, "but I knew he was stealing."

"Any more than you stole from Marvin Gaye? Or any more than Marvin Gaye stole from Sam Cooke? Or any more than Ray Charles stole from Charles Brown or Nat Cole?"

"When did you become such a musicologist, Brotha Guru?"

"Been loving music since before your mama ever met your daddy. And I know that in music there ain't nothing new. There are just new combinations. You combined something that had never been combined before. So did Prince. And I suspect that, because you're so musically savvy, you feared that he had the capacity to outdo you. So you tried to humiliate him whenever you could."

"That didn't take much."

"Whatever it took," says Brotha Guru, "you were eager to do it. I can understand that. I don't blame you. We all fear the next generation coming along and unseating us. That's human nature. I'm just pointing out your human nature."

"I still don't like the motherfucker."

"You don't have to. And since I've never met him, I have no opinion of his personality. At the same time, given his accomplishments, I'd have to say that anyone who doesn't recognize Prince's genius is something of a fool. And you, Rick James, are far from a fool."

"You want me to say that Prince is a genius?"

"Don't want you to say anything, boy. Just want you to go on with your story."

◆

Brotha Guru has insight into my story, because when I saw that Prince was stealing from me, I stole from him. During a break in the tour I took his OB-X synth—he was the first to have that model—and brought it with me to Miami, where I started fooling with my new record. When the tour continued, I put the synth back on the truck. Prince never knew I'd taken it.

At the end of the tour, I needed a break. Motown was clamoring for a new record but I decided to follow in the footsteps of Stevie and Marvin. They delivered their records in their own sweet time and I'd do the same. I was unhappy with Motown 'cause I thought my royalty checks, although large, should have been larger. I suspected they were scraping cream off the top.

Instead of rushing back to Buffalo to crank out a new record, I took the band to Miami, where we rented a mansion on one of those exclusive keys. The Bee Gees lived next door. When Miami got too hot, we went looking for some of those trade winds that you find in the Caribbean. With my acoustic guitar in hand, I hired a captain, rented a yacht, and drifted around St. Croix to St. Thomas, St. Maarten, and Martinique. Let the suits keep screaming at me in their ship-to-shore calls and their hysterical telegrams. When Berry Gordy tried to get hold of me, wanting to know why I wasn't in the studio, it felt good to send back a message that said, "Gone fishing."

The songs I wrote reflected my relaxation. Instead of my usual nine or ten songs, I recorded only six. Motown insisted I give them more material. I refused. I wanted this record to be sparse, not crowded. The stories coming through me were all about the sea and the sand and the beauty of the islands. I put in the sound of the waves and gave the tunes titles like "Island Lady," "Summer Love," and "Gettin' It On (In the Sunshine)." I wrote motifs and melodies that, to my mind, were some of the most haunting I had ever composed. I called the album *Garden of Love*. I was dead certain that I was presenting a side of Rick James that the public would like to know.

I was dead wrong. The only single that made any noise was "Big Time"—and it wasn't written by me. The deejays saw the other songs, the ones I viewed as so precious, as filler. The album barely went gold. By then I was so used to multiplatinum that gold equaled failure. Even worse, the album generated such little heat that the big Funky Island Tour I had planned for America and Europe was scrubbed. Promoters had lost their faith in my ability to draw big crowds.

I had to scratch my head. One day I was on top and then, with one underperforming record, the bottom fell out. Had my arrogance finally caught up with me? Was I too cocky for my own good? Had I lost my glow?

I decided I needed some time to reassess. Hawaii seemed the right place to do just that. I went to Maui, where my agent, Shep Gordon, had a house on the beach. During my stay he had a poolside dinner party. Among the guests was Salvador Dalí. I knew a little about art and was familiar with Dalí's far-out paintings. Like me, he had a crazy imagination.

During dinner he kept staring at me. I got a little uncomfortable until he finally blurted out, "Señor, I am mad about the way you look. Please allow me to sketch you."

"Hey, man," I said, "I'd love it."

He took his napkin and spent fifteen or twenty minutes doing this groovy portrait. When I saw it, I felt that he'd captured my soul.

"You can keep it, señor," he said.

"Wow. Thanks."

"You better be thankful," said Shep. "No telling what that thing is worth."

Next morning I awoke, fired up a joint, slipped on my shorts, and took a long walk along the beach. The waves were calm and the breezes delightful. At one point I decided to take a short dip. Soon as I dived into the sea, though, I had a terrible thought—that these were the shorts I'd worn last night. Dalí's portrait was still in my pocket. When I got out of the water and took out the napkin, Dalí's portrait was unrecognizable, just a pattern of blurs. They say pot destroys short-term memory. I sure could have used some sharp short-term memory that morning. Without it, I ruined the only known depiction of a famous funkster by an even more famous surrealist.

For the rest of that trip I discussed my career with Shep. He had lots of ideas for me. He thought I should be more pop and less street. He thought I should write songs that sounded more like Lionel Richie, who was threatening to be Motown's next big solo star. I thought Shep was wrong. I was convinced he just didn't get me—and I fired him.

My intention was to fly back to Buffalo from Hawaii with a very brief stopover in L.A. I hit my favorite spot, Carlos and Charlie's on the Strip, where I was greeted like a conquering hero. I wasn't sure what the hell I had conquered but that didn't matter. It was vintage champagne and primo blow. When I drove down Sunset Boulevard—I called it Ho Stroll—the ladies waved at me. I was their hero.

"If you're feeling so good," said Mom, calling from Buffalo, "why do you sound so bad?"

"My record flopped."

"Not every record can be number one, son. You been on a streak. All streaks come to an end."

"But I loved the last record, Mom. Didn't you?"

"I love everything you do, James, but I can see why it wasn't as popular as the others."

"Why?"

"You've been off the streets for a while."

"Wasn't that always the point of getting rich, Mom? Didn't we always wanna move outta the ghetto?"

"Sure we did. And it's fun to go sailing around those islands. It's fun to go to Hawaii. And I know that Hollywood is fun. But when I was out there with you, son, I saw how alone L.A. can make you feel. No one's on the streets. They don't even have sidewalks. There's something about them streets, boy. You don't ever wanna forget the streets."

Rick James and Art Stewart receiving Rick's first gold album for
Come Get It! with Skip Miller and Barney Ales, 1979.

Bobby Holland/Michael Ochs Archives/Getty Images.

Fire It Up tour, 1979.
Paul Natkin/WireImage.

Performance in Los Angeles, California, circa 1981.
Michael Ochs Archives/Stinger/Getty Images.

November 7, 1981: Rick performs on *Saturday Night Live*. The episode was hosted by Lauren Hutton.

NBCUniversal/Getty Images.

A performance at the International Amphitheater in Chicago, Illinois, 1982.

Raymond Boyd/Michael Ochs Archives/Getty Images.

Onstage during the *Cold Blooded* tour, 1983.

Paul Natkin/WireImage.

Rick James wins the American Music Award for Favorite
Soul Album for *Street Songs*, 1982.

Time & Life Pictures/The LIFE Pictures Collection/Getty Images.

That signature Rick James stare.
Kypros/Hulton Archive/Getty Images.

Linda Blair and Rick, October 1982.
New York Daily News *Archive/Getty Images.*

Backstage with Grace Jones at the 25th Annual Grammy Awards, 1983. Earlier in the evening, Rick presented Marvin Gaye with a Grammy for "Sexual Healing."

Ron Gallela/WireImage.

Rick with the Mary Jane Girls at the 1984 American Music Awards.

Ron Gallela/WireImage.

Eddie Murphy and Rick backstage following Murphy's
performance at Madison Square Garden, 1985.

David McGough/The LIFE Picture Collection/Getty Images.

Rick and Teena Marie perform at the House of Blues in LA, 1997.
Jim Steinfeldt/Michael Ochs Archives/Getty Images.

Onstage with Teena Marie at the *Standing in the Shadows of Motown* performance, 2002.
Michael Schwartz/WireImage.

Rick selects jewelry before his performance at Constitution Hall in Washington, DC, 1998. The Washington Post/*Getty Images.*

Rick and his daughter, Ty.
Tyenza Matthews.

Rick, Tanya, and son Tazman at the studio, 1993.
Tyenza Matthews.

Dear Tanya,

Just a short letter to let U know that Im Thinking about U, with every day that passes. Its Tuesday night and my day has gone by quick. But the time will never be short until I am in your loving arms. You sounded great tonight when we spoke, I am so proud of you baby, you are so very special to me and theres not a day that goes by where you are not a part of my every thought. I love you Tanya. More Then life itself. I am so proud to have you as my love and the mother —

Rick's letter to Tanya, written while serving time in prison.
Tyenza Matthews.

Clockwise from left to right: Tanya, Ty, Rick, Tazman, and
Ty's daughters, Charisma and Jasmin.
Tyenza Matthews.

Smiling on a Christmas morning.
Tyenza Matthews.

Early days in Buffalo.
Tyenza Matthews.

Rick with his beloved mother.
Tyenza Matthews.

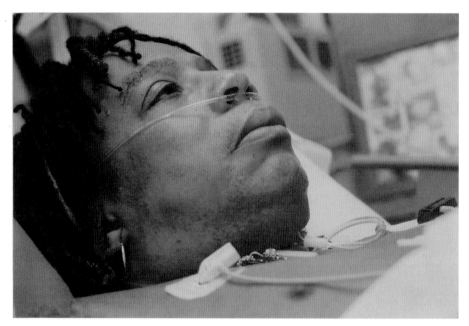

Rick in his hospital bed.
Tyenza Matthews.

THE STREETS

New York City is bigger, Chicago is windier, Atlanta is warmer, but of all the chocolate cities, Buffalo may be the baddest. You'd have to compare it to Detroit to get a sense of the down-and-out feeling that hangs over the inner city. Like Detroit, Buffalo was once a booming Great Lakes city. But unlike Detroit, it never even began to forge a comeback. It's the filthiest buckle in the center of the Rust Belt. The steel mills are shut down tight, the jobs long gone. The ghetto is one nasty liquor store after another. The bars are dirty holes-in-the-wall where the patrons are drinking themselves to death on cheap gin and rotgut wine.

When I got to the city of my birth, I gathered up my hair and hid it under an old baseball cap that had BUFFALO BILLS written across the front. I pulled it down on my face. I put on a sweatshirt, some old jeans, and hiking boots and went down to the old neighborhood. I walked through the projects and all the central scenes of my childhood. Places, people, and smells came back to me. My

mind was flooded with memories. I heard the music coming out of the ghetto blasters—Larry Graham's "One in a Million You," George Benson's "Give Me the Night," Kool and the Gang's "Celebration," the Gap Band's "Burn Rubber on Me." I absorbed all the sounds—the kids crying, the moms screaming, the dogs barking, the cats fighting. I absorbed all the life around me. I didn't judge it, didn't see it as good or bad. It just was. It was where I came from. It was me.

I made four or five of these secret trips, always in disguise and always alone. If I had gone with my entourage, everyone would have guessed that some big shot was coming through. For me to ingest what I needed to ingest, I couldn't afford to be a big shot. I had to be nobody. The only person I told about these excursions was Mom. After all, it was her idea.

"When I feel myself getting a little crazy," she said, "I go down there to where it all began just to look around. I'll just stop by some bar and hang out for a minute. I'll watch the number runner do what I did for so many years. Seeing that makes me smile. Can't explain it exactly, James, but you know what I mean."

I did. Mom was leading me back to the path where I'd begun. I needed to reconnect, remember, and write.

I could have written *Street Songs* in Buffalo, the city that inspired me, but after revisiting my old haunts I realized that I needed to distance myself from the memories. I needed to isolate in a setting where I wouldn't be disturbed. The Record Plant in Sausalito, where I'd cut the successful *Fire It Up*, seemed like the right spot. The studio prepared a bedroom where it was just me and my guitar, my bass, and a drum machine. I lived there for a week, writing nonstop. That's where I composed the core of *Street Songs*, a concept album that mirrored my life. The subjects were sex, drugs, fame, frustration, police brutality, passion, and determination. Marvin Gaye was

still my idol, and I wanted to create something along the lines of his *What's Going On*—only with more of an emphasis on sex.

"Give It to Me Baby," the first of several smashes off the album, was written first. If you read between the lines you'll see that the subtext concerns my problems with sexual performance. Some cats can screw on coke like there's no tomorrow. I can't. Because I love both fucking and coking in equal measure, it was a struggle. At a younger age, I managed to combine them. But the longer I snorted, the more it impaired my ability to ball. Many cats in the ghetto had this problem but lacked the guts to admit it.

Stevie Wonder, my other idol, came in and blew harp on "Mr. Policeman," the story of a friend gunned down in Buffalo by the cops. I gave it a reggae flavor because I had recently watched Jimmy Cliff's *The Harder They Come* for the second time. It's one of my favorite movies, filled with Jamaican grit and Jamaican grooves.

After one of my tours I'd flown to Paris, where I'd met an Ethiopian princess. I've always adored African women, and I was under this lady's spell for days. Her body was a living miracle. We didn't make love; we made a new universe in which she was queen and I was king. I wanted to bring her back to America but she knew I wouldn't be faithful. She saw me for who I was—a man incapable of fidelity. I give her credit for her intelligence and insight. But that same intelligence and insight made me want her even more. She left me in the Paris hotel, and though I was crushed, I knew I had met my match.

The whole episode came back to me that week I was writing in Sausalito. The experience became "Fire and Desire." I heard it as a duet and naturally thought of Teena, whose star continued to rise. When Teena arrived at the studio, though, she had a bad fever and couldn't sing. She went right to bed. When the doctor said she could be out for a week or more, I found a local singer who could do the job. Someone told Teena what I was about to do and, just like that, she got out of her sickbed and showed up at the studio.

"No way I'm gonna let some other bitch sing that song," she said.

"You sure you can handle it, feeling the way you do?"

"Just play the track, Rick, and give me the headphones."

Still sweating from her fever, Lady T marched into the booth and tore that shit up! I mean, she delivered a vocal performance that folks gonna be listening to as long as human beings are capable of love. I realized I had written a good song, but Teena turned it into a great song for the ages. More than a hit, it was soon put into that one category all songwriters dream of; "Fire and Desire" became a standard.

There were other songs on the record that I felt told my story—"Ghetto Life," "Below the Funk (Pass the J)," "Call Me Up," and "Make Love to Me." I looked over the tunes and felt that I was nearly finished. I had seven strong songs. Even though some of them were long-form, they could each be edited down for under-four-minutes radio play. But satisfied as I was, I knew something was missing.

It was about three in the morning. We had just put the horn parts on "Give It to Me Baby" when I was sitting in front of the console with my bass. I wasn't trying to write. I was just noodling. This bass line came out of nowhere. Four descending notes. Nothing particularly striking. It was cheesy, but it was also catchy. I couldn't stop playing it. At the same time, I started singing, "She's a very kinky girl . . ." I was about to stop—the whole thing sounded a little dumb—when one of my cats said, "Cut it, Rick."

"You crazy?" I asked.

"No man, it's cool. It's hypnotic."

I kept playing the riff and realized that it *was* hypnotic. Right then and there I had the engineer hook up a mic and started singing the story as it came to me—this story of a super freak. I never wrote down a word. Made it up on the spot. It just kinda grew out of me.

When I started arranging it, bringing in the musicians and calling out their parts, I began to see that I really did have something. I got excited. Rather than call in the usual background singers, I used the greatest singing group in the world, the Temptations, to sing behind me. I told them, "It's not as funky as my usual stuff, but maybe that'll mean white people will dance to it."

Alonzo Miller, a deejay friend, said that the lyrics were too raunchy to get airplay and helped me clean them up. Ironically, after "Super Freak" was released as the second single off *Street Songs*, Alonzo got complaints from prudes and took it out of his rotation. I raised hell until he started playing it again. When he did, his request line blew up. "Super Freak" became the crossover hit Motown had been looking for. I was suddenly a crossover artist. Suddenly I had more white fans than black fans. Suddenly I had shown that *Garden of Love*, with its poor sales, was just an aberration. Not only was I back making hits, I was making history. Motown hadn't seen sales like this since the days of Stevie's *Songs in the Key of Life*. I had reclaimed my glow—and then some.

The question became, how much bigger and brighter could my glow ever get?

At Studio 54 in New York, I had carte blanche. The new owner, Mark Fleischman, treated me like royalty. Grace Jones was my best friend. Peter Max was my best friend. Tanya Tucker was my best friend. Iman, the gorgeous Somalian supermodel, was my girlfriend. I had walked through high cotton before, but this was the highest.

The acts I was developing were also super-hot. I helped my protégée Teena Marie with her fourth studio album, *It Must Be Magic*, though it was mainly her production and her songs. "Square

Biz" was a huge hit off the record. Along with New Edition, the Gap Band, Luther Vandross, and Grandmaster Flash, Teena became one of my opening acts.

Then came Funk Fest, George Clinton's operation, a battle of the bands. I did several dates in stadiums that held sixty thousand people. I remembered how George had forgotten to help me back in the day, so when I agreed it was with a reason. Other acts were on the show—Bootsy, the Isley Brothers, Maze, Con Funk Shun—but it was George's ass that I was after.

These groups were great. After all, they were the culmination of the Golden Age of Funk, which, like the Big Band era of Count Basie and Duke Ellington, brought out the best musicianship. Everyone was throwing down. I loved these groups but was not intimidated by any of them. I wouldn't have minded following any of them. But I did have a goal—and that was to go on before Clinton. If that could be arranged, I'd wear out those fans with the most ferocious funk the world had ever heard. I'd hurt them so bad that they'd have nothing left for George. And that's exactly what happened—not once but twice. By the time Clinton's funksters wandered out onstage, the exhausted crowd was on its way up the aisles and out of the stadium. Once they heard our jams, they'd heard enough.

Revenge. How sweet it is!

And yet, for all the satisfaction that comes with payback, I felt something missing deep in the center of my soul.

"It's a soul mate," my mother was quick to say when I told her that despite all the crazy success, I was still feeling a little down. "You need someone who loves you for who you are, baby—not for your money."

Mom was right. My flings were all over before they began. I'd become Mr. Hit It and Quit It. My addictive mind was focused on good pussy as opposed to good women. I was looking at ladies the way I was looking at blow—as objects to consume. My thinking was fucked, and I knew it.

At the same time I was reassessing my messed-up approach to sex, I knew that Marvin Gaye and his wife, Jan, were splitsville. When I first met Jan in Marvin's studio, I saw her as a princess to his prince. They were soul royalty. I was in awe of their great poise, charm, and intelligence. I was a gentleman in Jan's presence but was secretly attracted to her. Who wouldn't be? She was gorgeous, hip, and an altogether wonderful woman. I wasn't about to hit on Marvin's woman. But when I learned that they were living apart, I figured it was perfectly appropriate to invite Jan to one of my concerts.

I chose the biggest Funk Fest of all—the one at the L.A. Coliseum. I invited Jan to my trailer, where she showed up with two of her friends. I was disappointed that she hadn't come alone but still happy to see her. I didn't get into the details of what was happening between her and Marvin, but I could tell she felt neglected by him. I wasn't about to neglect her. We drank a little champagne, shared a joint, and snorted a little blow. I made sure that she and her friends had the best seats in the house. After the show, we partied a little more and that was it. I gave her a hug and kissed her on the cheek.

"You're an outta-sight chick, Jan," I said, "and you deserve the best."

"Thank you, Rick. Thank you for all your thoughtfulness."

That was it. I could have asked for more, but I didn't. Since she was still married to Marvin, I had mixed feelings. Motown was a place that fostered ferocious competition. I'd seen that back in Detroit, where the producers, like Mickey Stevenson and Norman Whitfield, would fight like demons to get their songs cut by the hot artists. That didn't change when Motown moved to L.A. Berry Gordy is the most competitive motherfucker the world has ever known. He was a boxer and views the music biz as one big battle. I fit into that mode myself. One of the reasons I prospered was because I wanted to take on cats like George Clinton and prove my funk was fiercer than theirs.

I say all this to admit that I had competitive feelings about Marvin. I saw him as the old prince of Motown. I was the new prince. In a good-natured way, he used to needle me that my songs all sounded the same. And in an equally good-natured way, I'd needle him that he hadn't had a hit since "Got to Give It Up." While I was going up, Marvin was going down. His autobiographical piece about his ex-wife, Anna, *Here, My Dear*, was an artistic triumph but a commercial flop. Because it was critical of Anna, the Chairman's sister, it put him at further odds with Berry. He kept saying that he didn't care about whether his shit sold or not; he just wanted to follow his muse. His muse had him writing strange songs about the end of the world and the nuclear holocaust. When I heard his new stuff, I knew he was lost at sea. No matter how loudly an artist claims that he doesn't care about having hits, I know he's lying. Everyone wants hits, Marvin Gaye included.

As Marvin's musical mojo was dwindling and mine was expanding, he was also losing his personal mojo. He was sinking into deeper depressions and disrespecting Jan big-time. I saw an opportunity to move in. So before the start of my *Street Songs* tour, I invited Jan to meet me at a five-star hotel in Maui. She accepted, we became lovers, and it was a beautiful thing.

Because Jan is an intellectual chick with a strong spiritual bent, she brought out the best in me. We'd discuss movies and books, religion and politics. Her mind was as amazing as her body. She loved drugs as much as I did, but the drugs never stopped us from going deep into conversations about the heart and mind. I felt like this was a woman I could live with the rest of my life. The only problem, of course, was that she was still married to Marvin. Beyond that, she still loved the man. No matter how she cared for me, Marvin would always come first. If he hadn't neglected and mistreated her, she never would have come to me for consolation.

"Go back to Marvin," I told her. "Try and work it out. I know he's the love of your life. I just want you to be happy."

"Thank you, Rick," she said. "You're a good guy."

"If I thought I really had a chance with you, I wouldn't be all that good."

Saying that, I was sure that I had come to the bittersweet end of my brief romance with Jan. In fact, I was sure wrong.

THE KING IS DEAD! LONG LIVE THE KING!

The *Street Songs* tour was my biggest ever. Every twenty-thousand-seater in every city was sold out for a minimum of two nights. Even in a place like Memphis scalpers were making a fortune off our shows. Memphis was a trip in and of itself.

No one can forget that Memphis is where they got Dr. King. Turned out that Memphis was also where I'd been getting death threats. That's why when I arrived fifteen plainclothes cops immediately surrounded me. It didn't help that the newspaper was talking about how my three sold-out shows at the Mid-South Coliseum would break Elvis's record. Making matters worse were firebombings at a couple of record stores that displayed my poster in the window. Haters didn't want a pot-smoking, wise-ass nigger coming to town.

That didn't stop me from going to Graceland. On the afternoon before my last show I went there with my entourage and police escort in tow. I'm not one of those people who think Elvis is even close to the musical genius of artists like Charlie Parker, Miles Davis, Ray Charles, or Marvin Gaye, but I have to respect his accomplishment. He took R & B and made it acceptable to white people. Plus I had heard from B. B. King, who knew Elvis personally, that he was quick to acknowledge and respect the black artists who showed him the way. I was curious to see his crib, an international tourist attraction.

When we got there and I went in the house, which was much smaller than I expected, someone saw me and yelled out, "The King is dead! Long live the King!" It was a Rick James fan. I smiled and didn't think anything of it when he came over for my autograph. Soon a number of other people lined up for my signature. The Graceland officials didn't like that. They said to take it outside. Not to disappoint the fans, I took it outside and started autographing in an area behind the house. The officials didn't like that either.

"Sorry, fans," I said, "but I'm here to pay my respects to Elvis. No more autographs." When I started to go back in to see the rest of the house, the officials blocked the door. They asked me to leave. I started to protest but knew it wasn't worth it. They didn't want me there.

That night onstage I told a little bit of the story. I said, "Today I went to Elvis's house and guess what I learned?"

"*What?*" the crowd roared back at me.

"That the motherfucker wasn't home!"

Then I took a rebel flag and ripped it in half.

Everyone cheered. Next day the press criticized my ass for disrespecting the King. I never bothered telling the press how the King's people disrespected me.

Things got even crazier in Dallas. Because of a sleazeball promoter who tried to book my tour and sued me when I rejected his offer, legal beagles had been on my tail trying to serve me. My main security guy—we called him Big Motherfuckin' Moe—was super savvy at keeping them away from me. Moe had me ducking and hiding in and out of freight elevators and service doors. In Dallas the servers got to the city cops, who were working with them to bust me. Keep in mind that nearly every hour of the day I was blasted on smoke and coke.

Before I got onstage, the chief cop told me, "I know you smoke pot during your show—but not here. Do it here and we'll bust your ass."

"Fuck you," was my only reply.

"Mary Jane" was the tune where I stood before twenty-foot joints made out of papier-mâché with smoke coming out the tips. I'd always fire up. So did the rest of the crowd. It was our big bonding moment. On this night I told the fans, "The cops say if I light up they'll haul my ass off to jail."

The crowd let out a gigantic "*Boooooooooo!*"

"Y'all gonna let them do that?" I asked.

"Hell, no!" "Fuck, no!" "We'll tear this place apart!" "We'll riot all night!"

The cops got the message loud and clear. I smoked and they didn't do shit.

The next night in Dallas that same cop told me that this time he was prepared. He had brought along the SWAT team and there was no way I was getting outta there if I smoked a joint onstage.

"What do you have to say about that, Mr. James?" he asked.

"Fuck you."

During "Mary Jane" I smoked my joint. At the end of the show, all my roadies came out onstage and surrounded me. In the middle of the circle, I switched clothes with one of the mechanics. I put on these greasy overalls, put my braids inside a Rasta hat, and ran out of the place with Big Moe beside me.

We jumped in a cab and had dinner at Denny's.

Pittsburgh was memorable because it was the first time Teena Marie and I made love. Like the record says, it was wild and peaceful. Don't know whether Teena was just trying to flatter me, but she claimed I was the first man who made her come. She also claimed that she had feelings for women. My feelings for Teena were always positive—I loved her talent, I loved her openness, I loved her willingness to let me help her. If they'll admit it, most people have a complicated sexual agenda. Teena simply had the guts to talk about it. Our lovemaking brought us closer together, but we also understood that we could never be boyfriend and girlfriend. We loved each other without being in love. We were so close musically that we had to take that closeness to the limit.

Fucking changes a relationship. Doesn't matter if both people say that the fuck was just for fun. Once you've had serious sex, the balance of power shifts. That certainly happened with me and Teena. Not long after our encounter, she started demanding more money for her appearances on my tour. It pissed me off that she had recruited my sister Penny, who was extremely close to Teena, and my brother Roy to back her up. Once my docile student, Lady T suddenly turned into an independent woman making demands. Maybe that's because after we'd made love she secretly wanted to be my exclusive girlfriend. When I refused, she got angry. That's when she found the strength to take me on. Eventually I saw that she deserved my respect. The Vanilla Child was coming of age. Good for her.

Bad for me was the discovery of freebasing. That happened in Chicago. I ain't naming names and giving numbers. Doesn't matter who turned me on, because if it hadn't been this "friend" it would have been another. Base was sweeping through the black hoods of America. I'd heard reports it was the highest high of all. No way I wasn't gonna hit it and see for myself.

When I hit it that first time, sirens went off. Rockets were launched. I was sent reeling through space. I wanted to run up to the roof of the hotel and scream the good news to all of Chicago.

The good news, of course, would turn into tragic news. The tragic news would eventually lead me to where I am now—jail. But at the time, the physical exhilaration of smoking coke in pure form overpowered any semblance of sense I had ever once possessed. I wasn't thinking. I was just feeling. And like millions of fuckin' fools who came both before and after me, I fell. I submitted. I got on my hands and knees and sucked the devil's glass dick.

It's not lost on me that a great triumph, the *Street Songs* success, coincided with a great catastrophe: my introduction to base.

◆

"The way you see it now is one thing," says Brotha Guru, who's just heard my long description of what happened during that long tour. "But there was no way you could have seen it with such detachment while it was happening."

"Why not? I'm smart."

"Very smart. But no one's smart enough to take on the Me Monster when the Me Monster is fueled not only by balls-out adulation—tens of thousands of people screaming your name—but by an incredibly potent chemical as well. When you're high on base, it's nothing but ego."

"You've done it?" I ask.

"I couldn't be talking this way if I hadn't," Brotha Guru admits. "I think of myself as a pretty centered person. I like to listen, I like to help other people, I believe in service. But when I was on base it was all about me and my pleasures. There was no consideration—not the least goddamn bit—for any other living thing except me."

"You're singing my song," I say.

"And yet even after I sobered up the next day and realized how selfish I'd been, the first thing I did was reach for the phone to get more."

"You've been there."

"And it isn't just base. It can be weed, it can be booze, it sure as hell can be sex. And God knows it's control. The main thing the Me Monster is hooked on is more. Whatever it is, just give me more. And then, sadly, more is never enough."

I sigh a deep sigh.

As my story continues, it becomes clear that I wanted more, more, and more.

✦

I wanted more of a connection with a woman I could call my own. I thought that might have happened on a couple of occasions when Seville showed up without Ty. I got the idea that Seville was interested in reconciliation. We even renewed our sexual relationship, which was even better than I had remembered. In the end, though, I came to the opinion that Seville's mother was behind the maneuver. It was her way to get money out of me.

Seville hinted that she also had a son by me. I didn't know what to make of that. I asked her to show me pictures but she wouldn't. Was that the truth or just a way of getting more bread? Things got confused and nasty between us. Seville demanded a huge settlement. I told her if she didn't back off I'd sue her for custody of Ty. That frightened Seville, who took Ty and disappeared. Through private detectives, I tried to find them. But Seville changed her name and couldn't be located.

I fooled myself into thinking that I could put together some kind of family. But who I was kidding? No judge in his or her right mind would have awarded me custody of a child. And even if I were awarded custody, I didn't have the time or—I admit—the inclination to do any full-time or even part-time fathering. The Me Monster doesn't make for a great dad.

And yet the idea of a happy, united family didn't go away. Some of my siblings would travel with me—and that would help. The Stone City Band was a form of family, although personnel changes made it a family under continual change. Motown liked to describe the "family nature" of the label, but that was utter bullshit. Motown was a backbiting dog-eat-dog company that liked to pit artist against artist and producer against producer. I was always convinced that Motown was holding back major royalties. Our relationship had gone from good to bad to worse.

The one woman who kept coming to mind was Jan Gaye. And even though she was still attached to Marvin emotionally, he was doing everything to push her away while I was doing everything to draw her in.

I invited her to spend a weekend in Buffalo with me and Mom. Mom was as crazy about Jan as I was. She saw her as a daughter.

When my driver picked Jan up at the airport and brought her to the house, she was shook up. She looked frightened.

"What's wrong, baby?" I asked.

"The plane was about to take off in L.A. when someone brought me a bouquet of flowers," she said. "They were from Marvin. His note said, 'Have a good time.'"

"You told him you were coming here?"

"No. We haven't spoken in weeks. But somehow he found out. Holding those flowers in my lap, I got paranoid, Rick. I fantasized he'd planted a bomb on the plane."

Just about then, the phone rang. It was Marvin. He wanted to know why his wife was visiting me. I said it was because she and I were friends. He asked if we had been lovers. I lied and said no. Then he said he wanted to talk to Jan. They spoke for a long while. When the conversation was over, she said, "I need to get back to L.A."

"You just got here, honey."

"I know, Rick. But I don't want to get Marvin any more upset."

I didn't argue.

Before she left, though, friends called and told me to turn on WBLK, the soul radio station. Marvin was on the air saying, "I just want to say hello to my friend Rick James, who's hosting my wife, Janis, this weekend in Buffalo at his home. I want to wish them both the best—now and in the future."

He spoke in the sweetest tone you can imagine.

◆

For many months Jan and I had no contact. She tried her best to work out her marriage with Marvin. I respected that. But Marvin's world was even more chaotic than mine. Because he hadn't had a hit in years, he owed massive back taxes. He also owed Motown an album that was way overdue. He decided to flee L.A. and fly to Hawaii without Jan or their two kids. At one point, his family surreptitiously arranged a "kidnapping" of the son he had with Jan and brought him to Hawaii. That broke Jan's heart. I tried my best to comfort her during that period. It wasn't sexual then; it was just friendship. Marvin had cut off her money. She needed a job and I gave her one in my office. Mary Jane Productions was a going concern where Jan was supposed to work as a secretary and planner. Because she's a brilliant woman, I wanted her on staff. But, as painful as it is to admit, I mainly used her to pick up and deliver my drugs. Jan was willing, not only because she was desperate for income but because, like me and Marvin, she was hooked on drugs herself.

Privately, my life was not a pretty picture. Professionally, my life looked like a masterpiece in the making.

Street Songs won Dick Clark's American Music Award for Favorite Album—Soul/R & B. Dick threw an after-party. I took Mom as my date. In these settings, Mom was beautiful. She was impressed with stars and never tried to hide it. In fact, she collected autographs.

"Guess who I just saw, James?" she said to me.

"Who?"

"Prince."

"You didn't ask him for his autograph, did you?"

"I sure did."

"Why?"

"Because I like his music, son. I think he's great."

"Okay. So now you have Prince's autograph."

"Wish I did. When I asked him, he just turned around and walked away."

"You're kidding."

"No, I guess he don't like giving out autographs."

That's all I needed to hear. I chased after that little turd. I caught up with him and was about to lay him out when his manager stepped in.

"What the hell is wrong with you, Rick?" asked the manager.

I told him Prince had dissed Mom and that I was gonna kick his scrawny ass. Prince explained that he didn't know who Mom was.

"Well, now you know, motherfucker," I said.

"Prince will be happy to apologize to your mother," said the manager, "and he will be happy to apologize to you."

Prince apologized to Mom and apologized to me. I was a little disappointed 'cause I really did wanna kick his ass.

At that same party I was hanging out with Grace Jones, who'd become a close friend. There's never been a groovier chick than Grace. She's a nervy lady who says what she wants when she wants to say it. So when a reporter asked about why her videos weren't played on MTV, she said MTV was prejudiced against blacks.

"How do you feel about that, Rick?"

"I feel the same as Grace. It's racist bullshit, pure and simple. I spend a fortune on my videos and MTV won't play them because they're too black. If they did, I'd sell tens of millions more records. So I say, fuck MTV."

That statement caused all sorts of shit. I didn't care. I welcomed a war on MTV—a war I was not about to lose.

MAN IN THE MOON

Street Songs became a pop culture phenomenon. The last stop on the tour was *Saturday Night Live*, where the producer, Lorne Michaels, kicked a young comic named Eddie Murphy out of his dressing room so I could use it. Dan Aykroyd took me to dinner and afterward showed me an early cut of a new film, *Dr. Detroit.* He wanted me to do the soundtrack. I appreciated the offer but made up some excuse 'cause I just didn't think it was funny.

"How 'bout if we use 'Super Freak' for one scene?" he asked.

"No problem," I said.

I got a check for thirty thousand dollars.

I was getting checks from everywhere and everyone. I took the bread and bought Mom a bigger house in Buffalo that used to be owned by the Albrights, one of the richest and most aristocratic families in the city's history.

I flew the Concorde to Europe on a promotional whirlwind tour of Paris, Rome, Amsterdam, Milan, and London. It was in London that I scored a mess of pure Peruvian coke at an embassy party, picked up two superfine English chicks, took them back to my suite, and partied all night. I got so high I missed my all-important BBC interview. I didn't care. BBC tried to reschedule but I said I had no time. I was too busy making the London nightclub scene with these beauties on my arm. Before I left the country an English newspaper ran a list of the world's most terrible people. I was number three, under Idi Amin.

With an entourage of thirty-seven, I ran down to Jamaica to headline the World Music Fest, which included the Beach Boys, the Clash, Jimmy Buffett, and Gladys Knight. Jimmy Cliff, Sly & Robbie, and Peter Tosh came to my room with gifts of ganja. Black Uhuru came onstage and presented me with a spliff that I passed around to the band. They said the shit was so potent they started hallucinating. I looked at the full moon and saw my face. I was the man in the moon.

Back in L.A. I moved into a bungalow at the Chateau Marmont, the hippest scene in dope-crazed, decadent Hollywood. Rod Stewart became my best friend. Timothy Hutton became my best friend. Robin Williams became my best friend. Elisabeth Shue became my girlfriend. Someone showed me a magazine article where Linda Blair, who had starred in *The Exorcist* and was now a full-grown voluptuous woman, called me the sexiest man in the world. The next thing I knew we were in touch and about to meet in New York.

Linda was incredible. A free spirit. A beautiful mind. A mind-blowing body. She liked getting high and getting down as much as I did. We posed topless for a photograph that showed up everywhere. We didn't care. We were doing our own thing in our own way. It was a love affair that I hoped would last. It didn't.

At Caesars Palace in Vegas, Diana Ross introduced me as the King of Punk Funk. The *Rockpalast* show in Essen, Germany—the one I already told you about—was televised around the world and being called the biggest triumph of my career.

What more could I do?

Produce the Temptations—that's what. They were reuniting with some of the original members and calling their new album *Reunion*. The Chairman asked me to write and produce a song for them. He also wanted me to sing on it. The idea that the Temptations needed me to boost their appeal was music to my ears. What a thrill! For the first time, lead singers David Ruffin, Dennis Edwards, and Eddie Kendricks would be on the same record—plus Otis Williams, Richard Street, Glenn Leonard, and my man Melvin Franklin.

When we recorded the song "Standing on the Top" the studio was filled with celebrities. Jim Brown, the great running back, who'd become a close friend, dropped by, as well as Berry Gordy and Timothy Hutton. I gave the Tempts their harmony notes and wrote the vocal arrangement. For all I had done, I still couldn't get over the idea that I was directing the Tempts. I didn't see it at the time, but the lyrics were prophetic. I wrote, "Standing on the top there's no place you can really go but down, down, down." If you read between the lines, the story is really about the fall of a superstar. Ironically, the song was a hit, bringing the Temptations back to the spotlight and magnifying my own stardom, even as I predicted my downfall.

On a conscious level, I saw my power increasing, while my subconscious saw it decreasing. My power was enough to take on MTV's racist policy in a campaign that I consciously conducted through the press. Everywhere I went I denounced their policy. In every interview I gave, I called them out. I named names—especially one asshole executive who had it out for me. When he heard me bashing him, he made sure to play the video of my rival—Prince— and keep mine off the air. That's how "Little Red Corvette" blew up so big. It was MTV's way of shooting me the shaft. But MTV was on the wrong side of history. It wasn't just the pressure of my mouthing off to the press. It was the fact that in 1982 Michael Jackson had released *Thriller*, and there was no way they could keep those videos off the air. Columbia, Michael's label, gave MTV all kinds of shit. I credit them with helping to break down the color barrier. But I know that I did my part. I called those bastards racists every chance I had, and I don't regret that for a minute.

Because I was increasingly being seen as the Super Freak, I felt a need to be taken more seriously. Granted, my stuff didn't carry the intellectual or spiritual weight of Marvin Gaye, but I was a sincere and deep artist. I didn't want to be dismissed as superficial or fleeting. It took a while for the critics to come around, but when they did I couldn't help but feel satisfaction. When *Street Songs* was put into a special edition years after its initial release, Craig Werner, a professor of African-American studies at the University of Wisconsin, wrote, "In the summer of 1981, no one was keeping the faith with more fire than Rick James. Invoking Miles Davis and John Coltrane as well as James Brown and Sly Stone, the fiery funk sermon he preached on *Street Songs* provided a frontline report from the blues-haunted streets of black America while opening a jazz vision of a new and better world."

Reading that shit made me feel good.

✦

In the summer of 1982, Marvin Gaye finally found his way back onto the charts. "Sexual Healing" proved one of the biggest hits of his long career. By then Marvin had gone from Hawaii to England to Belgium. He'd been in exile for two years, and during that time, he and Jan finally divorced. I took that as a sign that Jan and I could finally be together—and we were, for a time. She no longer worked for me but would come to see me at the Chateau Marmont or at my home in Buffalo. There was never a time that I didn't love Jan's company. And there were many times when we discussed marriage. I'm not sure why it didn't happen. She certainly understood me as deeply as any woman I've ever known. And I certainly appreciated her intellect and beauty. Maybe it was because Jan was a little too sane for me. Maybe I needed a crazier life than the one she wanted. After what she'd gone through with Marvin, she needed less chaos, not more.

It also didn't help that one time when Jan was staying with me in Buffalo I received word that Linda Blair was coming to visit. I had my people move Jan into a room down in the basement. I didn't want Linda to know that Jan was there, and Jan was cool enough to let me pull of the charade. I know Jan wasn't happy about that—what woman would be?—and I was always grateful to her for not busting me in front of Linda.

The player played on. The chicks kept arriving and leaving. One chick was a brainy English major at the State University of New York at Buffalo. I was convinced her real major was giving head. She had a PhD in blow jobs. She also loved poetry. She kept reading "The Love Song of J. Alfred Prufrock" by T. S. Eliot, which said, "In the room the women come and go, speaking of Michelangelo." She told me that she wanted to change the poem to "In the room the women come and go, looking to snort Rick James's blow."

By then it was more than snorting. My bottom line in Buffalo had become base. Idiot that I was, I was certain freebase was setting me free even as it was imprisoning me. For a long while I was happy when I was high. I knew about certain jazz musicians who had lived long and productive lives high on drugs. I figured I was one of them. I was different from your average addict. My body could take it. My mind could absorb it. I was special, I was invincible, but I was also crying myself to sleep every night. I'd wake up in a panic over the nightmares haunting my unconscious. In those dreams I saw images of children who looked like me. I dreamed of children falling into a sea of fire, children being struck by freight trains and chased down by vicious wolves. These were my children, and every time I tried to help them, I was stopped. I was impotent to do a fuckin' thing.

When I awoke, I realized I had to do something. I sprang into action, but not even the best detectives could find Seville. I must have gone through six different agencies when something wonderful happened. A friend had a daughter who went to a ghetto school in the San Fernando Valley outside L.A. That girl said her schoolmate claimed to be Rick James's son. I immediately hired a detective to go to the school and photograph the boy. When I saw the pictures I was looking at myself. Seville had, in fact, given birth to our son. I had two children and I needed to see them. By then my brother Roy, a lawyer, was working with me. I told him to find Seville and forge some financial settlement that would let me see my kids. I wanted them to fly to Buffalo so that Mom and I could see them together. At that moment, I knew I'd need Mom by my side.

Roy did it. Seville agreed to send Ty, eleven, and the boy she had named Ricky, nine, to see me. I counted the days until their arrival. Mom and I got to the Buffalo airport a full hour before they were due in. I kept watching the clock, kept looking out on the runway for the plane to land. I worried that it might crash and with it all my hopes and dreams.

It didn't. The plane landed safely. I stood by the door as the passengers entered the terminal. At the sight of a young black girl holding hands with a little boy who seemed to be her brother, I rushed over to them and hugged them both. They looked shocked.

"Who are you?" said the voice of a large black woman who was standing behind them.

"Their father."

"The hell you are. These are my kids and their dad is back in Burbank. Get out of our way."

I had hugged the wrong kids!

I stood back with Mom and waited awhile until the right kids finally came through the door. They were both gorgeous. Their eyes were bright. They had the glow. Ty was a poised young lady. Ricky was a handsome young man. I introduced them to their grandmother, who showered them with kisses. We went home, where I had gone to great lengths to prepare a boy's bedroom filled with sports for Rick and a girl's bedroom filled with flowers and dresses for Ty. Even though I tried hard to buy their love with all sorts of presents, they were too cool to accept them. They had beautiful manners and strong values. Seville had raised them right.

It took a while before they went from calling me "Mr. James" to calling me "Daddy," but I understood. It was a shock for all of us. I saw that Ricky drew beautifully; he had real talent as an artist. Ty wrote beautifully; I knew she'd be a poet. These two precious blessings had walked back into my life and given me new hope. When they flew back to their mother I felt that Ty, Ricky, and I had developed a close bond. I wanted to make sure that bond was never broken. I wanted my children to become as much a part of my life as my music, my women, my drugs, and my career.

In that regard, I failed miserably.

PART FOUR

BREAKING DOWN

COLD BLOODED

When one of the cats in Stone City saw the cover of my new album, *Throwin' Down*, he said I looked like a freaky funky Aztec warrior. I was photographed wearing animal-skin shorts, studded leather boots, and open-toed black sandals. In my left hand I was holding a big battle shield. I was ready to take on the world. That was my attitude. "Dance Wit' Me" was a huge R & B hit off *Throwin' Down*, proving that my star status was more potent than ever.

Defiance continued to define me—even though I'm not sure what the hell I was still defiant about. Hadn't I already proven everything that needed to be proven?

Brotha Guru talks about how we've got to give our defiance up to God, but I wasn't ready to hear that kind of talk when I was standing on the top.

"Defiance doesn't need a reason or even a target," says Brotha Guru. "It just is. None of us want to be told what to do."

"Do you know Jim Brown?" I ask the good brother.

"Never met the man, but I hear he's a good cat."

"The best," I say. "Jim talks a lot like you. He's a man of reason and a man of God. He was coming around the studio when I was cutting *Throwin' Down*. He knew I was basing and he knew 'throwin' down' was my code expression for smoking cocaine. He told me flat-out that I was destroying myself and about to destroy my career. I love Jim. Ain't no one I respect more. But I was defiant—even in the presence of a soul as gentle and wise and Jim."

"That's the thing about defiance," says Brotha Guru. "It wipes out any trace of humility. And without humility, our spiritual life is fucked. A spiritual life is based on submission to something outside of ourselves."

"I understand, brotha. But you gotta understand that when I was cutting *Throwin' Down* I was also putting together other acts and helping other artists."

"That's great. And I'm sure those people remain grateful to you. But in the end, weren't they extensions of you?"

"I wasn't thinking that way at the time."

"How were you thinking at the time?"

◆

It wasn't enough for me to outsell my idols, like Marvin Gaye, Stevie Wonder, and Smokey Robinson. Wasn't enough to produce and bring the Tempts back to the top of the charts. I needed to outdo Berry Gordy. Berry had the Supremes—well, I'd have the Colored Girls, named after that line in Lou Reed's great "Walk on the Wild Side." In forming the Colored Girls, I wanted to reinvent the image of a girl group. I wanted four chicks—a Valley girl, a classy vamp, a leather queen, and a Rick James bitch.

But then I made a foolish mistake: I talked about my concept with Prince's manager, and the next thing I knew Vanity 6 was out there parading around in their lingerie. That motivated me even more. I saw it as another chance to outdo Prince.

Even though the Colored Girls required my grooming and training, they were great to begin with. Joanne "JoJo" McDuffie sang sexy lead. She was a female version of me. Kimberly "Maxi" Wuletich was a white chick who played the part of a dominatrix. Candice "Candi" Ghant was the classy vamp and Cheri Wells the Valley Girl. I personally picked out their costumes, gave them their moves, and sent them to the famous vocal coach Seth Riggs, who helped build their chops. Mom didn't like the name Colored Girls. She said to call them the Mary Jane Girls instead, a label that went well with my image. I agreed, and soon four new stars were born.

We shot their first two videos in Buffalo, where Mom helped put the finishing touches on their costumes. Both songs—"Candy Man" and "Boy"—were hits, along with "All Night Long," whose groove turned out to be one of the most-sampled I've ever done.

They opened for me on the *Throwin' Down* tour and caused a sensation. Unlike Ray Charles, who said that to be a Raelette you had to "let Ray," I didn't want to blur the boundaries. I was their mentor and father, not their lover. On tour, I had them under lockdown. Didn't want other cats messin' with them, not while they were working with me. They needed to concentrate on the show.

My franchise widened when I also wrote and produced two albums for a fine singer named Val Young, who'd sung backup for George Clinton and for me on *Street Songs*. Also got Motown to sign a blazing new tenor player, Bobby Militello, who I'd heard at his brother's club in Buffalo. To help Bobby further, I got Lenny White from Return to Forever to play on his album and called it *Rick James Presents Bobby M: Blow.*

I also wanted a doo-wop group in my stable. I knew that high tenor Bunty Hawkins, who sang background for me, could sing dynamite lead. After auditioning hundreds of cats in Buffalo I chose four to harmonize and, with Mom's help, gave them an image out of her era, the forties and fifties: slicked-down process do's, vintage wide double-breasted suits, stingy-brim hats, two-toned gator shoes. So I named them Process and the Doo Rags. I flew in Cholly Atkins, the famous choreographer to the Tempts and the Miracles, who taught them their steps. Eddie Murphy came to their opening at the Cotton Club in Buffalo and liked 'em so much he put 'em on his tour when he was selling out arenas. I showcased them in L.A. and got 'em a deal at Columbia. Their debut album, *Too Sharp*, got rave reviews.

I was sponsoring artists other than myself. I was going out of my way for new talent. I was helping my friends when they needed a hand. I was doing my best not to stay loaded. I was trying to own up to the responsibility that comes with power in showbiz.

In a surreal moment at the Grammy Awards in 1983, with Grace Jones by my side, I announced to an international audience the winner of the award for Rhythm and Blues Vocal Performance, "Sexual Healing." As Marvin came onstage to accept the award, my mind was swimming with thoughts. I hadn't seen Marvin since I'd gotten involved with Jan. I wondered if he'd take a swing at me. If so, I was ready. My fists were clenched. I also wondered if he'd make some cutting remark. But Marvin could not have been more charming. He gave a beautiful speech. Turned out that this was his first Grammy. Unbelievable as it might sound, *What's Going On, Let's Get It On, I Want You, Here, My Dear*—none of his masterpieces had ever won. Understandably, he was a happy man that night. Before he left the stage, he whispered in my ear, "She gave me the happiest years of my life."

✦

When I called my new album *Cold Blooded* I wasn't talking about my personality. I didn't see myself that way. I was warm-blooded. I was a guy who needed other people. I also needed other people to need me. No, "cold-blooded" was a description of the music. "Cold Blooded," which turned into a number-one R & B hit, was about my steamy affair with Linda Blair. It was about how Linda could freeze my blood. The title might also have referred to the fact that Linda had an abortion. She told me that it was our child but gave me no voice in her decision. I call that cold-blooded.

I wrote and recorded my album in the state-of-the-art recording studio I'd put into my home in Buffalo. I was mindful of doing something because Quincy Jones, a cat I respect, told me it was time to switch up my shit since everyone and his mother was biting it off. I was the most copied artist out there. Having my own studio gave me time to reflect and experiment. I knew I had to slim down the sound, make it more economical and striking. Having a new guitarist—Kenny Hawkins, the brother of Bunt, the Doo Rags' lead singer—was a blessing. Kenny and my new keyboardist Treadwell came up with some blistering tracks. Danny LeMelle and Tom McDermott also helped sculpt a leaner and meaner instrumental attitude.

"U Bring the Freak Out" was the follow-up hit to "Cold Blooded." The third smash was a ballad that I wrote and sang as a duet with Smokey Robinson, "Ebony Eyes." Like Marvin and Stevie, Smokey was a man I deeply admired. Wasn't easy for me to find the authority to produce his vocal. It was easy for Smokey, though, because, for all his genius accomplishments, he's a humble cat who allowed me to direct the whole operation. I'll always love him for that.

Cold Blooded contained the first rap I'd ever written. It was delivered by Grandmaster Flash's Melle Mel, Scorpio, and Rahiem and called "P.I.M.P. the S.I.M.P." Then I went from the street to the bedroom and asked my buddy Billy Dee Williams to read my romantic rap over "Tell Me (What You Want)."

I wanted the cover to be as different as the music. Enough with the thigh-high boots! I wanted something more soulful. After a dream in which I saw a pyramid, I decided to use that image behind a photograph of me. I saw the pyramid as a symbol of racial unity. I later learned that the image was the logo for twelve-step recovery. I had no idea at the time. At the time I was spending five thousand dollars a week on freebase.

The *Cold Blooded* tour was my biggest yet. The Mary Jane Girls tore it up and so did two new dancers I hired—a brotha named Bobby Sepheus and a beautiful sista called T. Bobby. When we hit L.A., we were the hottest ticket in town. The Universal Amphitheatre had been sold out months in advance. That's where I got word Prince was coming to the show.

I'd been told that Prince had this habit of going to other artists' concerts and leaving early in order to disrupt the show. To undermine his undermining plan, I gave his four front-row seats to Rod Stewart, Rod's wife Alana, Tina Sinatra, and her boyfriend. When Prince arrived with his entourage, Alana, a gutsy chick, told him to kiss her ass. The little prick had to split. I got a good chuckle out of that.

While I was laughing at Prince I could well have been laughing at myself. I could laugh at a guy who, standing on the top, was about to hit bottom. I could laugh at someone who had all the control he wanted over his professional life and no control whatsoever over his personal life. I could laugh at a cat with less self-control than anyone in the universe. And yet I wasn't laughing. I was chasing—and catching—drop-dead beautiful soap opera actresses who, in their fictitious soap operas, didn't have nearly the drama I was creating in my real life.

At the end of the tour I experienced shock and outrage when I looked out in the audience and saw little girls sticking out their tongues at me like snakes. They couldn't have been older than thirteen. They'd gyrate sexually and even pull up their tops to reveal their small budding breasts. It wasn't that they disgusted me; I disgusted myself. I was disgusted by how my music was prompting young girls to do this kind of thing. I felt deep and shameful guilt. I'd always reasoned that the message in my songs was directed at adults. I didn't think how it was corrupting some youth—girls young enough to be my own daughters. I vowed that if this was the influence I was having on these kids, I would never tour again.

That moment of moral self-recrimination, though, wasn't enough to get me to change my lifestyle. I still found myself devouring women as obsessively as I devoured blow, bouncing from one crazed celebrity party to another, living off of adulation, pride, chemical-fueled ego, flying so fuckin' high that nothing except the news of a tragedy could make me think that maybe I should quit laughing and figure out how to stop self-destructing.

The call came on April Fool's Day 1984. It was from Jan Gaye, the one woman I could have loved forever but the woman whose heart had been given to another.

"Marvin's gone," she said.

"How do you mean 'gone'?"

"Dead."

"How?"

"His daddy shot him."

"What!"

"It's the truth. He's dead. Tomorrow was his birthday. He would have been forty-five."

The pipe. I knew that Marvin had been on the pipe.

When Jan had called, I was in the middle of basing. So I put down the freebase pipe I was smoking and swore I'd never touch it again.

My pledge lasted nearly twenty-four hours.

✦

Fear is not sobriety's friend. After hearing about Marvin, fear was all over me—fear for my dear friend Jan and the welfare of her children; fear that I, addicted to the same shit that turned Marvin's brilliant mind to madness, might go mad myself; fear that I didn't have the guts to look cold-blooded reality in the face. On the day after Marvin's death, all this fear got me to go back to the thing I both feared and craved the most—the devil's dick.

I had OD'd a couple of times in L.A. but was able to keep that secret. After those episodes, I easily found a Dr. Feelgood who prescribed pain pills to get me back on my feet while keeping me loaded in a legal way. The streets of downtown Beverly Hills are lined with the fancy offices of dozens of Dr. Feelgoods. They'll give you whatever you need, especially if you let them take a picture with you to hang in their reception area. My Dr. Feelgood used to give me song lyrics, hoping we'd collaborate. His lyrics sucked but his pain pills were strong. Those were the pills that eventually led me back to the best pain pill of all—the pipe.

After Marvin's death, rather than go north to recovery, I went south to collapse. I went on a wild binge. The result was that I OD'd at home in Buffalo—something that had never happened before. They rushed me to the hospital, where I was told to stay for several weeks. The thought was that I'd get a head start on recovery if I stayed confined.

I didn't want to stay confined. I wanted to get back out on the street.

"Don't you think you've hit bottom?" Jim Brown asked me on the phone from L.A. He was concerned for my life.

The answer was no. I knew I could get farther down, and—don't ask me to explain it—I wanted to get farther down.

"Isn't there anyone who could knock some sense in your head?" asked Jim.

The answer was my mother, but I had kept her from coming to the hospital. I didn't want her to see me like this. But I'm guessing it was Jim who called her. I'm guessing it was Jim who told her that she was the only one who could convince me to stay confined.

By the time Mom arrived, I'd been in the hospital for a full two days and was going stir-crazy. I had to get out. In fact, I was already dressed in my street clothes and was on my way out the door when Mom walked in.

"Where do you think you're going, James?"

"I'm outta here, Mom."

"You just got here."

"Forty-eight hours is all I needed to get my strength back."

"You look terrible, son. You need to put on that hospital gown and get back in bed."

"Sorry, Mom. My energy is taking me somewhere else."

"I don't wanna hear none of that mumbo jumbo crap. Your energy is what got you in here in the first place. Your energy can wait. Your body's got to heal, boy, and it ain't gonna heal if you keep feeding it that dope poison."

"I don't need no more dope," I lied. "That's not why I'm leaving. I'm leaving 'cause there's nothing more these doctors can do for me."

"I talked to the head doctor and he don't agree with you. He says you need rest and after that you need some rehabilitation facility."

"He's saying that 'cause he gets a cut of the money I'll have to pay that facility. All these rehabs are rackets."

"What difference does it make to you if he does get a cut? All you should care about is getting well. I've talked to a lot of people who say that rehab is a good thing. You read a lot of stories about big stars getting off dope by going to those places."

"Mom, there's no use arguing with me. I'm not staying here."

"You're not walking out that door, James."

"Mom, don't make me push you out the way."

"If you're gonna leave, that's what you're gonna have to do, son."

I couldn't believe what I did next—I pushed my mother out of the way, pushed her so firmly that she fell to the floor. My beautiful little mother was lying on the floor. Thank God she wasn't hurt. When I went down to pick her up, she held up her hand.

"Don't touch me, James. Just get outta my sight. You're my son and I love you, but you're stubborn and willful and I just pray that one of these days you'll stop serving Satan and start serving God."

I felt awful. How could I have knocked my mother to the floor? I felt guiltier than at any time in my life. I never forgave myself for what I'd done. But those feelings didn't stop me from going out, buying an ounce of cocaine, and freebasing that shit for two straight days. When it was all smoked up and I was coked out of my mind, I prayed for my death. Death didn't come, but something else did— new ideas for songs.

STORM WARNINGS

After my habit got to the point where I was shoving my own mother out of the way so I could get to the dope man, I decided I needed to talk to an addict who'd gotten cured. I wanted someone I could relate to—a musician I respected. I thought of Ray Charles, because there's no one I respect more. I arranged the meeting through Ray's best friend, Quincy Jones, who said, "He won't give you a lot of time, but you won't need a lot of time. Brother Ray says what he needs to say quicker than anyone."

I flew to L.A. and went straight to Ray's small office building on Washington Boulevard right in the middle of funky town. They had me go back to the studio, where the lights were out and I couldn't see my way in. When Ray heard me stumbling around, he said, "Switch is on the right." He was working alone, so naturally he didn't need any light. He was seated in front of his twenty-four-track console, doing his own engineering. I was amazed to watch his fingers flying over the dials and knobs. His voice was booming over the speakers.

"Hey, Rick," he said. "Q said you wanted to ask me something."

He was friendly, but I could see that he was in a hurry. I was clearly interrupting his work. I jumped right in, telling him what a hard time I was having giving up blow.

"I don't know nothing about no blow," said Ray as he took sips out of the biggest coffee mug I'd ever seen. "Tried cocaine once and it didn't do shit for me. Heroin was my thing. And the only reason I stopped was because it was either that or go to jail."

"Wasn't it hurting your work?"

"I hate to tell people this, Rick, but I cut all my big hits when I was high. I'm not saying they wouldn't have been bigger hits if I had done them sober, but they were pretty goddamn big hits anyway. Dope kills people every day of the week. Dope ain't nothing that I'd recommend to anyone. Dope cost me a fortune. I had to spend all sorts of money on high-priced lawyers to solve my legal problems brought on by dope. But no, sir—dope never slowed down my writing, my singing, or any of my shows. Some people need to write and sing no matter how high or low they may be. I'm one of those fools. I don't say that with pride, because it would have been easier to give up dope if dope had ruined my career. But if you're a fool like me, Rick, and you can work when you're loaded, you're gonna have a hard time giving it up. I know that ain't what you came to hear from me, but I'm giving it to you straight, son. I been there."

I thanked Ray for his time and left. On my way out, I saw one of his assistants washing out Ray's mug in the little kitchen area. I was curious, so I stayed to watch her fill half the mug with coffee and the other half with gin before adding five heaping spoonfuls of sugar.

"How many of those does he drink a day?" I asked the lady.

"Oh, about one every ninety minutes," she said.

◆

I couldn't help but relate to Ray, especially when back in Buffalo I left the hospital only to get high, and then only to find myself writing again. It was crazy that my addiction wasn't killing my music, but Ray had explained why. Some of us can work fucked-up, and some of us can't. Ray had also explained how my ability to work fucked-up was no blessing. In many ways, the notion that I could do my art fucked-up only fucked me up more.

There's another factor. One of Ray's hits, "Let's Go Get Stoned," was about getting high. But hell, at least two-thirds of my hits had to do with dope. Dope was not only the content of my life, it was the content of my songs. Dope was interwoven into everything I did.

I was high when Motown called and said they needed another album from me. At that point I had three songs, hardly enough for a new record.

"Fine," said Jay Lasker, Motown's old-school president and one of Berry's many minions. "We'll put out a greatest hits and not give you a cent."

"I don't have to remind you, Jay—I get a million dollars a record."

"Not if there aren't any new songs. Your contract lets us put out a greatest hits without giving you an advance."

"Do that and I'll never record another motherfuckin' thing for Motown again."

"Then what do you want?"

"A million dollars for three new songs you can stick on a greatest hits."

"That's crazy. You think I'm going to give you three hundred thirty-three thousand dollars for each song?"

"Yes, I do."

And yes, I was right. Motown paid me the cool million and I delivered the songs.

The one that hit big on the R & B charts, "17," was the most personal. It was based on a torrid love affair I had with a seventeen-year-old model in New York. Here's the story:

"Seventeen" and another young model fell into a crazy ménage with me. It went on for months. We were kicked out of the best and worst hotels in New York City. The whole thing was a blur of bliss. In the middle of the madness, Debbie Allen, a dear friend, called and insisted I go to her show on Broadway.

"I can't," I said as I looked over at these two naked beauties on either side of me in bed.

"You can. And you will. I'm sending a limo. Come tonight."

I went but was so drained from all the fucking and sucking that I slumped over and fell asleep during the show.

Afterward, Debbie dragged me into her dressing room and slammed the door. She threw me into a seat and actually sat on top of me so I couldn't move.

"You're killing yourself," she said. "You're throwing your life away. You can't even stay awake to see a friend's show. Do you know how pathetic that is, Rick? You're looking at someone who loves you and cares about you, someone who knows you're a serious artist with serious ideas and serious talent. Yet all you do is get high and have sex. Don't you realize that sex is just as much an addiction as cocaine? Don't you see how blind you are to all the things sapping your soul?"

All I could say was, "Please get off me, Debbie."

"Only if you promise to change your ways."

"I promise."

I broke my promise later that night.

In breaking that promise, though, I came up with "17," the story of the affair with my honey model. In addition to lyrics that spoke about how she was "sexy sexy sexy" and "almost jailbait," I also wrote about her "glow." That wonderful young woman had an incandescent glow and helped me reignite the glow that had once shone brightly inside me.

Something else helped bring me back from the darkness of depression that followed my OD in Buffalo: Eddie Murphy.

✦

Eddie's a comic on and offstage. His upbeat personality always kept me on a natural high. That's the only kind of high Eddie was interested in. He didn't have any of my dope habits. Like me, Eddie loved funky music and wanted a career outside stand-up comedy and movies. He wanted to sing—and I encouraged him. He had a good voice with the ability to imitate all sorts of singers, including me. He also had a great feel for funk.

When Eddie first approached me to produce him, I was off on a base binge and never responded. So he went and sought out Prince. After that, he called me again.

"I'd love to work with you, Rick," he said.

"What happened to Prince?"

"He made me uncomfortable. I didn't like the way he sat there and looked at me. I'm not working with him."

That was music to my ears. There wasn't anything I'd rather have done than write a hit for Eddie—and stick it in Prince's ear.

We decided it was best to work in my home studio in Buffalo. Eddie flew in during the dead of winter. I had my entire fleet of six cars drive to the airport to greet him. I wanted him to feel like royalty. I personally drove him back to my crib in my Rolls. We started gossiping like old ladies, to the point that I got into a little fender bender.

"Hope that isn't an omen of things to come," said Eddie.

"Don't worry, bro," I said. "I'll be driving you all the way up to the top of the charts."

Because I respected Eddie for not drinking or drugging, I stayed clean during our working session. (Well, not entirely clean. I did smoke some weed and drink some wine.) First day we got hit by a killer blizzard that kept us inside. We both loved the fact that we were cooped up in the studio.

With snow piling up outside, we got busy in a hurry and worked nonstop for days. Eddie was a dream to produce, a real pro. The only challenge was finding his true voice. He could imitate Michael Jackson and Al Green to a T. But getting him to relax was the key. When he kicked back I finally heard the true Eddie. He had a good high tenor.

I came up with a story based on a chick Eddie knew in New York who liked to party without him. I called it "Party All the Time." The track was a motherfucker, and vocally, Eddie killed it. I put my own voice on some of the refrains 'cause I thought it'd help us get airplay.

When Eddie left Buffalo he thanked me graciously. He said he was having Stevie Wonder produce some tracks as well. Given Stevie's genius, I was sure one of his songs would be picked as the first single. When the album was completed, Columbia had a huge listening party in a fancy Malibu beach house to choose the single. Turned out "Party All the Time" was the cut that got the crowd dancing—and it was released first. Went number one all over the world. Beyond the toughness of the song itself, the release did something else for me. It got my ass on MTV.

I'd been fighting those MTV bastards all this time, and while I'd helped other acts get their videos played, they still refused to air mine. Eddie changed all that. He shot the video to "Party All the Time" at Electric Lady, Jimi Hendrix's studio in Greenwich Village, and Eddie insisted that I get lots of camera time in my producing role. At the time my hair was dyed red. Some friends said I stole the show from Eddie. I didn't. It was his singing and performance that sold the song. It was also the fact that Eddie was going to host the MTV Video Music Awards that finally got them to put one of my productions in rotation. A little later MTV aired the Mary Jane Girls' "In My House" video. I hadn't kicked down the door yet, but it was starting to open.

✦

If that door was opening, the door to my bedroom was closing. After "Party All the Time" went to the top, months passed—maybe years—before I went out in sunlight. I became a vampire—sleeping all day and hitting the base pipe at night. I had my bedroom windows covered with aluminum foil so not a single ray of sunlight could get through.

If I came out at all it was only to fly down to New York, where I found those two model chicks and fell back into the ménage à trois. That meant another week or two of drug-induced stupefaction.

God knows I can't remember everything during this period. Certain scenes, though, are perceptible through the fog. One of my chicks knew Billy Idol and brought him over to our suite at Le Parker Meridien. I dug Billy. I didn't know his music but he had a shy, easy-to-be-with vibe. He invited us down to his crib in the Village. When we got there he said he was trying to kick freebase. I told him that I had stopped trying. I was hopelessly hooked. Rather than tempt him, I got out of there. In the culture of drugs, it was one of my rare acts of kindness.

Christmas was coming and Mom called to ask when I was coming home to Buffalo. I wanted to tell her that I was too fucked-up to go anywhere but invented some lame lie about business I was doing in Manhattan. Mom was too sharp to believe me. If I was lying to my mama, I was also lying to myself.

The thought of suicide came back to mind. The more I smoked, the more I wanted to smoke myself to death. One day I couldn't take it anymore. I wanted to see if I had the balls to jump in front of a speeding bus. I wanted to put an end to it all. I was drowning in a sea of confusion. With my head spinning, I stuffed my hair under a Rasta cap and hit the streets. I walked and walked and walked. With its lavish decorations, New York City was beautiful at Christmastime, but somehow the thought of the holidays, when everyone was happy, just reinforced my loneliness. Every time a speeding bus passed by, I thought about stepping in its path. I walked down to a subway platform and got close to the edge. As the train roared into the station, I thought how easy it'd be to fall on the tracks. Except it wasn't easy at all. I was frightened, and I was angry at myself for being frightened, angry at my lack of courage to do what my dark mind was telling me had to be done. I got on the subway and rode to Greenwich Village. Walked back up the stairs to the streets. It started to snow. I stopped in a bar and had a couple of shots. That made me feel worse. I was walking through some park when miraculously I heard two cats call out my name: "Rick! Hey, man, it's us!" It was Melle Mel and Scorpio from Grandmaster Flash and the Furious Five. I loved those guys but I ignored them. Just pushed my chin into the collar of my coat and walked away. I couldn't look anyone in the eye, couldn't speak, couldn't explain, couldn't lose what felt like the heaviest fuckin' blues of my life.

The feeling got heavier. At some point I must have copped some shit, because the rest of the night became a blackout. All I remember is lying on the street with some chick looking down at me. She was a beautiful sista with coal-black skin and dark brown eyes. She was an angel. I guess she knew who I was because she kept asking how I'd fallen so low. The way she asked it, though, wasn't harsh. It was loving. She took me to her pad and made a pot of coffee. The smell of brewing coffee was stimulating. She helped me drink it and let me sleep in her bed. Nothing sexual happened. She just watched over me. In the morning she fed me breakfast and asked what else she could do. She didn't want money, she didn't want credit, she didn't even want an ongoing relationship with me. She had done this one single deed and that was enough. I kissed her on the cheek and told her that God was good. She was a manifestation of God's goodness. Inexplicably she had saved me. I still don't know why.

I took a cab back to my hotel and there, sitting in the lobby, waiting for me, was another angel: my mother. I'd never been so happy to see anyone. We embraced for a long time. That's when I lost it. I broke down and cried.

"It's okay, baby," she said as she wiped away my tears. "I'm here."

"How did you know to come?"

"Well, tomorrow's Christmas, James, and I didn't want you to be alone. When you called me and I heard how lonely you were, I knew I had to be here."

"What about the family back in Buffalo?"

"The family is fine. And they can have this one Christmas without me."

In between sobs, I could only say, "Thank you, Mom."

Mom raised my spirits so that the darkness diminished. In Mom's eyes I saw the hope of a life lived in love. Chico Ross, Diana's brother and my good buddy, invited us to Diana's place in Connecticut for Christmas dinner. Eddie Murphy also told us to stop by his place.

Christmas day was beautiful. I'd gone from hell to heaven in an instant. First Mom and I went to Eddie's, where we shot pool and listened to records. Then we drove out to Diana's spread. Diana seemed happier than I had ever seen her. She and Mom loved each other dearly. Because Diana had lost her own mother a few years earlier, I could see how much she related to this small, world-wise, loving woman from Buffalo. They chatted for hours. Diana wouldn't let Mom out of her sight. At one point, she asked me, "Can I adopt your mother?"

"She'll probably adopt you first," I told Diana.

At that same happy Christmas evening I met Catherine Oxenberg, an actress on *Dynasty,* the nighttime soap opera. I was more interested in Catherine's mother, Princess Elizabeth of Yugoslavia. Turned out Elizabeth was real-life royalty and a fascinating woman. We became fast friends. She was twelve years older than me, but you couldn't tell that by her firm body and youthful face. Naturally I was flattered that she took a liking to me. She was serious lady involved in all sorts of human rights causes. We fell into a deep discussion about religion and politics. She said I had a supple mind and wanted to get to know me better. We exchanged numbers.

After that evening Elizabeth and I met several times. I never got high in front of her but told her about my struggles with dope. She encouraged me to stop and said she'd gladly hook me up with rehab centers in Europe. She considered them far superior to the ones in America.

At one point Elizabeth was in my hotel suite and expressed interest in seeing Eddie Murphy in concert. He was appearing that night. I said I'd take her, but did she have any idea how nasty Eddie's comedy could be? I had hesitations about exposing a princess to such vulgarity.

"Let me ease your mind by asking you this, Rick," she said. "Do you know why a dog licks his own dick?"

"No."

"Because he can," said the princess.

"I guess you're ready for Eddie," I said.

We went to the concert, where we met up with her son and daughter and had a ball. Our relationship continued to blossom, and as it did, I had to step back and marvel at what had happened to me. A couple of days before Christmas and meeting the princess, I was toying with suicide. I was at the lowest point of my life. The appearance of this black angel lady who scooped me off the street, the appearance of my mother, and the appearance of Elizabeth had completely turned me around. Just like that, I got off the pipe and felt my spirits renewed. The princess made me feel worthwhile, like I had a worthy intellect. She kept telling me that I was a person who had something to give to the world. I wanted to believe her. And for a while I did. Yet—and this is the part that kills me—I eventually stopped taking her calls and cut her out of my life.

"How you getting along with that princess of yours?" Mom asked me one day when I was back home in Buffalo.

"I'm not seeing her anymore."

"Why is that, son?"

"I don't wanna hurt her. She's too good for me. The last thing she needs in her life is a loser like me."

THE FABLE

It came to me in a dream. In the dead of night a little boy went into a forest, where he got lost. A cloud-covered moon yielded no light. Absolute darkness prevailed. The little boy stumbled over tree trunks. Sharp branches scratched his face. The sound of wild animals frightened him. He didn't know where to go. There were no paths, no signs, no directions to lead him home. He began to cry out in despair. And then, just as all hope was lost, he saw a faint glimmer through the trees. At first it was a flickering light, but then the light turned steady. It was a glow. The glow seemed to call to him, and when he followed it, the glow got brighter, the glow kept moving before him, leading him through the thick forest until it showed him the path home.

After that dream, I knew that I had to call my new album *Glow*. That was the glow that had illuminated my life from the very start, the glow I had lost. But even after the inspiration came to me, even after I knew that my record would have this beautiful theme and title, even after I had actually started writing and working in the studio, I lost the glow. The base pipe snuffed it out.

I wish my story didn't have to dwell so long on dope and the impact it had on me. I wish I could cut this section short and tell you that I had quit for good. I wish I could report that once I saw the glow, I left the darkness behind. To say so, though, would be a lie. This goddamn pipe continued to kick my ass. I continued to plaster aluminum on my windows to keep out any glow. I continued to light up between the hours of midnight and five A.M. If I couldn't jump in front of the bus or fall on the subway tracks, at least I could base until there was nothing left of my rotting brain.

Then came the day in Buffalo when I heard a knock on my door. It was Mom.

"You have visitors," she said.

It was four P.M. and I just was getting up.

"I don't want any visitors," I said.

"They've come all the way from L.A."

"Who let 'em in?"

"I did."

"Why?"

"Because they're your lawyers and your accountants."

That got my attention. Why should my lawyers and accountants have flown all the way to Buffalo? I knew I'd been buying base like a fiend, but I wasn't broke. Royalties were still rolling in. What the fuck could they want?

I put on a robe and went downstairs, where they were seated in my living room. These guys were in black suits, black shoes, white shirts, and black ties. Motherfuckers looked like undertakers. Naturally I knew them—they were my legal and money men—but I wasn't all that close to them. I employed them to protect my business interests.

"To what do I owe this honor?" I asked.

They got right down to business. They were resigning if I didn't go to rehab. They could no longer represent me.

Can't tell you what an impression this made. Other friends—Jim Brown, Debbie Allen, Princess Elizabeth, Teena Marie, my sister Penny, Eddie Murphy—had all told me that I was killing myself. Hearing it from these cold-blooded professionals, though, made a difference. I had to take note, and in the end, I took action.

Went off to McLean Hospital outside Boston, a psychiatric facility that had a celebrated rehab unit. It's where Brother Ray went to kick smack. The place had beautiful grounds. The doctors were cool. Being a natural born rebel, I still wasn't happy having people tell me what to do. I was still giving everyone a hard time. But then I got a big boost. I saw my old friend Steven Tyler. He told me he'd been there for a while and dug it completely. He looked happy and healthy and gave me hope that I could get my shit together.

The twelve-step program they preached said you had to admit you were out of control—an easy thing for me to acknowledge—but I also had to surrender to a higher power. A former altar boy, I'd run away from the church a long time ago. I wasn't sure I was ready for this new twelve-step church.

"It isn't like a regular church," said Steven. "You can define God any way you want. You just have to admit that there's something greater in this world than you. For lead singers and superstars like us, that's not such an easy admission."

My first instinct was to leave after a week. Not only was I experiencing extreme physical withdrawals, I got bored with the meetings. I wanted out. I was told, though, that I couldn't leave until my twenty-eight-day stint was over. That felt like the military. Having no choice, I stuck with it. They said get a sponsor. I got a cat called Chuck, a speaker I heard at a meeting. They called Chuck a Step

Nazi, which meant he was strict as hell about making me work those twelve steps. Far as I understood, they represented a method to cleanse your soul of all the bad shit you'd ever done. I don't have to tell you that I did a whole lot of bad shit. They also gave me a chance to make amends to people I'd hurt. My amends list went on for pages. So did my list of resentments, going back to where the hell was my father and why did he choose to walk out of my life.

Aside from the group, I had individual therapy. I didn't mind that 'cause I got to talk about myself. But I wasn't impressed with the lady shrink. She had a homely face but big tits and great legs. I was sure she had the hots for me 'cause she kept asking about my sex life. When I gave her the details, she said I was describing too much. But wasn't that what she wanted? No, she said she was just trying to get me to understand how I was using sex like drugs—as a way to escape and dull my pain. Maybe, but I still thought she wanted me to dull her pain. If she had asked me, I probably would have boned her. I had fantasies about putting her on her desk and fucking her right there in the office. I even wrote a song about it. "Shrink Freak" never made it on any of my albums, but I still remember the line that said, "She talks psychology but I know she craves sexuality."

One way or the other I made it through the twenty-eight days clean and sober. I stayed in Boston for a minute because I wanted to be around my sponsor, Chuck T. He took me to a bunch of meetings, where I was able to discuss my nervousness about reentering the world. When I finally went home Mom gave me a welcome party—a sober party—where all my friends showed up with soft drinks and cake. Not even a joint was smoked. Might have been my first party where drugs weren't part of the action. Mom had the boys take the aluminum off my windows. The sun was out in force. Everyone kept saying how good I looked. The bags under my eyes were gone and I could work during the days and sleep at night—a minor miracle.

I refocused on *Glow*, a concept that made even more sense since I had relocated the glow, thanks to McLean and my sponsor, who I called every day. I went to meetings in Buffalo and found a strong support group I could trust.

I relocated my groove as a producer. That was helped by the arrival of Steve Ferrone, the black English drummer famous for the funk he put on Average White Band and the great Chaka Khan. Steve has a beautiful smile. When he's around, the chicks come running and the party's on. I give Steve mad props for coming up with pocket grooves and nasty moves few percussion men can match.

My sobriety also let me focus on more spiritual feelings. I wrote the song "Moon Child," for example, for my beloved assistant Linda Hunt, my most loyal friend.

My productions usually start with a bass line of my invention. Because I think in bass, my songs are born from the bottom up. Then I'll have the rhythm guitarist double what I've done on bass. From there I build up the production in my own unique fashion. Yet none of my classic hits—not even "In My House" for the Mary Jane Girls—gained me the reputation as a master producer that I felt I deserved.

"That's because your sex-and-drug shit overwhelms everything else about you," said my sponsor, Chuck. "You're more famous for being a freak than a musician."

Chuck was right. That's why I wanted to address that issue once and for all. *Glow* was the vehicle.

The long-form video for the title cut showed me drunk on booze. When I shot it, I was sober as a nun but had to act drunk. The story had me walking onstage, a liquor bottle in hand, and then stumbling to the floor. Defiantly I kicked the bottle out of my way—an act symbolic of my recovery—and sang the hell outta the song. Without drugs and drink, I was able to find my glow.

I was high on not being high. I had to tell everyone I met how sobriety was giving me back my sanity. When I went down to L.A. I made sure to set up a twelve-step meeting schedule before I arrived. Jan Gaye came by my suite at the Chateau Marmont. I could see she'd been using.

"I wanna tell you something, Jan," I told her. "With the exception of Mom there's no woman in the world I love more than you. I'd do anything for you. But if you keep getting fucked-up, I never want to see you again. I never want you to call me. I never want to have any more contact with you."

Jan looked at me like I was kidding.

"You mean it, don't you?" she asked.

"It's the only way I can show you love," I said.

Jan took what I said to heart. She started going to meetings and got sober. Sobriety changed her life. It sure changed mine.

I did the Johnny Carson show when Joan Rivers was hosting. Joan's a crazy bitch, but a sweet one. She encouraged me to talk about my addiction and recovery in front of the entire country.

I stayed strong for three, then four, then five months. In the sixth month of my sobriety, my friend Carrie Fisher—another crazy bitch I loved—cohosted a party with me for all our Hollywood friends. I'd met Carrie at the meetings and thought she was one groovy chick. Like Joan, she was a comic and used humor to take the sting out of life. Both those ladies cracked me up.

We held the party at Carrie's beautiful house in the hills. Harrison Ford came. So did Jack Nicholson and Timothy Leary, the "turn on, tune in, drop out" guru. The only turn-on I needed was the recognition by all these famous people that I had done what I'd set out to do—I slayed the dope dragon. I felt proud.

I'd forgotten the proverb that says pride goeth before the fall. I'd forgotten that it wasn't me who facilitated my sobriety; it was my higher power. I'd surrendered to something besides myself, yet here I was at a fancy Hollywood party showing off my sobriety to all the stars.

Showing off my sobriety! Now ain't that a bitch!

When I walked outside and smelled weed from some folks smoking in the yard, I turned right away and went back inside.

When I went to the bathroom and saw fools snorting up a pile of blow, I marched right out of there.

Drugs were out. I could resist. I could turn my back on the flakiest, most potent Peruvian shit out there. I was beyond that. I was better than that.

But when, later in the evening, I hooked up with a lady I'd been wanting for months, and when that lady invited me to her crib, and when on the coffee table was a bag of blow, and when she sat across from me on the couch and spread her legs so I could see that under her black leather miniskirt she was wearing no panties, the sight of her pussy and the proximity of the blow was too much. She went down on the blow. I went down on her. She went down on me. And I went down on the blow. Before long, we were going and blowing like two wild animals.

Good-bye, recovery. Hello, addiction.

Me being me, I didn't just go back incrementally. I dived into the pussy pool, into the dope den, into the whole fuckin' world of depravity.

A week later, Jim Brown called.

"I heard what happened," he said. "I heard you were doing good until that sobriety party."

"It's the irony of ironies, Jim," I said. "The evening started out as a celebration of me getting clean and wound up with me getting dirty."

"Don't matter, Rick. You proved you can do it. You had some

clean months under your belt. You can do it again. I want you to come over and meet someone who I think will help."

"Who's that?"

"Minister Louis Farrakhan."

I respected the minister and was honored that he wanted to meet me. I showed up at Jim's early. The minister was warm and gracious. I could feel his positive spirit. He spoke of Allah and Allah's ability to heal all wounds, physical and psychological. He talked about darkness and lightness and the moral polarities that we must somehow negotiate. He spoke about patience and forgiveness. He said I had to forgive myself for those many times I had tried and failed. He couldn't have been more supportive. When our meeting was over, he hugged me like a father. He said he loved me. I said I loved him. And then I went out and got high.

Teena Marie and my sister Penny tried to reach me with reason. I kept them away. I didn't wanna hear about no reason.

Television offers came my way, but I managed to fuck them up. *The A-Team,* with George Peppard and Mr. T, offered me a costarring role with Isaac Hayes, the Black Moses. I loved Isaac and loved the idea of us duetting on James Taylor's "Steamroller Blues." I also had speaking lines. My plan was to learn those lines, get a good night's sleep, and show up at the set at six A.M. A kinky fox upset those plans. I wound up wilding with her. She was into asphyxiation. I dug her, but in the morning I was wasted. I messed up my lines so bad that George Peppard walked off the set.

The only reason I didn't screw up my next TV appearance, on *One Life to Live,* was because it was Mom's favorite soap opera. I sobered up long enough to learn my lines and make Mom proud. After the shoot, I flew home, where I started toying with ideas for my new album.

When Jan Gaye came to Buffalo she looked gorgeous. Her eyes were clear and her mind was sharper than ever.

"What's that in your hand?" she asked.

"A drink," I said.

"Of what?"

"Gin."

"You're drinking?"

"And smoking a little—and tooting too, if you must know."

She looked at me like I was the Grinch who ate Christmas.

"So you've given up on sobriety?" Jan asked.

"Temporarily."

Since I was the guy who had inspired her to stop drugs, I knew I was breaking her heart. But I couldn't lie. I'd never lie to Jan.

"I'm sorry," I said. "My motivation is strong but my willpower is weak."

"They keep telling me that it isn't a matter of willpower. It's willingness."

"They tell me a lot of stuff—and it's true. Program platitudes are great, but right now I'm enjoying my drink."

By the time Jan left Buffalo, she had succumbed to the temptations in my house. She got loaded on blow. I felt bad, but not bad enough to stop her—mainly because we were snorting together. Much to her credit, she got back into the program when she returned to California.

"I'm not going back to that life," she told me over the phone. "I'm not letting one slip throw me."

That's just what I needed to hear. If I inspired Jan the first time to get clean, it was she who inspired me this time. I went back to McLean for another month of rehab. Can't tell you how happy I was to see Steven Tyler, who had also slipped and needed another hospital stay. Steven's the most exuberant motherfucker on earth. Minute he saw me he jumped on my back. I carried him around the ward like he was a baby. You gotta love Steven's enthusiasm and love for life. That love came at a time when I sorely needed it. Tyler's the best recovery buddy I ever had. He's the one cat who can outtalk me and actually makes those meetings fun. Half of what he says is bullshit, but his bullshit is so brilliant I don't care if it's true or not. I say God bless Steven Tyler.

And I say God bless McLean and the staff who put up with me again. Yes, I went back; but yes, I also went back with my rebellious questioning attitude that challenged everyone and everything. I went back to my sponsor, Chuck, who said, "Problem with you is that no one knows—not even you—how low your goddamn bottom really is. Just when you think you've hit bottom, the bottom gets lower."

No truer words have ever been spoken.

"Rick, I think you need to see someone with supernatural powers," said Chuck. "I think you see need to see this woman who's a certified witch."

"Chuck, do you know how many goddamn witches I've already seen in my life? Damn near every bitch I've gone with has claimed to be a witch or a clairvoyant. I've seen all those tarot cards and I Ching coins. I've been told I'd be dead at twenty-eight and here I am nearly thirty-eight. I've been told I'd move to Tibet and live in a cage. Then some weird Gypsy looked into a crystal ball and saw me leading an African country to liberation. I've been damn well told everything."

"This woman's different," said Chuck. "The Boston police use her to solve cases. Her paranormal powers of perception have been documented."

"Why even mention her, Chuck?" I asked.

"She mentioned you. She said she knew I had a friend with the initials RJ and that she needed to talk to you."

"She wants money."

"Everyone wants money. It's more than that, though. There's no way in the world she could have known that you're my sponsee. I've never mentioned your name to a soul."

"All right, let's go see what the witch has to say."

The witch was an extra-large Italian woman with shiny black hair. From head to toe, she was dressed in black. She had a big booming voice and a howl of a laugh. She was earthy. She looked right into my eyes. I liked her. Somehow I trusted her.

She started telling me her story. Her husband had been a criminal who died and left her and their two sons destitute. She cursed his dead soul. Then one day she heard a spirit voice telling her to bust up her favorite lamp. It seemed crazy, but she obeyed the voice. Inside the lamp was eighty thousand dollars. Since then she had kept listening to this spirit voice.

The spirit voice had directed her to meet me. In her hand was a velvet package meant for me.

"Do you know what's in the package?" she asked.

"Yes," I said. "Tarot cards."

"You're right."

"Where have you kept them?"

"Buried in a quiet place."

The witch passed the first test. I knew tarot cards can't be properly read if you keep them in your home. It's too confusing. They require the shelter and quietude of Mother Earth.

When she took the cards out of the package, I saw they were tied in three knots. She passed the second test. Tarot cards must be tied in a certain way. She was gaining more of my confidence.

"I know you understand tarot," she said. "I know you've studied the Egyptian Book of the Dead, the Secret Scrolls, and the pyramids. I know when you were trying to purge yourself of your demons you read deeply into mysticism from all cultures."

She was right. During both stays at McLean, I had studied the occult. I'd reached no conclusions but I loved seeing how cultures dealt with the mysteries of human life and death.

She then started telling me the story of my life. She had all the specific names and places exactly right. She knew about Mom and Mom's work as a numbers runner. She knew all about my run-ins with the law. She talked about my time in Toronto as though she had been there to witness it all. She talked about a person I had worked with who went on to great fame. She couldn't say his name but said his initials—NY. That had to be Neil Young. She also mentioned that I had been in love with a woman whose husband had died at the hands of his father and whose initials were MG. That had to be Marvin Gaye. She named my children, named many of my former girlfriends, and even named BG—Berry Gordy—as a man who would soon oppose me.

I realized that the witch could see the future, but I also realized I was not ready for that knowledge. I was afraid of that knowledge. I was afraid of the witch's perception and wanted to leave.

"Not before I give you this," she said.

She handed me a beautiful crystal that she claimed had extraordinary healing powers. I asked her how much money I needed to give her. She said whatever I thought was fair. She gave me her phone number and said I could contact her anytime. I got up, left several hundred dollars on the table, and told her I'd call her sometime soon. I never did. The witch knew too much.

BEGINNING OF THE END/END OF THE BEGINNING

I thought I'd stay sober forever. I thought I had it beat. I thought I'd gotten into a righteous rhythm of recovery. Call my sponsor every day. Go to a meeting every night. Write out my resentments. Make an amend. Drink water. Eat healthy. Stay in the studio. Write. And then write some more.

Had a concept for a new album I wanted to call *The Flag*, a serious reflection of the hypocrisy of the American empire. These were the Reagan years, when a dumb-ass Grade B actor was ruling the roost. Much as I loved Michael Jackson, when I saw him going to the White House and standing next to Ridiculous Ronnie, I nearly puked. I wrote a song called "Funk in America/Silly Little Man," referring to our president and all the power maniacs out there with their fingers on the button. Also wrote a song called "Free to Be Me" about the freedom in recovery.

I worked like a demon and got the tracks where I wanted them. The funk was thick and was I ready to put on final vocals. Then came the shock: I couldn't sing. My lungs weren't working right. I flew to see a specialist in New York City, who took X-rays and called me into an office.

"Have you ever smoked cocaine?" he asked, knowing damn well that the answer was yes.

"I have."

"A lot, I presume."

"Yes, a lot."

"Are you still smoking?"

"Cigarettes, doctor, not cocaine."

"The effects of the cocaine are still there. Smoke it again and you'll permanently lose your singing voice."

That's all I needed to hear. The good doctor scared me shitless. I threw away my cigarettes, rented a fifty-foot yacht, and sailed the Caribbean from the port of St. Maarten. I wanted clear sea air to fill my lungs. Even running into my buddy Jimmy Cliff on that trip didn't break my sobriety. The ganja smelled mighty sweet, but the clear sea air was sweeter. I wanted to breathe. I wanted to sing. I took my guitar along and wrote songs under the light of the low-hanging moon. I brought along ladies who loved me in all sorts of wonderful ways. We said yes to sucking and fucking, no to smoking and coking. The trip put me back $100,000—the gas bill alone was $30,000—but it was worth it. I needed this newfound peace of mind to contend with the news that greeted me on dry land.

Motown didn't like my song concepts. They thought it was too serious. They wanted another "Party All the Time." My point was that I'd already done that. I wanted to go forward. They wanted me to go back. This was the same shit Berry Gordy was telling Marvin when he did *What's Going On.* Berry said it was too political, and politics and music don't mix. Motown had no social conscience, just a money conscience.

At the same time, Motown was trying to steal the Mary Jane Girls from me. Some of the girls had gone behind my back and told all kinds of untrue stories on me. The press depicted me as some kind of Svengali. Meanwhile, I was the cat who put the group together, gave them their sound, and turned them into stars. Now Motown was looking to snatch them from my production camp.

I ignored all this by going into the studio and, with my Caribbean-cleansed voice, putting my vocals on *The Flag*. I cut my hair for the cover shot, which had me looking sober. No gimmicks, no half-naked chicks. Then, without telling me, Motown released "Sweet and Sexy Thing" as the first single—the most obvious party cut off the record. I loved the groove-and-grind of that song but didn't think it really represented what I was going for. I wanted "Funk in America/Silly Little Man" as the first single.

Things got ugly between me and Motown. I'd always had a good relationship with Berry. I saw him as a cordial cat. He usually had time for me to air my complaints. Since we were fighting on two fronts—the Mary Jane Girls and the promotion of my own material—I figured I deserved a hearing. But Berry went MIA. I got word that he wanted me to work through his underlings. Well, fuck his underlings. His underlings were saying that I technically owed Motown another album when I felt I had damn well honored the contract and could go wherever I wanted. The underlings warned me they would sue. Then sue they did. I sued them back. I claimed they stole millions of dollars in royalties from me—and I also sued them for trying to steal the Mary Jane Girls.

The lawsuits were on and poppin'. They'd go for four, five, maybe six years. I stopped counting. I fell into depression and back into drugs.

In this epic period of endless legal battles, there were some good moments. After assuring me that black farmers would benefit as well as whites, Willie Nelson had me perform at a Farm Aid concert, where I reunited with Neil Young, jammed with Taj Mahal, and hung out with Dennis Hopper. During the show I called President Reagan an asshole. I got criticized for that remark but didn't give a shit. President Reagan was an asshole.

Not long after, I was sitting at a booth across from Reagan at Chasen's, the famous Beverly Hills celeb hangout. Someone introduced him to me, saying, "Mr. President, meet the King of Punk Funk." Reagan just smiled. His eyes were vacant. He didn't say a word. I said, "You know my cousin, Congressman Louis Stokes." Reagan still didn't say anything. He just looked at me with this idiot smile. An idiot was running our country.

But look who's calling someone an idiot. My idiotic reasoning was that I was actually cutting down on blow by doing what I called baby basin'. That's smoking coco puffs—cocaine mixed into cigarettes. All this in spite of the doctor's warning. For the next several years I found myself sliding on a downward slope. I still got invited to high-profile parties and the occasional orgy, but the invitations weren't what they used to be. I had some stylish girlfriends and could still gig when I wanted, but my power was definitely on the decline. I wouldn't record for Motown and Motown wouldn't let me record for anyone else.

My Me Monster was reinforced by my long string of girlfriends—Catherine Bach, who played Daisy Duke on *The Dukes of Hazzard*; Ola Ray, who played Michael Jackson's girlfriend in the video for "Thriller"—the list went on and on. I liked them. They liked me. Maybe they loved me. Maybe I loved them. Who knew?

"Get out of L.A.," Mom said when she called from Buffalo. "Come home. You were doing okay in Buffalo."

I went home for a week or a month but always wound up back in Hollywood. I told myself I wanted to be close to my lawyers and stay on top of my legal issues. That was a lie. I just wanted to be close to the edge.

Geoffrey Moore, son of James Bond actor Roger Moore, hired me to produce him. He was a nice-looking kid with a decent voice. He gave me money that I badly needed. He let me live in his luxurious guesthouse with its own two-car garage. He was dating Farrah Fawcett behind Ryan O'Neal's back. I was dating Merete Van Kamp, the internationally famous model who'd starred in the movie *Princess Daisy.* I was living in the middle of a Hollywood soap opera, and I was loving it. I was loving going down to Jack Nicholson's club, Helena's, and picking up the newest tallest skinniest hippest most beautiful majestic models from Milan or Paris and taking them back to the Moore mansion, where the after-parties never stopped. From there we might go to Richard Perry's crib in the hills, where the combination of good weed and willing women was irresistible. Richard was a premier producer who'd done the Pointer Sisters, Carly Simon, and Leo Sayer. He was also a chick magnet of the highest order.

Maybe if I heard a tape of my jam sessions at the China Club during this period I'd be horrified. Maybe I wasn't singing and playing as good as I remember. At the time, though, in spite of the drugs, I felt that those jams with Chaka Khan, Nile Rodgers, Elton John, John Entwistle of the Who, Chris Squire of Yes, and the Tower of Power horns were some of the most exciting musical nights of my life. Those jams kept my creative juices going.

One night at the China Club, Herbie Hancock and I were getting tipsy on another kind of juice—tequila—when we decided to get onstage and see what we could do together. I was feeling no pain when suddenly I felt nothing but pain. Damn if I didn't fall through a hole in the stage and break three ribs. An ambulance rushed me to Cedars Sinai; the next day the party continued at the hospital on the celebrity floor, where they stocked champagne in the refrigerators. The female guests kept coming through and the morphine shots kept me high as a kite. Recuperation continued in Palm Springs, where a friend put me up in his spectacularly modern all-glass home in the middle of the desert that looked like something out of *Architectural Digest*.

✦

Her name was Tanya Hijazi. When I met her she was seventeen, around the same age as Janis Gaye when she first met Marvin. I'd written that song "17" about a model I had met, but Tanya was different. She came to the Moore guesthouse, where I was staying with another chick. The minute I met Tanya I felt serious vibes—vibes that made me put down the pipe. Usually I passed the pipe to a woman who attracted me. I wanted her high as me. But I didn't want Tanya high. I just wanted her, yet I didn't make a move. We simply sat on my bed and talked for hours. Something about the sincerity in her voice, something about the sweetness in her eyes, something about the innocence of her personality—I was straight-up smitten. In the world of jaded Hollywood, she wasn't jaded at all. She lived with her mom. She didn't curse. She didn't badmouth anyone. She was pure.

"Can you come back and visit me tomorrow?" I asked her.

"I'd love to. I love talking to you."

True to her word, she returned and we spent the entire day just talking. No getting high. No sex. Just two souls getting to know each other.

Strange, but after that second day I let her go. I didn't call her, I didn't pursue the relationship. I'm not sure why. Maybe I didn't want to corrupt her. Maybe it was something like my feeling for Princess Elizabeth, only chronologically reversed. The princess was much older than me and Tanya much younger, but in both I saw beautiful human beings deserving of something better than the dark life I was living.

I met Tanya during the period when legal warfare with Motown had me on edge. I was trapped in a position where even if I did make new music, there was no way to put it out. All the majors wanted me, but until my battles with Berry were over, no one would touch me. I needed to concentrate on resolving the disputes and getting back to work, and the last thing I needed was the distraction of a serious love affair.

And yet "love" was the word. More than a light infatuation, more than a slight curiosity, it was love that I felt for Tanya. In spite of that love, I withdrew. I went back to Buffalo, back to my mother and the security of her always-calm presence. Surprisingly, Tanya came to visit me there. I was touched but also alarmed. We still hadn't made love, I still hadn't introduced her to the pipe, and I still hadn't declared my true feelings for her. I wanted to avoid a deep relationship, yet I was overjoyed to see her.

My daughter, Ty, was in Buffalo at the time. Ty was the same age as Tanya. How would they handle that? They handled it well. They met; they got along; they had no problems relating to each other.

How would I handle that? My love interest was the exact contemporary of my daughter. On one hand that made me feel strange. It gave me pause about pursuing the relationship with Tanya. But on the other hand love is an ageless thing. When you fall, you fall.

I was falling. I still kept the pipe away from Tanya, but we did make love. She wasn't a virgin but she also wasn't experienced. I wasn't into teaching her the fine art of fucking. I used her inexperience as an excuse to stop the affair before it started. I couldn't take on someone this young; I couldn't take on a student. I sent her back to Hollywood. She left with no hard feelings. She said she loved me.

I was about to say I loved her but I stopped myself. Inside my heart, though, I spoke those words. I knew that I loved her deeply.

The next time I flew out to L.A. I saw Tanya at a club. She had changed. She no longer looked innocent. Her hair was teased; her makeup was heavy; her outfit was over-the-top provocative. She'd gone Hollywood. I hated to see that. I knew that wasn't her true nature but I still restrained myself from getting involved.

Then came the call from a friend saying that Tanya had moved to Las Vegas. The thought of her working in Vegas hurt me. But my head was in charge; my head was saying let her be.

My head was also saying that I needed money. The lawsuits had stopped my income flow. My savings had been squandered on drugs. So when Merete Van Kamp told me that her new boyfriend, some rich old Frenchman, was willing to give me fifty thousand dollars to write and produce three songs on her, I agreed. I promised her boyfriend that if she came to Buffalo to record, I would concentrate on music, not sex. I gave him my word that I wouldn't fuck her.

Merete wasn't interested in my keeping my word. She wanted me, and it didn't take long to bring out my freak. We got fucked-up on drugs and did it on my living room floor. Two animals in heat. I felt guilty. Not only was I going behind her old man's back, but it was her old man who was financing me. I called the cat in France and confessed. He said not to worry. He understood the situation. He couldn't have cared less.

When we finished the production, which wasn't half-bad, Merete flew back to Hollywood. I realized that, beyond the music and the drugs and the wild sex on the floor, I had deep feelings for her. I'd see her again, but our love never blossomed. The love that did blossom, though, was the love I felt for Tanya. I thought of her during the day and dreamed of her at night. What was she doing in Vegas? Why wasn't she calling me? Shouldn't I go out there to see her?

Time was flying by. Years had passed without a new Rick James product in the marketplace. The lawyers kept doing what lawyers do—building up their hourly charges on all sorts of bullshit. When I asked for them to explain their bills, I never understood a fuckin' word they said. But what choice did I have? I had to pursue these suits so I could be free from Motown. I couldn't give up. I also couldn't stop believing that the fates had turned against me. I started feeling like a victim. I couldn't face the fact that I and I alone had created this situation. It was easier to blame someone else. The last thing in the world I wanted to do was look in the mirror.

HAPPY BIRTHDAY

As I approached the year 1988 and my fortieth birthday, I didn't want to take stock. I didn't want to admit that I was broke. I didn't want to remember that I gave my brother Roy power of attorney after my second stint in rehab because I no longer trusted myself with money. I didn't want to believe Roy when he said all my funds were exhausted. I didn't want to accept the fact that he—and most everyone I knew—would give me no money, believing that it would go for drugs (as it surely would have). I didn't want to see myself as a man living off women. And yet I was.

To keep up with my legal bills, I sold my Rolls and Excalibur. I desperately wanted to maintain my image, but that wasn't easy. I was living at a fancy French-style hotel in Hollywood where the management was about to kick me out because of unpaid bills. What would homelessness do to my image? I had to turn to women friends.

With her income from modeling and money from her rich French boyfriend, Merete paid up my hotel bill in L.A. when the management threatened to throw me out. Eventually Merete moved me into her hillside mansion while Frenchie was back in Paris. There were maids and butlers, and although broke as a bum, I was still living like a king.

My next enabler was a wonderful woman I'll call Madam Fine. She might have been a few years older than me, but she looked younger. She was a lifesaver. At the time I was suffering from cocaine dick. That's when blow makes an erection impossible. Months had passed since my last hard-on. Madam Fine changed all that. In her beautiful presence, I was good to go. And we went for hours.

Madam Fine was also a brilliant businesswoman who'd gained financial independence by virtue of her shrewdness. She had two daughters—sixteen and twenty-one—and was even a grandmother. I called her "Ma" and she called me "Dad." We became obsessed with each other. We'd get high and fuck in dark closets. We'd get kinky crazy for days on end. Madam Fine spent so much time with me that she eventually lost her business. But that didn't stop her. She talked her way into a big-time corporate gig, making sure to take care of me all the while. I've known hustlers my entire life, but none as classy as Madam Fine.

I was on the outs with my brother Roy because I thought he was withholding my money. I was on the outs with my sister Penny because she wouldn't loan me a dime. I got so mad at Penny that I pushed her down on the ground, just as I had shoved Mom. I was fucked-up when I did it, but that's no excuse. Being high brought out a devil in me, but being high and broke brought a double devil.

Back in Buffalo, there were only three people I felt I could trust—Mom; Linda Hunt, my loyal assistant; and Mildred, my cook. These women would never leave me, no matter how down-and-out I might be. They were bottom-line protectors. It did get to the point where I couldn't pay Linda and Mildred, but they stayed anyway. Mom kept saying that soon the legal nightmares would be over. She said it was just a matter of patience.

After years the suit was resolved and I had won, at least in my mind. I'd beaten Berry Gordy. Motown was offering me a huge settlement. In a matter of minutes, I'd gone from poor to rich. First thing I did was take Mom out for a lavish Christmas dinner. It was the time of year to count my blessings.

I paid off the world—the ladies I'd borrowed from as well as my attorneys, whose bill was a cool half million. I broke out of my relationship with brother Roy. I decided family and business didn't mix. I also decided that I needed a vacation.

Flew down to Coconut Grove and checked into the Mutiny, a hangout for international drug dealers. The hotel was about to close down for good and honored me as the last guest. Even after the official closing, they let me stay. I sent Madam Fine a first-class ticket to meet me, and for three days in the swanky Presidential Suite we fucked and doped our way into nirvana.

From nirvana I went to New York to visit the label chiefs who had been courting me. I started off with Clive Davis, supposedly the smartest of the lot. When I was shopping the Mary Jane Girls back in the day, Clive had passed. He didn't hear any hits. I reminded him that he'd been wrong. He reminded me of all the hits he had scored—everyone from Janis Joplin to Barry Manilow. He also went on about how he had made Whitney Houston into a superstar. Strange, but all this time I thought it was Whitney's voice that made her a star, not some stuffy executive sitting behind a desk. The problem with Clive was that his ego was bigger than mine—and that's pretty fuckin' big. Sure, he told me how great I was, but his praise for me went on for five minutes; his recitation of his own accomplishments went on for nearly two hours. I couldn't take it anymore. I lost it when he was deep into a monologue where he claimed to have personally picked every one of Air Supply's eight top-ten hits. Fuck Air Supply. I got up and left.

Next I met Bob Krasnow at Elektra, another cool character who wanted me on his label, but it wasn't until I met Mo Ostin at Warner that I found the kind of father figure I needed. Mo was the opposite of Clive. No ego at all. He didn't need to talk about himself. He wanted to hear about me. What concerns did I have about signing with Warner? My main concern was Prince. Warner was Prince's label and I was afraid they'd give him more attention than me. Mo assured me that wouldn't be the case. They'd give me all the promotional muscle I needed—and then some. They were completely committed to reviving my career and putting me back on top. When I asked him if he was worried about my reputation as a drug taker, he said no. He told me that he saw me as the kind of artist who always put his art first.

"I made a lot of hit records for Motown while I was on drugs," I said.

"Give me half the number of hit records you gave Motown and I'll be thrilled."

That's all I needed to hear. Mo was my man. I walked out of that meeting with a guarantee that Warner would pay $850,000 an album. For all the shit I'd been through, I could still demand big-time bread. Besides that, they were reviving their Reprise subsidary, the label that put out Jimi Hendrix's albums. I was honored to have my name associated with Jimi.

On my own, I had stopped basing. I was still smoking a little weed and snorting a little blow, but nothing compared to the past. I wanted my energy focused on making hits for Mo, who assigned Benny Medina as my A & R man. I'd known Benny when he was at Motown and had no problems with the brotha. Later, I'd have nothing but problems with the brotha.

◆

Lisa Keeter was a sweet girlfriend of mine from back in the day in New York City. She was a fine white chick from down south. She described her mom as a serious Christian and her dad as a redneck. For a long while I was certain that she was the woman of my dreams and even proposed to her. She said that her father, seeing she was about to marry a black, would kill me first. I said I'd find a way to charm him; I told Lisa that he'd wind up hugging me and offering me a cup of coffee. "Not in this lifetime!" said Lisa.

Later in my lifetime, after I'd worked with Eddie Murphy, gone through my dark and dismal lawsuit, and fought my way back, I reconnected with Lisa. In spite of my pledge to stay off the pipe, I had a couple of slips. I was already late in completing my first Warner record and feared that my dope addiction was, once again, about to take me down.

Because Lisa was always a friend, I called her to voice my fears.

"You need to talk to Mom," she said.

"I called to talk to you, Lisa."

"I'm happy to talk to you all night, Rick, but Mom can help you. She really can."

"Put her on the phone."

Lisa was right. Liz, Lisa's mom, had the power. She had the power of Christ. She spoke with such love and conviction that I felt my hard heart softening. She quoted scripture that said every bad thing I had done—every terrible sin, every evil wrong—could be washed away by the blood of the Lord. I could be forgiven. I could have all the guilt that weighed on me like concrete blocks lifted by the miraculous grace of God. Why was I fighting God?

I had no answer, so I kept listening to Liz. She explained that God wasn't interested in punishing me. God was interested in saving me. This was so different from the God I had learned about as a little boy in Catholic school. That God frightened me. Liz said that the real God loved me.

"This is the good news of the gospel," said Liz. "The good news of Christ. The bad news is all over. It's over if you accept Christ into your heart."

This was only the first of many conversations I had with Liz. The others were even better. I started praying, I started calling out the name of Jesus.

Miracle of miracles, my burden was lifted. I felt renewed, felt light, felt that I had, in fact, been forgiven. I read the Bible from start to finish. I studied the Word. I bought concordances that explained especially difficult passages. I read about the life of Christ. I came to see that he was the ultimate guru, a teacher who was God incarnate, a teacher whose message was love for all. Marvin Gaye had often spoken of Jesus and so had Stevie Wonder. But I'd been too high and haughty to really listen. Now I was ready for the transformation I had long sought.

Hardly a day passed that I didn't speak to both Liz and Lisa—Liz for spiritual direction, Lisa for a romantic reconnection. I invited Lisa to visit me in Buffalo, and she did. I told her that the desire to get high was no longer there. I also told her I thought it more appropriate if we slept in separate rooms. She understood. I also told her that I wanted to go to North Carolina to speak with her mom in person. She reminded me that her dad was a bigot, but I reminded her that I already knew that and was convinced he'd embrace me.

Lisa and I flew to North Carolina, where—praise God!—my prediction came true. Her dad hugged me and even offered me a cup of coffee! He had seen how his wife had brought me to Christ. His prejudice had melted in the same way as my crack addiction. God's love was overwhelming everything.

Liz was an even more powerful instrument of God in person. She took me outside, where, seated on their patio, we prayed. We thanked God for my deliverance and healing. She suggested I go to church with them and I gladly accepted. It was an integrated congregation, something I'd never seen before, where the Holy Ghost was strongly present. Folks were waving and shouting, crying and stomping. It was a beautiful thing. Most beautiful of all was speaking in tongues. Many people in that church had the gift. I wanted the gift. Congregants laid their hands on me and prayed that I'd be given the gift. I shut my eyes tight and felt something electric passing through me. I felt fantastic, but I still could not speak in tongues. Because speaking in tongues is proof that God is truly inside you, I couldn't wait for that experience.

That night in my hotel room I kept praying for the gift. Must have prayed for hours. Discouraged, I finally went to bed, only to be awoken by some joker in the next room rambling so loud in a strange foreign language that he'd startled me awake. I was about to call security to bust him but I realized that the joker had been me. I'd been given the gift. Praise the holy name of Jesus!

I praised God, I proposed to Lisa, Lisa accepted, and suddenly I was the happiest man on earth.

I flew back to Buffalo to complete work on my album. I took Lisa and her parents with me for inspiration. The tracks flowed. The melodies poured out of me like fresh water. The lyrics seemed to be written by God Himself. The lyrics were all about the glorification of God. Lisa, Liz, and Liz's husband all wept when they heard the songs. I had no doubt that this was my best work. God had come into my life and now I would bring God into the life of others. Spread the Word. Spread the blessings. Spread love.

Benny Medina, representing Warner, came to Buffalo to hear what I'd done. At that time Benny was especially powerful. The Will

Smith sitcom *The Fresh Prince of Bel Air* was based on his life. Benny was one of the show's producers. He was also Mo Ostin's golden boy. He sat in my studio and listened to every song. When the music had played, he said one word, "cool," before getting up to leave.

"That's all you have to say?" I asked.

"Let me think about it and get back to you."

Two weeks passed before he called from L.A.

"Warner doesn't want that album," Benny said. "That album is not Rick James."

"What are you talking about, man? That album *is* Rick James, the Rick James who's on fire for the Lord."

"That's not the Rick James we signed and promised eight hundred fifty thousand an album."

"This is the album God wants me to make."

"God isn't paying you. We are. And we don't intend to give you a cent if you don't give us some music we can sell. We didn't sign a gospel artist. We signed a secular artist—one of the sexiest secular artists who's ever sung. If you want to collect your advance, you're gonna have to deliver secular music. Short of that, it's back to the legal wars."

The legal wars were the last thing in the world I wanted. Those wars had nearly done me in. Besides that, I had nearly spent all the Motown settlement money and was on the verge of going broke again. I was counting on that $850,000 to sustain my lifestyle. Now Benny fuckin' Medina was telling me I'd have to abandon my spiritual music for something sexy and street.

I didn't know what to do. In the Bible, Christ told one rich guy to give up all his worldly possessions; he also told his disciples that it's easier for a camel to pass through the eye of a needle than for a rich man to get to heaven. Maybe I was meant to disown this world of dope and flesh, money and fame. Maybe this was the final crossroads. Stick up for God and stick it to the record execs. The record execs had no idea what my soul required. They merely wanted profits. But I had read Mark 8:36, which says, "For what shall it profit a man, if he shall gain the whole world, and lose his own soul." I didn't want to lose my soul. I wanted to do the music I wanted to do.

✦

And yet I caved. I submitted to man, not to God. I wanted the money more than integrity. As much as I loathed Benny Medina, I submitted to his demands. In essence I said, "Give me the check and I'll give you the music you want." Plain and simple, I sold out. And within a month of changing up those lyrics and rewriting those tracks, I broke up with Lisa, cut off communication with Liz, and was back sucking the glass dick.

WONDERFUL/HORRIBLE

You blame Benny Medina?" asks Brotha Guru when I tell him the story of how I turned from God.

"I blame the system," I say.

"The system that made you rich? The same system you embraced since you first tried to get a record deal?"

"I wanted to use that system to do God's work."

"Aren't there dozens of Christian labels you could have approached? Isn't gospel music a big business as well—an entire system of its own?"

"I'm sure it is, but I didn't know it."

"And chose not to learn it."

"I had a deal with Warner."

"And wanted that Warner money."

"I already told you that I did."

"So it's not the system that did you in. You used the system's insistence that you honor your contract as an excuse to go out and get loaded again."

"Damn right."

"It was either one thing or the other. Heaven or hell."

"I could never get in heaven, not with what I'd done. So I chose hell."

"Willingly," says Brother Guru.

"Free will is a motherfucker," I say. "It's a setup for the devil to grab your ass and keep you in his grip."

"I don't see it that way, Rick."

Brotha Guru always has a different way of seeing things. He likes to put a different spin on the ball.

"What does it look like to you?" I ask.

"You wanted to see how far down you could go. For a hot minute you felt the joy of what it was like serving the higher power. But then when you saw an out, you took it. You saw a chance to serve the lower power. In a weird way, I think you felt more comfortable in the devil's playground. The devil had you convinced that's where you really belong. You believed his lie that said you didn't really deserve to be anywhere else."

I have to accept Brotha Guru's words because they closely correspond to exactly what I was feeling at the time. I did want to test the limits of evil. In the battle between the spirit and the flesh, the flesh clearly won. Wasn't even a close contest. To think otherwise would be bullshit. I was through bullshitting myself. If I was meant to be Satan's servant, then I'd go ahead and worship the motherfucker. Besides, Satan was offering what I wanted most: crack and pussy.

Under the influence, I went back and rewrote the songs and called the record *Wonderful*. The circumstances under which I cut those tracks, though, were horrible. I was back to my old tricks, and the songs themselves—"Sexual Luv Affair," "So Tight," "In the Girls' Room," "Love's Fire"—were soaked in smoke and sex. The one hit off the record, "Loosey's Rap," is about a "freaky thang who's exotic, erotic, and X-rated."

I did everything that Warner wanted; I gave the label the tried-and-true Rick James. I wanted their bread; I wanted the biggest album of my career. For the album cover, I had my designer custom-sew a flowery suit and cape with matching wide-brimmed hat. With a wink to Prince, the basic color of the cover was purple. Around my neck I wore two symbols—a diamond-crusted cross and a diamond-crusted twelve-step triangle surrounded by a circle with "Rick" written at the bottom.

The album reached gold but never made it to platinum. I was disappointed. Some writers said that certain tracks, like "Loosey's Rap," were reminiscent of Prince. That hurt me to the quick since I was still convinced that Prince got his shit off me—not vice versa.

I did a second Warner album they never bothered to release. The label didn't think it measured up. That kind of criticism threw me into a deep funk. I was told that both my fan base and my creative powers were dwindling. Cats like Richard Perry tried to lift my spirits. He did a compilation called *Rock, Rhythm and Blues* comprised of jams from back in day reinterpreted by artists like Chaka and Mike McDonald. Perry had me sing "This Magic Moment" and "Dance with Me," old Drifters hits. I loved doing them and, for a moment, thought maybe I could get back my glow back.

When MC Hammer came out with "U Can't Touch This," I had to sue him to get writer's credit. He didn't merely sample me; he used the hook and heart of my song. I won the suit and wound up making a lot of money, but that took a lot of time. "U Can't Touch This" was one of the biggest hits of all time and, ironically, won me my only Grammy for best R & B song, an award I shared with MC and Alonzo Miller. I liked the recognition, but that didn't keep my spirits from sinking.

Seeing how far I was falling, friends rallied around me. Jan Gaye, who was successful in sobriety, valiantly tried to get me back into the twelve steps. Jim Brown practically kidnapped me. He had the Muslims talking to me; he had the reformed Crips and Bloods talking to me. Lisa and Liz kept calling me and speaking of grace. I heard all these people. I thanked them all. But I stayed loaded anyway.

Then came word that Mom was dealing with terminal cancer. I didn't want to hear that; I didn't want to believe that; I tried my best to hide from that fact. I flew Mom out to L.A. but wouldn't let her in my bedroom, where the windows were covered with aluminum and the crack pipes were on full display. Sometimes we'd talk in the kitchen and sometimes in the living room, but to be honest, I avoided her. Even though I had sent for her, the reality of seeing her sick was too much for me.

One night she came to my bedroom and knocked on the door.

"I know what you're doing in there, James," she said. "You ain't hiding nothing from me."

I knew she knew, but I still didn't want her in.

"I know you, son. I know you're trying to kill yourself so you can die before me."

Those words penetrated my heart like an arrow. She was right. I was trying to OD so I wouldn't have to face her death.

"Can we talk about it, James?" she asked.

I cracked open the door.

"I can't, Mom, I can't talk, I can't look at you, I can't look at myself. All I can say is that I love you."

"I love you too, son, but I'm not doing you any good in L.A. I'm going home."

I didn't try to stop her. That's how we said good-bye—with the door barely cracked open. No kisses, no hugs.

With Mom gone, there was nothing to keep me from descending

into the lowest level of hell. That meant orgies. That meant sado-masochism. That even meant bestiality. I was the Roman emperor Caligula. I was the Marquis de Sade.

Beyond the crack, I was ingesting seven or eight Halcion a day. I was losing my memory and walking around in a hypnotic state. I was in that state when Tanya—the woman I loved so deeply—came to rescue me. She said our love would save us. Our love would set us free. I wanted to believe her, but I also wanted her to share my pipe. If I couldn't raise myself out of this circle of hell where I was dwelling, I wanted her to join me there.

And she did. She succumbed to the madness that surrounded me. The madness was nothing short of murderous. The details are foggy, but one woman brought another woman to our crack den. She looked like a hooker and I wanted her. Within fifteen minutes of meeting, we were fucking on the floor. She not only loved fucking, she loved crack, she loved having her pussy eaten and loved eating pussy herself. She had come to the right place.

She stayed for many weeks. She was part of the sex circus that had become my life. When she left she went back to her pimp, who was pissed that she hadn't brought him any of my money. He beat her and burned her with a pipe. She came back to us looking half-dead. Out of the kindness of her heart, Tanya drove her to the emergency room in my Jaguar.

That night I had a funny feeling that we were in trouble. For the first time in months, I decided to clean up my place—vacuum the carpets, dump out the drugs and all the drug paraphernalia. That same night the cops—some thirty of them—broke down our door and put shotguns to our heads. Tanya was hysterical. I was cool. I'd seen it coming. The officials had written down the license of my Jag when Tanya brought the chick to the ER. They claimed that it was me and Tanya who had beaten her. We were charged with assault.

My bail was a million; Tanya's was set at seven hundred fifty thousand.

We spent a week in filthy county jail doing a hard detox. On the eighth day I was able to post bail for both of us. That's the day Penny called to say that Mom was dying. The court let me fly to Buffalo.

When Tanya and I arrived, the whole family was gathered around Mom's bed. Even my brother William, still serving a jail sentence, was there. He stood in shackles, a guard on either side of him.

I asked if everyone would leave so I could be alone with my mother. They granted me that courtesy. Even though Mom could no longer speak, her eyes said that she recognized me. Her eyes began to tear before she drifted in and out of consciousness. I felt that the evil of my life had somehow brought all this on. Because I had turned my back on God, God was punishing me by taking my precious mother. I began sobbing like a baby. Tanya came in to comfort me. She whispered that it was time for me to leave. I reached down, took Mom's rosary, and hung it around my neck.

A few minutes later, as I sat in the waiting room, word came that Mom was gone. I went back to see her, kiss her forehead, and speak one more time the words "I love you." Her face had a peaceful expression, and I knew she'd gone to a better place.

The funeral was huge. The press came looking for me. Paparazzi were everywhere. I was too broken up to speak. Cousin Louis Stokes delivered the eulogy. I was lost in a fog of grief. Mom was gone—the person I loved most in the world. The person who'd seen me come up from nothing and go back to nothing. How I hated that on her last trip to California I was too cracked out to leave my bedroom! How I hated that I had disappointed her! All that faith she had in me—and what I did do but squander my talent! I knew she was a forgiving soul, but the shit I'd done went way beyond forgiveness. "So," said the demon inside me, "you might as well do some more."

THE BLOOD ROOM

Before the room with the blood splattered on the walls, before the busted mirrors and shattered furniture, the vomit stains on the clothes that had been ripped in a moment of madness, the crack pipe burns on the couch, the half-eaten food rotting on the floor—before all this, the aftermath of a seven-day binge—there was our last-gasp rehab.

Our lawyers had said the obvious—we needed to be clean for our court date. We went to different rehabs—Tanya's was in the Valley, mine was at the beach—though I flipped out and had to be restrained. I couldn't stand to be away from Tanya and demanded she and I go through rehab together. The lawyers thought that might impress the judge. I got my way and we were both sent to a facility in Marina del Rey. On our first night a friend came to visit. He replaced the batteries in his beeper with rocks and got us loaded. Tanya got too high and flipped out. She was put in the psych ward for thirty days. From there the two of us went to a clean-living house, where we managed to stay straight.

Before our trial came up, I took Tanya and her mom on vacation to Maui. On our way to meet her mom at LAX, Tanya and I decided to stop at the corner of Argyle and Yucca, a hot Hollywood spot for dope deals. We wanted to buy some rocks and get blasted before the plane took off. We stopped at the corner when the boys jumped out and provided curb service. I bought eight rocks for about eighty bucks. Just as we pulled away from the curb, a couple of guys jumped out of their car and headed our way, their guns pointed at our heads. I guessed that they were plainclothes cops. Tanya began crying hysterically. She didn't want to go back to jail, and neither did I. So before the guy reached our car I turned my head and swallowed all eight rocks.

They took the car apart and didn't find anything.

"I know you bought something," one of the cops said. "I saw the transaction."

"I was just comparison-shopping," I said. "Just checking on prices. I didn't buy a thing."

"The hell you didn't."

And with that, the cops took the car apart again. When nothing showed up, they had to let us go.

Hawaii was cool and we were finally able to relax. No drugs. This marked a new period of sobriety. We learned that Tanya was pregnant, another motivation to stay clean. The birth of our son, Taz, was one of the great events of both our lives. Taz was my third child. While I had been too crazed and self-absorbed to stay really involved with my first two kids, I was determined to break that pattern with my third. I wanted to be there for him. He was, after all, the manifestation of the great love Tanya and I shared. We had to do better for him. We had no choice.

Or did we?

✦

Some months after Taz's birth, Tanya and I broke up. We decided that the love between us might be too powerful. The love was so strong it was toxic. When we were together, our combined spirits yearned for not only excessive physical passion but the insane passion of the pipe. We had to stay apart. We couldn't stay apart. We'd break up to make up and wound up in hotel room after hotel room, swearing we'd never see each other again, swearing we'd never leave each other again, swearing that we'd find a way out of the heavenly hell that was the domain of rock cocaine.

This pattern continued for months. Tanya became pregnant again, thus strengthening our bond. We wanted to celebrate and figured the best way was to rent a suite at the St. James, an art deco hotel on Sunset that symbolized the refined taste of old Hollywood. We would be refined; we would be restrained. For a few short hours we simply enjoyed the luxurious surroundings. Then the crack man called. Did we want a delivery?

No.

Yes.

No.

Well, why not?

The crack man arrived with a large supply. Thus began the weeklong deluge. We became happy, sad, sane, crazy, crazier, and craziest. A man came to see us. Probably a dealer. I can't remember. He sat across the room from me as I sucked up the crack. I started seeing him as Satan. I saw terrible evil behind his eyes. I sucked up more crack and suddenly he looked like God's only begotten son. His aura was all sweetness and light. He had a halo around his head. I pictured him playing a harp. I asked him to pray for me. When my request confused him, I suddenly saw the evil again. The halo was gone. He was there to rob and kill me. I kicked his ass out. That happened with not just him but many others who came by to see us as we slowly but surely tore apart our luxurious suite at the St. James hotel.

The visitor who helped bring me to my absolute rock bottom was a woman I'll call M. This was the bottom I had been reaching for, a bottom so low, so demoralizing, so absolutely destructive that not even I, with my conniving sense of survival, could dig my way out of it. This was the bloody tragic bottom that sponsors and counselors had been predicting for years. This was what I had been looking for, living for, dying for—the single act that would let me and the world know that I had come to the end of my rope, certain proof that I was beyond any and all redemption.

I saw M as someone with business sense. I saw her as someone who could facilitate my fucked-up half-baked notion of starting a record label. She entered our suite as an angel surrounded by light. After an hour or so of her disagreeing with me about my business plans, I saw her as a devil of darkness. Tanya began arguing with her as well. Their argument became vicious, then violent. She kicked pregnant Tanya in the stomach. M swung at me. I punched her face and proceeded to beat the shit out of her.

The beating I gave her was brutal. I have no excuses. I was bigger and stronger and I unmercifully unloaded on her. When I came to my senses, I helped her off the floor. Blood was everywhere. Her eyes were blackened. Her skin was bruised. She looked like she'd been run over by a truck.

"Sorry," was all I could say. "I got some more rock if you want some."

I offered her the peace pipe. She grabbed it and sucked it up like it was her mama's tit. And for the next two days, she, Tanya, and I smoked our brains out. Thanks to my ample supply of crack, we rebonded. It was as though the violence never happened.

When we finally left our suite at the St. James and went to

Agoura, where Tanya's parents were living, we crashed. I felt like I could sleep for a hundred years. Can't say how much time passed before Tanya woke me and said, "M's on the phone."

"What does that bitch want?" I asked.

"You talk to her," said Tanya.

"I want what's coming to me," M said when I got on the phone.

"I'll give you what's coming to you, bitch," I said.

"I could have died up in there. I can bring assault charges—and don't think I won't."

"No one asked you up to our suite. No one told you to smoke our shit. No one told you to attack my old lady. Bring up whatever charges you want."

Tanya, far wiser than me, whispered, "Find out what she wants, Rick. She could mean trouble."

"Okay," I said to M. "What do you want?"

"Two thousand in cash and a shopping spree in Beverly Hills."

I laughed. I thought she was gonna say two hundred thousand. She was thinking more in terms of five thousand. This was a nickel-dime shakedown, something I didn't need to worry about.

"I'm going to bed, bitch," I told M, "and when I wake up I ain't even gonna remember talking to you."

"Don't blow me off."

"I'm not blowing you off, I'm just going back to sleep."

Tanya and I probably slept thirty hours straight. When we woke up, we headed back to L.A. to score more dope. We went to a dealer in Inglewood. We were seated in front of his big-screen TV, blasted on blow and booze, when I felt Tanya stiffen up next to me. She had been listening to the TV while I'd been nodding out.

"Rick!" she cried. "They're talking about us!"

The reporter was saying that Rick James, "already facing charges of drug possession, kidnapping, and torture"—referring to our pending case—"has new legal problems. He and his twenty-one-year-old girlfriend, Tanya Hijazi, are being sought in another incident at a local hotel where James and Ms. Hijazi allegedly assaulted a thirty-two-year-old West Hollywood woman."

Inside my head, I went crazy. I wanted to go find M and murder her. What kind of bitch would file assault charges after smoking my crack and hanging out with me and Tanya for days after the assault? Later I learned that M's roommate was a lawyer looking to score. With this shit all over the TV screen—with mug shots of me and talk of the cops chasing me down—it was hard not to panic.

I called a few friends I could trust. They all confirmed my gut instinct. We had to turn ourselves in. If there was a dragnet, we'd never make it out of town. And even if we did, how long could we duck and hide? I was too well-known. Eventually someone would drop a dime on my ass.

Problem, though, was that it was Friday night. If we gave ourselves up we'd have to spend the weekend in the can. There'd be no hope of bail till Monday. Neither of us wanted to spend forty-eight hours in jail separated from each other—and separated from the pipe. So we copped as much of the dealer's dope as possible and planned on one more lost weekend.

We put on disguises, and rather than take a chance on driving, we walked the streets of Inglewood, a crazy crack couple in search of some anonymous hot-sheet motel. We found one just off the freeway. Forty bucks a night. Moth-eaten bedspreads and pee-stained rugs. Seedy as seedy gets. We didn't care. We had our stash and forty-eight hours to stay plastered.

The high was hell. We kept watching the broken-down TV for news flashes. Soon as the picture came on, it'd fade out. Same for the sound. We heard bits of our story and saw flashes of our faces. But we didn't catch it all. Paranoia attacked us like the flu. We were sweating and shaking. Around three A.M. we thought we heard sirens. Was it from the TV or real life? We saw flashing lights. I peeped through the curtains and saw that a SWAT team was surrounding the motel. The manager must have turned us in. What the fuck to do? We climbed out the bathroom window and dropped down into the shrubbery. We stayed there, expecting the SWAT to start screaming at us through a bullhorn. But those screams never came. The SWAT team went away. But maybe they hadn't been there to begin with. Maybe my fucked-up mind was seeing things.

When dawn broke, we were more trashed than at any time in our lives. All we had were a few Valiums. We swallowed them and waited for the calming effects. When the calm came we used it to walk to the nearest cop station to turn ourselves in. We slept in our jail cells for three straight days.

On the fourth day I posted bond. We moved in with Tanya's mother, our staunchest supporter, where we stayed while the long legal drama unfolded.

Everything was gone—my reputation, my money, my dignity. I had lost my self-respect long ago. Now it was nothing but self-disgust. I had my woman Tanya but knew that I was the one who'd dragged her down into the pits of hell.

What was there worth fighting for?

What was there worth living for?

I looked at the big picture:

This adventure began in 1948 in Buffalo, New York, when a boychild was born to a wonderful woman who worked hard so that he might have a life easier than hers. The boychild became a manchild who managed to turn that life from triumph to tragedy. In 1993, in the forty-fifth year of that life, the manchild was down to two choices—suicide and jail.

JAIL

ell me how you managed to get such little time for such big convictions," Brotha Guru says to me as we sit in a corner of the yard of Folsom prison. The Northern California sky is overcast, but the chill in the air feels good. It feels good to breathe fresh air.

"First of all, the bastards tried to get Tanya to testify against me, and she wouldn't."

"She proved loyal."

"She proved strong. When that bitch kicked Tanya in the stomach, we lost our baby, but that motivated Tanya even more to be a good mother to Taz. So she took a deal that's gonna get her out in two years."

"What about your deal?" asks Brotha Guru. "How did it come down?"

"The original court, in Malibu, was liberal as a motherfucker. But at the last minute I was switched to San Fernando, which had a ninety-eight percent conviction rate. I was nailed on two charges—

assault and kidnapping. They wanted to get me on torture but that was dropped. Torture could have gotten me life. Then the negotiations started. I was offered eight years, but something told me to turn that down. I had this gut feeling I could do better. I did do better, thanks to a cat I met through Jim Brown—Dwayne Moody. Dwayne had had similar legal problems to mine and hooked me up with Tom Owens, a private detective, who gathered evidence that the chicks who had testified against me had been compensated in one form or another. It was Tom's badass detective work that got my sentence reduced to five years. With good behavior, I was told I'd be out in two."

"And here you are, almost at the end of your prison journey."

"Did I tell you about the beginning of the journey?" I ask Brotha Guru.

"You said you started out in L.A. County."

✦

Prison wasn't anything new for me. I'd been in before and I knew how to deal with the shit. Because I'm a celebrity, I knew I'd have certain protections and privileges—and I did. I also knew I needed to get clean, and prison was the only way. Prison would only make me stronger. I had no doubt I'd get through twenty-four months without breaking down.

My breakdown happened on January 17, 1994, at four thirty in the morning. The walls of the prison began to shake violently. The floor began to sway. I was thrown out of my bunk. Prisoners—hardened criminals—began screaming like frightened babies. An earthquake was rocking the massive building from side to side. The corrections officers ran outside, leaving us alone. I was certain the ceiling would cave in on my head. I was certain I'd be trapped in this fuckin' cell and die a slow and agonizing death. I began sobbing and praying. I completely lost it. And even when the shaking stopped,

I was still covered in fear. The aftershocks only reinforced the fear. It's one thing to be in an earthquake; it's another to be in a tiny jail cell, locked up and unable to run, when the quake hits. It took me weeks to lose this horrible feeling of impending doom. I was a nervous wreck.

What saved me was a transfer from county to the California Rehabilitation Center, a minimum-security prison they call Camp Snoopy. I lived in a dorm, got to play sports all day, and attended decent therapy sessions, group and individual. It was a humane situation.

The only bad day at Camp Snoopy happened courtesy of an Aryan-power fucker. He didn't like that I was recruited on his baseball team. After a game he suckered me into the bathroom. He thought he'd teach me a lesson. But I drew on my experience as a YMCA boxer back in Buffalo and beat the shit out of him. Once he was down, I was about to kick in his ribs when a brotha stopped me and said, "Rick, you got short time here. Don't mess up by putting this cat in the hospital." The brotha was right. I backed off. From that day on, though, my reputation was sealed. Don't fuck with Rick.

After nearly nine months, the woman warden sent me to Folsom. The bitch never liked me. She thought I had attitude.

"Did you?" asks Brotha Guru, interrupting my story.

"Sure. It's attitude that got me through."

"Or attitude that got you in."

"I've survived, haven't I?"

"When you got here, you made a helluva stir."

"You heard about that?"

"Who didn't? It was big news that Rick James had come to Folsom. Were you scared?"

"A little. County and Camp Snoopy had been a breeze. But Folsom had this reputation as the hard-core prison in the state. I remember walking through the yard my first day. All the cats stopped talking. They stopped lifting weights and turned to look at me. I didn't know what the fuck they were thinking. Then one guy yelled, 'Hey, Rick, come to Five Building,' and another screamed, 'No, man, Four Building is the jam. Have them put you in Four Building.' Soon everyone was shouting to get me into their building. They started singing 'Mary Jane' and 'You and I' and shouting my name like I was Muhammad Ali."

"Wasn't there some big commotion when you wound up here in Building Two?" asks Brotha Guru.

"That happened because of this fat redneck guard who brought me over here. When I asked him if I could call my lawyers, he gave me shit. He said, 'Sing me a song, boy, and maybe I'll let you.' Well, with all the prisoners listening, I made up a song on the spot:

Well, I guess here in Folsom I gotta figure
This big fat redneck guard don't like niggas

"The guys in their cells screamed and clapped. The guard was humiliated. A little later three female guards—one Puerto Rican, one black, one white—came to see me. They heard I'd just arrived and wanted to hear me sing. I went into 'Ebony Eyes' and they started swooning, 'That's my song!' I sang some more songs and by the time I was through every nigga in the joint was my best friend."

"That's when you became king of Folsom," says Brotha Guru.

"You know how it went down. All the power cats wanted to get next to me. They threw a blanket of love over me. The 415, the Crips, the Bloods, even the fuckin' Aryan cats thought I was cool. For a while I heard the Mexican Mafia had a hit out on me. That got me worried until the head Mexican came to me and said, 'That's bullshit, Rick. I've been locked up in this motherfucker for twenty-five years and your music helped me get through this shit. I ain't letting no one touch you.'"

"I heard that some of the guards had it out for you."

"They did until I let them know that my cousin Louis Stokes is one of the most powerful cats in the U.S. Congress."

"So now you're all set."

"One of the lady corrections officers got me an acoustic guitar and lets me play for hours in a room behind the library. She even snuck in a tape recorder for me. Since I been locked up, I've written over three hundred songs."

"That's beautiful."

"And I don't gotta tell you, Brotha Guru, that I got all the steak, escargot, and champagne I want."

"Doesn't that champagne mess with your sobriety, Rick?"

"Booze was never my problem. Blow was the problem. Haven't had any blow in my body for nearly two years."

"And soon you'll be outta here."

"In just a couple of weeks."

"You worried?"

"What should I be worried about?"

"That Me Monster."

"You still on that Me Monster kick?"

"I'm believing that you got to the truth. It wasn't no Mexican Mafia that had a hit out on you. It wasn't the Aryan Brotherhood. But it was—and it still is—someone. I think it's the Me Monster, Rick. I think that's the motherfucker that wants to do you in."

"Too late."

"What do you mean?"

"I've already gotten through this prison thing. If the earthquake didn't kill me, if the redneck guards and the crazy prisoners didn't kill me, I ain't worried about nothing."

"Not even going out on drugs again?"

"No, sir. I know better. That shit is behind me."

✦

The thing that made me confident was my new family. Tanya's mom had taken Taz to see me nearly every weekend at Folsom. He was a beautiful child and gave me reason to live. Tanya and I wrote each other hundreds of letters. Our love was stronger than ever, and we planned to marry soon as I was released. She got out first and started planning the wedding. She fucked up, though, when she got caught stealing a pair of shoes for her bridal shower. That parole violation sent her back to county jail. That meant I'd have to raise Taz alone until her release. Her mom would help, but I was still nervous. I'd been dreaming of freedom—but freedom meant I'd have a million choices. I wanted to make the right ones.

I wanted to get straight and stay straight.

STRAIGHT

Straight is the gate," said Jesus, "and narrow the way that leads unto life, and few there be that find it."

I wanted to find it.

One of the beautiful things I did in jail was to learn more about the great sages—Jesus, Buddha, Confucius. I studied the life of Muhammad. I read the Koran and felt myself deeply drawn to Islam. I realized that wisdom is required to get through this life. I knew that Brotha Guru, in his warnings about the Me Monster, was talking about the need to believe in something bigger than myself. I did believe. I was willing to submit to God. I wanted to be released, as they say in the program, from the burden of self.

And yet, upon release from prison, I needed to feel good about myself. I needed to know that I was still wanted by the public and loved by my fans. I needed to be reassured that my old friends were still there and ready to re-embrace me.

They were.

After Tanya's release from county jail, we married at the end of 1997. It was a small wedding at our house. Our marriage came as the result of deep love but also practicality. We were both felons, and felons aren't allowed to live together if either is on parole. My parole officer urged us to marry or else risk another prison sentence.

That same year saw the release of an album that gave me more satisfaction than any other. I was gratified that a major label, Mercury/Polygram, wanted me and was willing to let me produce it myself. They trusted me as an artist.

I recruited my main man, Danny LeMelle, to help me write, produce, and arrange the record. Danny had been with me for years and understood my music as well as anyone.

My concept was big. Following in the footsteps of Marvin Gaye, I wanted to do my own *What's Going On.* I wanted to create a suite of songs and tell a long-form story that would be a permanent part of our musical heritage. Where Marvin's concept album concerned his brother Frankie's return to America from Vietnam, mine would focus on my return from prison. I called it *Urban Rapsody.*

It opens with a Marvin-esque, Gershwin-esque mood piece, the title track, "Urban Rapsody." The rap is by 4-Tay, who lets you know that I'm using all the tools of cutting-edge hip-hop. For a long time I had an attitude about rap. I thought all the rapping and sampling was adopted by people who, because they couldn't sing, had to figure out some other shit. Over the years, though, I realized that rapping and sampling were their own art forms. Of course it helped that, years before, MC Hammer's use of "Super Freak" in "U Can't Touch This" made me a shitload of money. That did wonders for my appreciation of sampling. Beyond that, though, I realized that music always grows and I wanted to grow along with it. I wanted *Urban Rapsody* to go forward even as it referred to the past.

I saw "West Coast Thang" as my return to L.A., to the sunshine and the palm trees and yes, the fine bitches I'd missed in prison. I needed to let the world know that the Rick James character, the man who knew how to party, was back, "sippin' gin and juice, blowing some Mary Jane, and talking about our future."

"Somebody's Watching You" took the story back to my jail days when the corrections officers were giving me shit and I gave them shit back. The song's about the paranoia that clings to you during prison and the years that follow.

"Back in You Again" was a happy track written for the film *Money Talks.* I saw the preview with the movie's star, Chris Tucker. We became fast friends and the tune turned out to be, in part, the story of my love for Tanya: "Glad to say that I miss your sexy ways / Here I am girl back in you again / Since I've been gone I thought about you every day . . . One minute I'm in jail, the next I'm on the run . . . but suddenly I'm free." The song proved prophetic, at least in the short run.

Some songs, like "Turn It Out," were sex fantasies I had about Tanya when I was locked up, while other songs, like "Good Ol Days," sung with Charlie Wilson of the Gap Band and my girl Joanne from the Mary Jane Girls, were pure nostalgia.

Bobby Womack joined me on "Player's Way." Bobby's one of the baddest soul singers ever, and he helped me gain back the confidence I needed to put this jam in the pocket. I love Snoop Dogg, who wrote a super-hip rap that smoothed out the track with a cool contemporary feel.

I wrote "Never Say You Love Me" for me and Teena Marie. It was gonna be the next Rick/Teena big thing after "Fire and Desire." At the time Teena was living with my sister Penny. Penny and I got into an argument—can't even remember what about—and Teena wouldn't sing with me until I made up with Penny. I said, "Fuck it," and got JoJo McDuffie Funderburg, who sang it beautifully. Before the album came out though, I remembered how much I loved Teena and dedicated the song to her.

"So Soft So Wet" is more late-night jailhouse super-horny sex music, written when Tanya sent me some outrageous pictures of her. Instead of jacking off, I wrote this song. I saw it as a musical ejaculation.

"Bring on the Love" takes a serious turn. It's a meditation on violence in the ghetto, a lament for those children killed by stray bullets meant for gangstas. It also gives voice—my old voice—to those poor souls still screaming for crack, indifferent to the deadly consequences of the drug.

I had long wanted to write a song about my mother. My only regret was that when I finally recorded "Mama's Eyes," Mom was gone. I wanted her to see my recovery and rebirth into a world of freedom. It's a song that tells Mom, who's now living on the other side of time, that I love her more than life itself—and that all is well. I put a muted Miles-like trumpet behind my voice, reminding me of that time that Mom snuck me into a club in Buffalo to see Miles and Trane.

The other woman whose spirit demanded her own song was Tanya. I called hers "Soul Sista." It was written at Folsom on acoustic guitar. When I got to the studio, I used lots of instruments but somehow the feeling got drowned. So I went back to simplicity. I see love as simple. I call Tanya "the queen of my soul, the queen of my heart."

I did a small-scale tour behind *Urban Rapsody* with a band I put together with cats from Buffalo. The big warm-up gig was at the House of Blues in L.A. All Hollywood turned out—all my friends, like Wesley Snipes, Eddie Murphy, Paul Mooney, Chris Tucker, Denzel Washington. It'd been over ten years since I put out a new album. That's a long fuckin' time in the record business. I was nervous as hell, sweating bullets. I had flop fears. I worried about whether I'd be remembered. I worried about whether I'd get over. I didn't need to worry. The place was packed. Thousands of fans couldn't even get in. The evening was a triumph.

Urban Rapsody put me back where I wanted to be: in the middle of the mix. After it had been extinguished by the evils of cocaine and the confinement of prison, I had my glow back. In 1999, Eddie Murphy helped tremendously when he got me a role in the movie he did with Martin Lawrence, *Life*. I played the part of a big-time gangsta. Reviews were positive and one critic saw a movie career in my future. I had no doubt I could act. I'd been acting my entire life. Hope was—and remains—everywhere in my world.

◆

All this leads to my saying that at the end of this, my story so far, I'm still glowing. I'm still thinking that I have a long life in front of me and good times ahead. I know I have the right woman, and even though my track record at long-term relationships isn't great, I'm believing this time will be different.

This time I've become a grandfather. My beautiful daughter, Ty, has two beautiful daughters of her own, the bright lights of my life. My sons, Rick and Taz, mean the world to me. Family has never been more important. Family keeps me anchored in the reality of love, and love keeps me from straying off into the darkness that I know all too well.

Will I return to that darkness? In the words of Brotha Guru, will the Me Monster get hold of me again?

I can't make any guarantees. Who knows what direction I—or, for that matter, the world—am going in. George W. Bush is our post–9/11 president. He reminds me of Reagan. I don't like the guy and everything he represents. Feels to me like he's using this terror scare to rob us of our liberties. I hope we survive him. I hope the president who comes next has a clearer vision of the world situation.

I'm back in the studio working on *Deeper Still*, an album for my own Stone City Records. It's bad. And probably its baddest joint is a funky thing called "Stroke," an autobiographical groove that has me talking about my prison past as well as my promising future. "Stroke" lets you know that I got my stroke back.

In terms of my personal situation, I'm feeling pretty steady. I'm not back on crack. I'd be lying if I said that I didn't think about dabbling, but I've avoided it. An occasional joint, a sip of wine— nothing more. If I start to forget what blow did to my brain, all I have to do is the read the words that I have written here—my own horror story—to remember the pain and suffering. I don't want to repeat the mistakes of the past. I don't want to lose the glow. I pray that the glow will be with me forever, in this lifetime and the worlds that follow.

EPILOGUE

I n bodily form, the glow was extinguished on August 6, 2004, when Rick died of a heart attack at age fifty-six. The coroner's report indicated nine drugs in his body, including cocaine, Valium, Vicodin, and methamphetamine. He had been diagnosed years earlier with diabetes and had suffered a mild stroke in 1998. He had also been wearing a pacemaker. Since leaving jail eight years earlier, his health had steadily declined. His effort to find sobriety became a study in frustration.

"I never got more than a few weeks clean before I was looking to get high again," he told me. "I wanted relief from all sorts of pain, and the high was the quickest way."

"Rick called a few months before he passed," Jan Gaye told me. "I was in my car driving from LAX. He said he'd gone out on drugs but now was back and recommitted to sobriety. He sounded great, full of determination. He said that he had missed our deep discussions and was looking to reconnect with the people he called his intellectual friends. I was flattered. I was eager to renew our friendship. As he began describing this new awakening, I drove through a tunnel and lost the connection. I tried calling him back but didn't get through. That was the last time we spoke.

"The day after his death, Linda Hunt, who'd worked for Rick for years, called and asked me to come to the apartment where they'd been living. It was the Oakwood, a complex of furnished apartments on the hill above Burbank next to Forest Lawn Cemetery. The place was chaos. The entire aftermath of Rick's death was chaos. You die the way you live, and Rick lived in chaos. His family and friends had written an obituary to use in a program for the memorial service. They asked me to read it over. I told them that it wasn't right. At their request, I rewrote it. I wanted it to be about Rick's greatness. I wanted him to be remembered as a creative giant and a loving human being."

The service was held in the Hall of Liberty at Forest Lawn, where, a little more than twenty years earlier, Marvin Gaye had been eulogized. Two prominent ministers from two different faiths spoke. Bishop Noel Jones, brother of entertainer Grace Jones and a brilliant rhetorician, spoke from a Christian perspective. Minister Louis Farrakhan, who was both restrained and eloquent, spoke from the perspective of the Nation of Islam. In addition, Rick's sister Camille, a minister as well, described the disastrous effects of drugs on the life of her brother. Jan Gaye spoke lovingly of her dear friend, whom she called a student of all religions. Rick's Stone City Band played. Stevie Wonder sang. Teena Marie compared her musical partnership with Rick to Marvin Gaye/Tammi Terrell and Donny Hathaway/Roberta Flack. Berry Gordy was in attendance, along with Smokey Robinson.

During the service, a giant joint was placed atop one of the speakers facing the mourners. Someone lit it. The smell of weed began drifting over the hall. A few turned their heads to avoid the smoke; others opened their mouths and inhaled.

In the open casket, dressed in a regal outfit of moss green and embroidered gold, the lifeless body of Rick James remained the focal point—a symbol of the turbulent relationship between excess and success.

He had lived a life of extravagant complexity. He had sought and won the attention of the world. He had made a permanent and important mark on musical history. He had struggled for clarity, and at key moments, clarity had been realized. But those moments were few. The excitement of show business, the thrill of adulation, the intoxication of wealth, and a battery of lethal compulsions had driven him to dangerous places. Lost in an emotional wilderness, time and time again he looked for a way home.

In the Hall of Liberty, he had finally found that home. Disembodied, his spirit was free to live outside of time and space, a steady and inextinguishable glow.

The glow lives on in Rick's legacy. His place in history is secure. Fletcher Henderson is heralded for his seminal contribution to big band jazz; Louis Jordan is remembered as a forefather of small-group R & B; James Brown and George Clinton are recognized as pioneers in orchestrated funk; and, in that hallowed tradition, Rick James stands tall. He fused these three strains—jazz, R & B, and funk—into a sound of his own. Like other idiosyncratic geniuses—from Louis Jordan to Jackie Wilson, from Elvis Presley to Chubby Checker—he forged a wholly original voice. He created vital dance music. His public persona—defiant, daring, hedonistic—touched a deep nerve of our pop culture. In short, he became larger than life. His undisciplined life is a finite story with a beginning, middle, and end. But his art, so strangely and wildly satisfying, has no end. His art lives.

SELECTED DISCOGRAPHY

Albums

The Great White Cane, Lion, 1972

Come Get It!, Gordy, 1978

Bustin' Out of L Seven, Gordy, 1979

Fire It Up, Gordy, 1979

Rick James Presents the Stone City Band: In 'n' Out, Gordy, 1980

Garden of Love, Gordy, 1980

Street Songs, Gordy, 1981

The Boys Are Back: The Stone City Band, Gordy, 1981

Throwin' Down, Gordy, 1982

Cold Blooded, Gordy, 1983

Meet the Stone City Band! Out from the Shadow, Motown, 1983

Reflections, Gordy, 1984

The Flag, Gordy, 1986

Wonderful, Reprise, 1988

Rock, Rhythm and Blues, Warner, 1989

Bustin' Out: The Best of Rick James, Motown, 1994

Urban Rapsody, Private I, 1997

DVDs

Super Freak Live, Eagle Rock, 1982

The Best of Rick James: The 20th Century Masters DVD Collection, Motown, 2005

I'm Rick James: The Definitive DVD, Motown, 2009

INDEX